Experience the Freedom
You Already Have in Christ

Experience the Freedom
You Already Have in Christ

A personal or small group study for very tired Christians

PAULA NEALL COLEMAN

Experience the Freedom You Already Have in Christ

© 2024 Paula Neall Coleman
Printed in the United State of America
ISBN 978-0-9798487-3-5

All rights reserved. No part of this book may be reproduced in any form without permission in writing from the author, except in the case of brief quotations embodied in critical articles or reviews.

All Scripture quotations, unless otherwise indicated, are taken from the *Holy Bible, New International Version*®, NIV®. Copyright ©1973, 1978, 1984, 2011 by Biblica, Inc.™ Used by permission of Zondervan. All rights reserved worldwide. www.zondervan.com. The "NIV" and "New International Version" are trademarks registered in the United States Patent and Trademark Office by Biblica, Inc.™

Scripture quotations marked "KJV" are from the King James Version of the Bible.

Scripture quotations marked "ESV" are from The ESV® Bible (The Holy Bible, English Standard Version®), © 2001 by Crossway, a publishing ministry of Good News Publishers. Used by permission. All rights reserved.

Scripture quotations marked "NASB" are taken from the (NASB®) New American Standard Bible®, Copyright © 1960, 1971, 1977, 1995, 2020 by The Lockman Foundation. Used by permission. All rights reserved. lockman.org.

Scripture quotations marked "AMP" are taken from the *Amplified Bible,* Copyright © 1954, 1958, 1962, 1964, 1965, 1987 by The Lockman Foundation. Used by permission. lockman.org.

Scripture quotations marked "NKJV™" are taken from the New King James Version®. Copyright © 1982 by Thomas Nelson, Inc. Used by permission. All rights reserved.

Scripture quotations marked "GNT" are taken from the *Good News Translation - Second Edition* © 1992 by American Bible Society. Used by permission.

Cover design by Michelle Atkinson Creative Services

...you will know the truth, and the truth will set you free.

John 8:32

CONTENTS

Diagrams iii

Foreword v

Will *You* Benefit from Reading This Book? 1

How to Effectively Use This Book's Format 5

    1. Freedom from What ... and How? 9

    2. Freeing Truth about God the Father and God the Son 19

    3. Freeing Truth about God the Spirit 27

    4. Freeing Truth about Who You've Become and Why You Still Sin Anyway 35

    5. Freeing Truth about How Your Beliefs Motivate Your Behavior 49

    6. Freeing Truth about Your Emotions 63

    7. Freeing Truth about Some Specific, Especially Troubling Emotions 75

    8. Freeing Truth about Guilt, Shame, and Punishment 93

    9. Freeing Truth about Living by Rules and Standards 103

   10. Freeing Truth about Relationships 113

   11. Freeing Truth about Bad Things People Have Done to You 121

   12. Where Do You Go from Here? 129

Addendum One: *FatherCare* 141

Addendum Two: Transcript of "Self-Disciplined Religion," a recorded message by Malcolm Smith 189

Addendum Three: "Living Well" Handout by Ed and Donna Edwards 203

Addendum Four: Transcript of "Attitude of Gratitude," a recorded message by Bill Ewing 211

Addendum Five: Answer Keys 221

Addendum Six: Facilitator's Guide 225

Acknowledgments 229

Notes 231

About the Author 237

DIAGRAMS

What You Were Like before Trusting Christ	38
What You Are Like after Trusting Christ	39
Diving Deep with God	54
Resurfacing from the Deep with God	55
"REED"	71
Expectations, Anger, and Bitterness	76

FOREWORD

During the past 35 or so years, when encouraging stressed and struggling Christians, over and over again I've found myself relaying to each person certain basic biblical principles. Frequently the people I have the opportunity to encourage are contending with devastating defeat in the face of ongoing depression, anxiety, anger, and/or an inability to stop engaging in an unwanted behavior, such as immoral sexual activity, overeating, hair-pulling, or overspending.

Although the information I cover is relayed in ways so that each individual sees very personal application, the same biblical concepts are covered and almost always in the same order, before the struggling believer experiences the freedom he or she actually had all along but hadn't yet realized.

Certainly, the biblical truths that are foundational to living out the freedom in Christ we already have are not hidden or mysterious. Many authors have written on these topics. But I've not found a resource that gives these "basics" all in one volume, in the particular order I've found almost always applies, and with simple, practical "homework" that makes the concepts covered very personally pertinent. Therefore, mostly for my own sake in working with what I think of as "stuck Christians," I've written this workbook. My desire is that it also serves as a resource to individuals, mentors, and small group participants exploring biblical truths that set believers free from whatever "miry clay" in which they find themselves. And no one should be surprised by there being freeing power in God's Word that is effective for God's people, since "you will know the truth, and the truth will set you free"! (John 8:32)

But have I personally experienced the freedom that results from knowing God's truth? Well, let me first say that it is clear in Scripture that no one experiences total freedom on this side of heaven. (See Galatians 5:13-17 and Hebrews 10:14, for example.) However, I do know from very personal experience – as well as from observing the experiences of others I've encouraged – that freedom from deeply painful and harmful behaviors and emotions is where Jesus wants to take each of us.

Having survived a number of childhood traumas, such as sexual molestation, parental abandonment, and all the physical, verbal, and emotional assaults that came with having parents and stepparents who daily misused alcohol, I entered adulthood and the Christian life (at age 19) with a lot of "baggage." I engaged in binge-eating and compulsive exercising, felt angry constantly, woke up almost daily with the first thought of *I wish I were dead*, and at age 25 overachieved myself into a breakdown and total collapse that left me unemployed, unable to drive, and often unable to speak or move for hours at a time.

God allowed me to be crushed by my own coping mechanisms so he could raise up the real me from that ash heap. My gradual recovery was with the help of a biblical counseling ministry that introduced me to a new way of thinking about the character of God, what it means to be a "new creation in Christ," and how to address even overwhelming emotions in a healthy, biblical way. All of this healing guidance was clearly presented in Scripture but had never been part of the discipleship I'd received from the churches and parachurch organizations in which I'd previously participated. To be honest, though, even if I had been exposed to these biblical truths prior to my dramatic personal meltdown, I doubt I would have accepted them, since I was so

No one should be surprised by there being freeing power in God's Word that is effective for God's people, since "you will know the truth, and the truth will set you free"! (John 8:32)

determined to live the Christian life by means of objective goals and rules that provided me with a way to measure my "success."

Thankfully not everyone needs to experience a sudden, dramatic collapse to be profoundly changed by exposure to freeing scriptural insights. If you are exhausted by trying harder and harder but never permanently or significantly experiencing progress in your battle with certain behaviors, thoughts, and/or emotions, you are likely very ready for the refreshing good news that was lovingly presented to me and that I've repeatedly shared with tired, discouraged Christians over the years. And nearly every time I've had the privilege to point out to anyone the freedom he or she already has in Christ, the effects of God's Spirit applying the truth of God's Word have been an exhilarating joy to behold, proving over and over again that **"you will know the truth, and the truth will set you free"**! (John 8:32)

> *The effects of God's Spirit applying the truth of God's Word have been an exhilarating joy to behold.*

Experience the Freedom
You Already Have in Christ

WILL *YOU* BENEFIT FROM READING THIS BOOK?

You will be very relieved and encouraged by the information presented in this book if you identify with most of the following:

- You have tried harder and harder to overcome unwanted emotions or a pattern of negative behavior but never make much progress and often "relapse" or "backslide."
- You feel God is disgusted with you for having so little self-control and for not getting your act together.
- You often feel stymied or defeated by such emotions as rage, depression, shame, anxiety, and/or loneliness.
- You feel absolutely compelled to engage in a behavior you later regret, such as overeating, compulsive shopping, looking at pornography, binge-watching TV or videos, shoplifting, hair-pulling, face-picking, getting high, or drinking alcohol in excess. When the urge comes upon you, you know you're eventually going to have to engage in that behavior or the tension will be unbearable.
- You've resolved to read the Bible more, pray more, and attend church more regularly, but none of these activities have provided much help for what's really bothering you.
- You have told yourself to be obedient to God and have berated yourself for your disobedience, but you just don't ever change.

Even more important than these points is whether you are open to considering a new way of thinking about yourself, your emotions, what motivates your behavior, and how God fits into these areas of your life. If that is true, you are certainly going to find a lot of freedom as a result of applying the concepts presented in this book.

This Is Not a Behavior Modification Approach

There is a clear pattern in the New Testament epistles, most easily seen in the letters of the apostle Paul: He first presents truth about God, the world, and/or the Christian. Only after truth is presented, Paul spells out practical application, usually regarding the day-to-day behavior such truth would lead one to engage in. For example, Paul wrote at great length about deep truths in the first 11 chapters of Romans before addressing practical application in the remainder of the book. Many self-help books do not take this approach. Although there are 12 chapters in this book, they are not 12 easy steps to freedom that involve "if you just do this, then you'll be free." No, instead, this approach is about "if you know these truths and put faith in them, then you'll gradually be transformed by the Spirit of God." Scriptural truths are highlighted and the reader is encouraged to engage with God on a very personal level in light of these truths with the natural result being the experience of more and more freedom.

So, if your idea of freedom is behaving perfectly and getting things done, this is not the book for you. If, however, you are more interested in living by God's truth and in the freedom of his grace than you are in completing steps, you will find true success when you start applying the concepts presented in this book.

> *This approach is about "if you know these truths and put faith in them, then you'll gradually be transformed by the Spirit of God."*

Dive on In!

Two of my closest friends – I'll call them Jodi and Jane – started with me on the "journey" toward freedom from our unwanted behaviors and most troubling emotions at about the same time. A few years after we had "set out," we were comparing notes about our differing levels of "success." Jodi noted that, even though we were exposed to the same biblical concepts and literature, the three of us had taken three different approaches as we tackled our struggles. She likened each approach to a recreational activity. Jane was compared to a person taking a tour in a helicopter, looking down at the scenery as it whizzed past below. She had scanned several of the books each of us purchased, but she hadn't actually read any of them. She listened to what Jodi and I said about what we'd read and what we'd understood from Scripture, but she hadn't read or understood any of it on her own. She just flew by and observed with interest what was going on with us "down on the ground." It was about two and half years after we'd started down this road when we had this discussion about our progress, and Jane, the "helicopter rider," had experienced almost no freedom from fairly extreme anxiety and frequent episodes of compulsive eating and purging.

Jodi likened herself to a water skier. She had skimmed over the surface of the materials and the issues they raised. She felt frightened about going very slowly because she might fall into the water and not be able to swim to the shore. She kept on moving, reading all the books, but never really thinking through what was presented in them. Some of the books we were reading had exercises in each chapter. She skipped the exercises to move quickly through each book. She covered a lot of territory but never got very wet. As a result, Jodi's struggles weren't as intense as they had been before, but she was still far from free in several areas of her life.

Finally, Jodi compared me to a deep-sea diver. Over the course of about two years, I'd thoroughly plunged into the books, exercises, articles, and especially the Bible, and looked at everything there was "down there." I'd soaked myself in prayerfully considering the underlying issues. I'd gone very slowly, exploring and pondering each new concept I encountered. I'd stayed in the water until I looked like a prune! As a result of "diving in," I'd found lasting freedom from panic attacks, obsessing about my appearance and worth, and 24 years of binge-eating and compulsive dieting.

If you're reading this introductory section, there's hope for you.

If you're reading this introductory section, there's hope for you. You've already taken a dip into the water. People who skip the introduction of a book are probably going to fly or water ski over the rest of it. So, be encouraged, you're already a likely candidate for getting a great deal of benefit from this book!

Two Are Better than One

Each chapter in this book provides a weekly session for a small group experience that allows group participants to engage in discussion about the chapter's information. During this discussion – and when participants do the "homework" that is assigned in each chapter – a lot of "light bulbs" go on for group members. The benefit group participants receive from interacting with each other is reminiscent of Ephesians 4:15-16:

> …speaking the truth in love, we will grow to become in every respect the mature body of him who is the head, that is, Christ. From him the whole body, joined

and held together by every supporting ligament, grows and builds itself up in love, as each part does its work.

When we share truth, in love, with one another – when we contribute to one another's lives – we do grow spiritually. You'll get the most from this book if you go through it with at least one other person and discuss with one another the reflection questions and "homework" provided in each chapter. (There is more information about the book's format in the following brief section, "How to Effectively Use this Book's Format.")

An Open Bible Really Helps

God's Word has more effect on us than any other written document. Therefore, I hope you take the time to carefully read referenced Scripture passages. Take advantage of the Scripture's power to transform (Isaiah 55:11; John 17:17; Hebrews 4:12). It was in understanding Scripture that I realized and experienced the freedom I already had in Christ. My prayer is that you, too, will experience this same freedom.

God's Word has more effect on us than any other written document.

Do You Know Your ABC's?[1]

This book is directed to people who have faith in Jesus Christ. If you haven't yet put your faith and trust in Christ, let me encourage you that it is as simple as "**ABC**" – not necessarily easy, but simple.

Acknowledge that you have sinned.
The word "sin" actually means "missing the mark" God has set for you. We all have missed the mark at some time or another! This sin separates us from God, and it's why we need to accept his forgiveness to spend eternity with him.
Romans 3:23: For all have sinned and fall short of the glory of God.

Believe in Jesus.
Belief is more than "head knowledge" of Jesus. It's a belief that leads to an action – placing your total trust and faith in Jesus for forgiveness of your sins.
Acts 16:31: Believe in the Lord Jesus, and you will be saved.

Completely surrender your life to Jesus and follow him.
When you place your full trust in Jesus, you are surrendering control of your life to him, so it's only natural that you will want to live in a way that glorifies him. His Word in the Bible and the Holy Spirit who will live within you will guide you in living that life day-by-day.
Luke 9:23-24: Then he said to them all: "Whoever wants to be my disciple must deny themselves and take up their cross daily and follow me. For whoever wants to save their life will lose it, but whoever loses his life for me will save it."

Then **pray...**
Placing your trust in Jesus begins with a simple prayer telling God that you cannot live up to his holy standards and need him to guide your life. You can put your faith in Christ right now by simply talking with God, who is not as concerned with your words as he is with the attitude of your heart. Here is a suggested prayer:

Lord Jesus, I want to know you personally. Thank you for dying on the cross for my sins. I surrender my life to you and confess that you are my Savior and Lord. Thank you for forgiving me for my sins and giving me eternal life. Take control of my life. Make me the kind of person you want me to be.

Does that prayer express what you desire in your heart? If it does, pray a prayer like this right now, and Christ will come into your life as he promised!

HOW TO EFFECTIVELY USE THIS BOOK'S FORMAT

The information in this book is most effective when two or more individuals go through it together. Each chapter is structured to facilitate group interaction and is divided into the following sections: (A Facilitator's Guide is provided on pages 225-228.)

- *Presentation of Information*: The "lesson" portion for the chapter.
- *Reflection*: These are questions intended to help you apply the information presented in each chapter. Write your answers and later discuss them with others who are reading the book also. Whether you're working through this book on your own or with friends, writing your answers to questions will be helpful. When you commit answers to writing, you have to face exactly what you're thinking rather than having some vague ideas rolling around in your head. You'll get the most out of the reflection questions if you do not proceed to the next section of the chapter until you've answered the reflection questions.
- *What Others Have Experienced:* Once you've responded to the reflection questions, this section provides some food for thought that is based on my own experiences or on how others have answered the questions. No fair reading ahead into this section, though, until you've already answered the reflection questions for yourself!
- *Homework*: These are exercises for you to do on your own. Sometimes the homework consists of simply reading material provided in an addendum, or you may be asked to write down your thoughts or fill in short answers. Usually, the homework takes between one and three hours to complete and is best done in one or two sittings. Completing homework is a vital part of making the kind of personal application necessary for you to experience freedom.
- *Homework Follow-up:* These questions will enable you to meaningfully reflect on your homework and how it has affected your perspective. You'll benefit most from these questions if you write your answers and later discuss them with others who are also going through the book *before* moving on to the last section of the chapter.
- *Comments on the Homework:* This section discusses how others have responded to the homework and/or provides additional pertinent information.

Completing homework is a vital part of making the kind of personal application necessary for you to experience freedom.

Over and over again, I have seen this format really flow in a small group setting. Hearing what others say about the same information you're contemplating frequently sparks ideas about personal application you'd never think of on your own.

Small Group Dynamics and Guidelines

You're probably familiar with the common wisdom that a small group is best kept to 12 members or fewer. (Jesus knew this way before the psychologists figured it out.) A group size limit certainly holds true for this material. I've conducted a small group in which 16 women regularly attended, and I was amazed at how everyone managed to participate to some degree in discussion. However, these women were all well acquainted with one another and encouraged each other to speak up. But we rarely got to thoroughly discuss truly personal application for more than a few participants during any one session. The best interaction I've seen has been in groups with five to eight participants. We were able to get onto a more personal level, and each week each participant was able to discuss his or her personal application of the concepts presented in the chapter. Also, there were just enough of us to have a variety of experiences to discuss and compare. As an aid for small groups making use of this book, on page 7 are the small group guidelines I use for the groups I facilitate.

Even If It's Just You, Don't Go It Alone

Whether you are going through this book with a friend, in a small group, or on your own, the most important person to invite into the process with you is God. Before you read each chapter, ask God to show you how the information being presented applies to you *personally*. Ask him to help you to be honest with yourself and with him. Ask him to help you through any shame that may be keeping you from facing some of the circumstances and thought processes that have contributed to your struggles. Remember to apply the forgiveness of the Cross to areas where you have fallen short.

Ask God to show you how the information being presented applies to you personally.

Invite God to help you do your homework. Ask him to bring to your mind the real answers to the questions rather than the answers you think you *should* give. He knows much more about you than you do, and he remembers your life perfectly. He knows what's in the back of your mind that you don't admit to even yourself. This is where God helped me the most as I studied the Bible and read books – including doing the exercises in those books. There were a number of thoughts, beliefs, and feelings I hadn't admitted to myself and certainly to no one else. Once these came to light through prayer and what I call "prayerful pondering," I was able to change my mind about them. Also, once I started discussing with others some of my faulty thinking and the issues with which I struggled, I found that no one was repulsed or offended. Usually, others were relieved to know they weren't the only ones who had had thoughts and beliefs similar to mine. This type of sharing was enormously helpful in reinforcing the concepts I was learning and starting to apply.

As I write this, I am praying for you, each and every person who will use this workbook, and asking God to make this a journey that is not just a road to freedom, but even more importantly, a path to greater intimacy with him.

SMALL GROUP GUIDELINES

1. Every effort will be made to start and end on time.

2. Group members should discuss only the portion of each chapter they've read, the questions they've answered, and the homework they've completed. A good discussion of the information requires familiarity with the information.

3. Confidentiality:

   Nothing personal said in the group goes out of the group. When you discuss your group experience with a friend or spouse, share only what *you* gained or learned. Share no one else's experiences but your own. Do not share any names, descriptions of group members, occupations of members, etc., with people outside the group. During the week, do not discuss with fellow group members any other group members. We all need to feel free to express ourselves openly without the fear of being discussed later, even by other group members.

4. Communication with each other:

   - Don't try to "fix" anyone else. That's God's job.
   - Use "I" statements, not "you" statements. An example would be, "I feel you may have misunderstood me," instead of, "You got that wrong!"
   - Keep Ephesians 4:15 and Ephesians 4:29 in mind as you interact with one another: (emphasis added)

     *...speaking the truth **in love**, we will grow to become in every respect the mature body of him who is the head, that is, Christ.*

     *Do not let any unwholesome talk come out of your mouths, but only what is **helpful for building others up according to their needs**, that it may benefit those who listen.*

5. You will get more out of the group if you participate by sharing your thoughts, experiences, and feelings. All the group participants will benefit from one another, so don't deprive others of your input. Your transparency will help you. Go ahead and risk judgment; it's better to be transparent and risk disapproval than to keep your thoughts to yourself. Trust that each member of the group wants the best for the other members.

1 FREEDOM FROM WHAT ... AND HOW?

"My chains are gone, I've been set free."[1]
"...you will know the truth, and the truth will set you free."[2]
"So, how much do you still have to struggle every day with overeating?"[3]

It was embarrassing! No, it was humiliating and I felt terribly ashamed. I was standing in my own kitchen, staring at a cabinet that was locked shut with a bicycle lock! While I was at work, my roommate had moved all of her groceries into one cabinet, placed the lock on it, and hidden the key. It seemed so extreme, but I knew it was her only way of making sure she'd have something to eat for breakfast in the morning. Almost every night, I raided the fridge and the cabinets, eating "everything that wasn't nailed down." Actually, I left most of the canned vegetables, but Karen really didn't enjoy green beans with her coffee!

How did it get this bad?! I had been a Christian for many years. I'd been in Christian ministry for years, was active in church and Bible studies, and was constantly attending discipleship and evangelism conferences and seminars. Why then did I constantly fight – without ever winning for any length of time – the "battle of the bulge"? How many times had I pleaded with God to help me stick to a diet? How many times had I lost and regained the same 30 to 60 pounds?

Overeating and weight gain were not my only struggles. My insecurity seemed to have no bounds. Did I look okay? Was every hair in place? Were all of my fingernails even with no chips in the polish? Had I done enough "good" today? Was I witnessing enough? Praying enough? Having a long enough daily "quiet time"? Did God approve or disapprove of me? (Pretty much always disapproved.) Why was I still single? Was God waiting until I had my act together before he'd allow me to marry?

The contradictions I saw in my life were extremely painful and bewildering. On the one hand, I appeared to others to epitomize the "committed Christian" who "had it all together." But, on the inside, I felt like a failure. Far from living in Christian freedom, I was expending a tremendous amount of emotional energy on obsessing over my failure to be self-controlled (*It's a fruit of the Spirit; why don't I have it?*) and suppressing all my anger and depression to make sure I was living the "victorious Christian life."

I had a lot I wanted to be free from. How about you? Take a moment to write out the most painful, persistent emotions and behaviors from which you'd like to experience total freedom:

_____

_____

_____

_____

The contradictions I saw in my life were extremely painful and bewildering.

> *"Sin" is anything that we think, feel, or do that isn't in line with the thoughts, feelings, and actions that God knows are in accordance with how he designed us as his image bearers.*

There is a blanket term for all of our emotions and behaviors that are not godly, and that term is "sin." That word used to absolutely fill me with guilt and shame. But I've come to see it in a less painful way, in a way that is just factual and not necessarily shame producing. "Sin" is anything that we think, feel, or do that isn't in line with the thoughts, feelings, and actions that God knows are in accordance with how he designed us as his image bearers. For example, it is clear in Scripture that God designed sexual activity to be confined to a committed, covenant relationship (i.e., marriage), so when someone engages in extramarital sexual relations of any sort, that person sins. He or she is not living as God designed people to live and, in effect, telling God he doesn't know what's best for his creatures. Sin is akin to trying to operate a car without looking at the owner's manual. For example, engaging in sexual immorality is like putting diesel fuel into a car that was designed to use only unleaded gasoline.

Sin can also be described as any way we feel, think, or act by our own power, apart from relying on God. Let's face it, we really don't know how to rely on God in every situation. When I become frustrated with how slowly my phone is loading, demonstrating impatience that is not in line with the fruit of the Spirit, then I'm also demonstrating that I am not relying on the fact that God has given me enough time to accomplish all he desires me to accomplish. Instead, I want the phone to load quicker so I can get more done right now! I could see the slowness of the phone as an opportunity to reflect on how amazing it is God has given me a phone at all and feel contentment instead of frustration.

"Oh my," you might say. "That's really getting into the weeds! I don't care about deliverance from cell phone frustration. Doesn't this author know that people have real problems?" Yes, I do get that, but in understanding freedom, we have to clearly understand sin, because that's actually what underlies all of our painful emotions and whacky behaviors. And it is from sin that Jesus offers us freedom, as we see in John 8:32-36:

> "Then you will know the truth, and the truth will set you free." They answered him, "We are Abraham's descendants and have never been slaves of anyone. How can you say that we shall be set free?" Jesus replied, "Very truly I tell you, everyone who sins is a slave to sin. Now a slave has no permanent place in the family, but a son belongs to it forever. So if the Son sets you free, you will be free indeed."

When Jesus said that knowing the truth would set you free, he was talking specifically about being set free from sin, the very thing that is at the heart of everything that you can't stand about yourself and results in extremely distressing emotions and behaviors. (For the context, see John 8:23-24.)

Okay, you can see how *what* you really need is freedom from sin. If you have freedom from sin, you'll be free from the overeating, flares of rage and cursing, wanting to slap your child silly, hating your mother-in-law, stealing just those tiny little trinkets you sneak into your purse, or cruising the sexually explicit websites where you know you have no business going. But HOW?! *How* do we find freedom from sin?!

In John 8, Jesus told us not only what we need freedom from – *sin* – but also how to obtain that freedom – *by knowing the truth*. It is apparent that his apostles "got" this when they wrote their epistles. They told the truth to the people to whom they wrote. They started with the truth and then expected those who heard or read their letters to respond to the truth by walking in freedom from sinful behavior. Here's a really plain example from one of Paul's letters to the Corinthians:

> Do you not know that your bodies are temples of the Holy Spirit, who is in you, whom you have received from God? You are not your own; you were bought at a price. Therefore honor God with your bodies. (1 Corinthians 6:19-20)

The context here is a discussion of sexual immorality in the lives of believers. Paul tells the Corinthians a few very important facts about them: that they are each a dwelling place of the Holy Spirit, that they have received the Spirit from God, that they belong to God, and that he paid a (very high) price to purchase them. Only *after* Paul tells them these truths, which he apparently doubted had really sunk in yet ("Do you not know…"), does he then conclude that they would quite naturally respond to such amazing truth by honoring God with their bodies by not engaging in sexual immorality. Duh!

Let's face it, not all the things we believe, much of which we've so taken for granted that we've never even questioned it, are actually based on the truth from God; i.e., the truth found in God's Word, the Bible. Even if you came to know Christ at a very early age, not everything you believed to be true after that was actually true according to Scripture. Here's an example: How many times did you hear godly older Christians say, "I'm just a dirty, rotten sinner saved by grace"? But that wasn't really a true statement. If you're saved by grace, you're a new creation in Christ with a new heart. Yes, you're saved by grace, but you're no longer dirty and rotten! If you truly believe you're still a dirty, rotten sinner, guess what? You'll find yourself acting like one. If, instead, you believe you're no longer dirty or rotten or even primarily a sinner, you are much more likely to behave in accordance with who you really are, which is "created to be like God in true righteousness and holiness" (Ephesians 4:24). (We'll look at what it means to be a new creation in Christ more thoroughly in Chapter 4.)

If believing the truth is what sets us free, yet we also believe in a whole lot of things that are *not* based on the truth, such as what our peers, culture, parents, schools, and even some churches have told us, then we're sunk! No truth, no freedom!

Oh, but there's hope. God has provided a means for us to replace all the erroneous beliefs we have that are motivating our painful emotions and ungodly behavior. Look at Romans 12:2.

> Do not conform to the pattern of this world, but be transformed by the renewing of your mind. Then you will be able to test and approve what God's will is—his good, pleasing and perfect will.

What is "the world"? It is the culture, institutions, media, and all people under the influence of sin and Satan – and it wants us to conform to *its* way of thinking. When we no longer let the world and its so-called "truths" press us into its mold[4], but instead change our thinking to align with the truth from God's Word, then we are able to discern God's will, which is pleasing and perfect…and frees us to be our true selves in Christ.

When we see and are convinced of reality as God sees it – when we believe in what is actually true – we are freed from the erroneous beliefs that are keeping us in bondage to painful emotions and the sinful behaviors we use to cope with our painful emotions. By renewing our minds, we reverse the process that led to slavery to sin as spelled out in Romans 1 – people exchanged the

If believing in the truth is what sets us free, but we believe in a whole lot of things that are not based on the truth, then we're sunk!

truth about God for a lie. We can now exchange the incorrect information we believe for the truth about and from God. And then we are set free from bondage to sin.

So, freedom from what? Sin, especially as manifested in our unbiblical thinking and beliefs that result in ungodly feelings and behaviors. And freedom how? By exchanging our erroneous thoughts and beliefs for God's truth as seen in his Word, the Bible; in other words, repentance.

A Word about "Repentance"

What does the word "repentance" mean to you? For many, "repentance" is a very loaded word, loaded with defeat and shame. However, the Bible's use of "repentance" is not meant to heap shame on a wrongdoer. In fact, true repentance is a simple recognition of how God's ways are far superior to any and all the ways we think might be best for us. I've heard several speakers and preachers refer to Romans 12:2 as the definition of true repentance – turning away from the "wisdom" of the world (including your own wisdom apart from Christ) and renewing your mind to agree with what God says. Too often people see repentance as "admit it and quit it"; i.e., recognize what you're doing is wrong and stop doing it. (I've heard this referred to as the "just do it gospel.") But this is an incomplete concept of repentance, especially since we are so often quite powerless to stop doing what we know we shouldn't be doing.

Romans 12:2 is the definition of true repentance.

When we understand, as the apostle Paul obviously did (see the example, above, from 1 Corinthians 6), that our actions are motivated by our beliefs, then we will humbly ask God to show us what erroneous beliefs are driving the negative feelings we have and the sinful behaviors in which we're engaging. Only when we "repent" – in other words, change our minds to align with God's truth – will we experience freedom from the feelings and behaviors that are symptoms of what we're thinking and believing.

Freedom You Already Have

This book is about freedom that you already have but have not yet experienced. The truth is that no one experiences *complete* freedom from sin and its consequences until glorification in heaven. However, we are able to experience more and more freedom as we grow in our understanding of God's truth and in our dependence upon God's Spirit to guide us into that truth. In Romans 6, the apostle Paul makes a startling statement about our identification with the death and eternal life of Jesus Christ.

> We are those who have died to sin; how can we live in it any longer? Or don't you know that all of us who were baptized into Christ Jesus were baptized into his death? We were therefore buried with him through baptism into death in order that, just as Christ was raised from the dead through the glory of the Father, we too may live a new life. ... For we know that our old self was crucified with him so that the body ruled by sin might be done away with, that we should no longer be slaves to sin—because anyone who has died has been set free from sin. ... The death he died, he died to sin once for all; but the life he lives, he lives to God. In the same way, count yourselves dead to sin but alive to God in Christ Jesus. (Romans 6:2-4, 6-7, 10-11. See also verses 12-18.)

In Romans 6:11, Paul uses an accounting-related term, translated "count." The word also has to do with logic. In fact, the root of *logizomai* is the same root used for our English word "logic."[5] I like the King James Version's rendering of that Greek word as "reckon" because it brings to mind a tallying up or an accountant's ledger. My personal paraphrase of Romans 6:11 is, "Put it down on your ledger that you are dead to sin (in the debit column) and alive to God (in the credit column)." Until you actually realize you have the money in your checking account, you won't spend it. (Well, you shouldn't spend it, but some do, so this analogy is quite limited!) Once you know it's there, you can spend it. I've "put it down" that I'm dead to sin and no longer have to do it! It no longer has power over me. As Romans 6:14 says, "...sin shall no longer be your master." In fact, because we died, we're no longer slaves to sin (the debit column), but we're now "slaves to righteousness" (the credit column – Romans 6:18).

Put it down on your ledger that you are dead to sin.

You are already free from sin (dead to sin), but you may not have "reckoned" that fully in your mental ledger. As you come to believe more and more in that truth, you will experience more and more the freedom you already have.

Because You're Already Free, You're Not an Addict

Most of the people I know who struggle with a persistent unwanted behavior, such as excessive online gaming, binge-watching TV, overeating, hair-pulling, or viewing pornography, refer to their "besetting sin" as an "addiction." Over recent decades, the idea of "addiction" has grown to encompass more and more behaviors and not just physiological dependence, such as with heroine or nicotine. In this book, the term "addiction" will not be used in reference to most of the sinful behaviors with which people struggle. I'm chuckling right now as I think of how many readers may respond to this with, "Well, you're in denial!" People identifying themselves as "addicts" do so in part to prove they are not in denial about an all-consuming, problematic, less-than-God-honoring behavior. However, for "new creations in Christ," behavior does not define us; God does. Anything upon which we rely other than Christ – for salvation or to make it through the day – is sinful and from the "flesh." (We'll discuss the flesh more in Chapter 4.) Although we are still contending with our flesh daily, we are not defined by our flesh and we are not defined by what we do. If we're in Christ, we are saints (1 Corinthians 1:2, ESV; "holy people," NIV), adopted sons of God (Galatians 4:5), children of God (1 John 3:2), the bride of Christ (2 Corinthians 11:2), and many other wonderful identifiers, thanks to what God has done for us in Christ. We are not just freed from something – the power of sin – but also we are freed to be something – our true selves, "created to be like God in true righteousness and holiness" (Ephesians 4:24).

For "new creations in Christ," behavior does not define us; God does.

Yes, there are physiological addictions – substances upon which the body can become dependent and without which the body goes into withdrawal. For some, surrender to Christ rids even the body of the power of such addiction, but for others medical intervention is needed. However, no amount of medical intervention is truly successful for the Christian unless the underlying motivations for using the addicting substance are addressed through renewing the mind – trading lies believed for truth revealed in Scripture. Whether a person is physiologically or emotionally dependent on any substance or behavior, the ultimate answer is the same – understanding how *you* are trying to meet your needs your way and trading that in for how *God* has provided to meet those needs his way. According to Romans 12:2 and Ephesians 4:23, this is the only way that enables you to experience true freedom to be the person God "rebirthed" you to be.

Reflection

You'll get the most from the following reflection questions if you discuss them with one or more individuals who are going through this book too. If you don't have someone with whom to discuss these questions, be sure to at least write down your answers (and don't worry about grammar or spelling). Only after you have talked over these questions with others or written your answers, move on to the next section of this chapter, "What Others Have Experienced."

1. From your list on page 9, choose one emotion or behavior from which you'd like to find freedom. Do you remember when this first became an issue for you? What was happening at that time? If you can't recall, ask God to remind you.

2. Given what was happening when you first started struggling with that particular emotion or behavior, what is a likely belief that you had at the time about yourself or about God or about how life works? Be sure to ask God to help you discern what your thinking was at the time.

3. Ask God to reveal to you a way in which your thinking was not in line with Scripture. Write your thoughts.

What Others Have Experienced

Many people I've asked to answer the questions, above, have said what amounts to this: "God doesn't speak to me." In fact, many have believed it was not biblical to expect God to personally remind them about an event or reveal their thinking about it. "Isn't that just psychological therapy?" "God doesn't speak personally to people. He has spoken in the Bible and that's all we need." And yet the Bible provides instance after instance of God very personally reminding his people of his truth. This is especially easy to see in the aptly-named Psalms of Lament. The authors of these psalms are in distress and having thoughts about their circumstances and about God that make their distress even worse. However, when they turn to

God for inspiration, he provides! Psalm 77 is a straightforward example. Asaph was groaning and sighing and even growing faint at the very thought of God (v. 3). However, he then prayerfully reflected: "My heart meditated and my spirit asked" (v. 6). God reminded Asaph of all the ways he had shown up for his people in the past, and Asaph was reassured and heartened.

There are many ways in which God speaks to us personally. How many times have you heard a sermon and known God was speaking directly to you? You were personally encouraged or saw a first step in a new direction. God also speaks to us by applying to our hearts what we read in Scripture or by reminding us of a passage with which we're familiar and now see a new application. He speaks to us through his people and his songs – see Colossians 3:16. In fact, when we speak the truth in love to one another, we actually grow in Christ (Ephesians 4:15-16).

It is my experience – and the experience of many people I've encouraged – that when we prayerfully and humbly ask for God's help in discerning how our thinking has departed from his thinking, God makes that clear. (See James 1:5.) The clarity may not come at the very moment we ask, but sometimes it does! Sometimes a few days or even weeks later, we hear a sermon or a hymn, or a friend says something, that the Holy Spirit uses to address our request for very particular wisdom.

When we prayerfully and humbly ask for God's help in discerning how our thinking has departed from his thinking, God makes that clear.

A very strange example of this occurred when I was struggling to overcome a persistent self-loathing that frequently led to my not wanting to even get out of bed in the morning. I had begun to "prayerfully ponder" what beliefs might be resulting in such a painful pattern. While preparing for a Bible study, I read the passage in Luke where Pilate, against his better judgment, succumbed to the loud, insistent shouts of the people to crucify an innocent Jesus. As I read this, it popped into my head that I, too, was allowing "insistent shouts" to influence me. The shouts were from my culture, trying to tempt me to consider myself ugly and unworthy because I don't fit into a size 9 skirt. I was a little shocked by what seemed to be a trivial application of so grave an event in the life of Christ. Nevertheless, I believe the Holy Spirit was willing to use the passage I was reading to speak to me about how I was letting myself be controlled by false beliefs.

If you found it difficult to answer the reflection questions, ask others who know you to suggest what they think might have been the beliefs that arose at the time you first started struggling with that troubling emotion or unwanted behavior. If you're going through this book with others, consider how others answered the reflection questions and see if someone else's experience might be similar to yours. Listening to the experiences of others can be a boon to each person who is working through this book in a small group context.

Homework

Take a piece of paper – this might take more than one piece! – and divide the paper into three columns with these headers:

Significant Event   *Lie(s) I Believed*   *God's Truth*[6]

Ask God to bring to your mind whatever events have led to you believing something that doesn't align with the truth about God, yourself, or life. Write those events in the first column. Then "prayerfully ponder" what you may have believed as a result of each event and write those beliefs in the second column. Again, ask God to bring to your mind Scripture passages that correct erroneous beliefs. Here's an example:

Significant Event	Lie(s) I Believed	God's Truth
Mom said I'm just like Dad and have no creativity.	*I do not have any creativity and never will.*	*Genesis 1:27* *Philippians 4:13*

Homework Follow-up

1. What was a stunning lie you believed to be true?

2. How might one of your beliefs motivate negative emotions and/or unwanted behaviors?

3. What reassurances from Scripture counter your erroneous belief?

Comments on the Homework

When small group members or individuals I'm mentoring insist, "God's not telling me anything about what my false beliefs are," my temptation is to make very pointed suggestions about what I suspect are the underlying beliefs. However, as much as I believe Christ uses fellow members of his body as a means of communicating with his people (exhortation, admonishing, teaching, preaching, etc.), I also believe it's very important for Christians to take care that they don't try to do the Holy Spirit's job for him, so I don't always offer my opinions. God is working in different areas of people's lives at different times. If now is not the time for a "word" from God about the beliefs that underlie an area of struggle, you can bet now *is* the time that God is at work in some other area within that person. Forcing the issue may actually be opposing God.

That said, here are a few suggestions if you feel you're not getting anywhere with hearing from God about your erroneous beliefs. First, honestly assess whether you are truly in submission to God. This does not mean that you absolutely never sin. This means that your desire is for God to have his way in your life.

Surrender to God is intimidating for many folks – it is for me. But to experience freedom, we must come to accept that God wants what is best for us and give him the access to our souls that he needs in order to change us. You may have to pray a prayer similar to the one I often pray: "Lord, you know I'm afraid of what you may do, but I'm totally at your disposal. I'm yours and

It's very important for Christians to take care that they don't try to do the Holy Spirit's job for him.

want you to work in me and through me in whatever ways you see fit." God is still working on some of my erroneous beliefs about him. Even though it is sometimes frightening, I am acknowledging that God is the Potter and I am the clay. Just as the old hymn says, my prayer is, "Have thine own way, Lord."[7]

Another barrier to hearing from God about the beliefs that are motivating your emotions and behaviors is engaging in willful, blatant sin. There are some activities in which we can be involved that result in our getting so spiritually out of whack that we cannot hear from God. Or, we can be under God's discipline, which may include his not speaking to us about those areas where we most want to hear from him until we accept what he is already telling us about the areas in which we have refused to obey. (For an example, see 1 Samuel 28:6-18.) But, hyper-conscientious people, beware! Do not think you have to quit every "besetting sin" before you can hear from God. Examples of the types of activities that disrupt our hearing from God are sins such as willful sexual immorality, involvement in the occult, or stealing. Experience tells me that God tends to deal with such "biggies" before working on the struggles that we may find most bothersome.

A barrier to hearing from God about the beliefs that are motivating emotions and behaviors is engaging in willful, blatant sin.

2   FREEING TRUTH ABOUT GOD THE FATHER AND GOD THE SON

"Let's start at the very beginning. A very good place to start."[1]
"In the beginning God…[2]   "In the beginning was the Word, and the Word was with God, and the Word was God."[3]
"I can't even think about God as Father; I think of him as Shepherd."[4]

Not only does all of creation start with God, but also all of your perceptions about yourself and how to go about life start with who you believe God to be and how you relate to him – or, more importantly, how you think God relates to you. Most of the discouraged Christians I've met did not realize they were operating under some false assumptions about God, his character, his purposes, and his feelings about them. Wait, I'm not going to say "most"; it's actually ALL, including me. On this side of heaven, we really can't fully know God, can we? That means it's not all that shocking to think we might not have a totally accurate view of God as he really is. (See 1 Corinthians 13:12.)

Fabulously, graciously, God has provided us with all we really need to know about him through his Word, the Bible. And the greatest revelation he gives us in the Bible is about Jesus. This is what Jesus said to his disciples about himself and his Father:

> If you really know me, you will know my Father as well. From now on, you do know him and have seen him. … Anyone who has seen me has seen the Father. (John 14: 7, 9)

When we see Jesus in the pages of the New Testament, we are actually looking at God in the flesh! But our preconceived notions about God can really distort what we see about God when we read about Jesus. I used to read nearly every red-lettered word in the Bible as Jesus yelling at people, being impatient with them, and heaving huge sighs of disappointment. Now, if you'd asked me to name aspects of the character of God, I'd have given you a very theologically accurate list: holy, sovereign, omnipotent, omniscient, omnipresent, immutable, merciful, and loving. However, my behavior betrayed what I really believed, that God is difficult to please, impatient, expects ever more of me, disdainful, and disgusted with me. I kept trying harder and harder to do what I thought would please him, but I never felt it was enough. I always saw myself as falling way short and hated myself for that.

When a biblical counselor asked me to write out adjectives that described how my father had related to me as a child and to compare those adjectives to how I believed God related to me, that was quite an eye-opener. I had been imposing onto God what I had experienced with significant authority figures. My dad had always been a faithful financial provider, and I had no problem believing God would supply my material needs. Also, my dad had a very tough life and was pretty easily irritated by "stupid kid stuff," often telling me, "You should have known better than that." But frequently I really hadn't known better because no one had told me. I had to try to keep one step ahead of whatever I thought Dad would want me to do or not do, and I frequently

Our preconceived notions about God can really distort what we see about God when we read about Jesus.

guessed wrong. This was exactly how I was trying to behave with God, guessing at what might make him happier with me.

Not only do we have a tendency to confuse our heavenly Father with our earthly fathers, but also there are a number of other factors that set us up for seeing God as less loving, trustworthy, and interested in our struggles than he truly is. First of all, as a result of our sinful nature, which we inherited from our distant ancestor Adam, we were born separated from God. In our most formative years, as any mother will tell you, we believed ourselves to be the center of the universe, and we did not have a close, dependent, personal relationship with God. For almost all of us, all we had to go on regarding understanding what God is like were the models our authority figures set for us and the messages we got from our environment.

If you did not grow up in a Christian home, it is likely that one of the few facts you learned about God was that God is almost always referred to as "he." You put two and two together to come up with the belief that God is probably a lot like the significant man or men in your life. This would be even more the case if you were exposed to references to God as "Father." Also, you probably drew many conclusions about God from the events in your life. When I was 16, after my stepmother attempted suicide, I wrote in my diary, "God, don't you see what a cruel game you're playing?" I interpreted the negative events I'd experienced as indicative of God being cruel. To this day, I struggle with that well-entrenched false belief about God.

You probably drew many conclusions about God from the events in your life.

If you grew up in a family that attended church, there are all sorts of inaccurate doctrines and ideas about the nature and character of God to which you may have been exposed. I have been a Christian for over 50 years and, as a result of working in interdenominational Christian organizations for many of those years, I've been exposed to dozens of Christian denominations and sects. Many denominations emphasize God's judgment over his mercy and his demand for holiness over his love and forgiveness. A lot of the preaching I've heard over the years has attempted to use guilt to motivate the believer to good works. The underlying message is that God is disapproving and expects much, much more than what we are giving to him or doing for him. My own feeling that I could never do enough to please God led to tremendous emotional difficulties for several years during the early part of my Christian walk.

But why do our perceptions about God matter when it comes to overcoming struggles with negative emotions and ungodly behaviors? Because without an accurate view of God and his role in every aspect of our lives, we do not access the only lasting solutions to our problems, which are all found in the context of a relationship with and reliance upon God. When we believe that God is disgusted and impatient with our failures, we find it difficult to invite God to help us with our struggles. We don't trust that God will do anything even if we do invite him to help. Often, we have prayed and prayed for God's help to have a more "victorious life" yet have seen no evidence that God has answered those prayers. This adds to the belief that God does not care. Because of erroneous beliefs about God, we are either not asking for God's help at all or are asking him to help in ways that do not provide permanent solutions to underlying spiritual and emotional issues. Therefore, the starting point for experiencing real freedom must be to overhaul one's view of God and his desire to be lovingly involved in every area of life.

So, if we admit to the possibility that our view of God is less than accurate and needs to change, how do we become acquainted with him as he truly is? The best place to start is in God's Word, the Bible. However, as mentioned above, many people, in reading the Bible, take it through their own mental filters that inadvertently lead them to interpret Scripture in such a way that it reinforces their negative perceptions about God. At a turning point in my Christian walk, I was asked by a counselor to read the Gospels assuming that Christ was always using a pleasant, understanding tone of voice.

Instead of looking at Scripture using only our own mental lens, which may be colored by erroneous assumptions or vague notions about God, we can see his true nature through Scripture when we ask him to illuminate what we're reading and when we remember to interpret whatever we read in the Bible through the filter of the Cross. If God so loved us that he sacrificed to the extent of suffering death on a cross, if the Cross is indeed the focal point of all history, then all that we read in Scripture about him should be colored by that immeasurable love. So often, the harsh tones and impatience we attribute to God are really the product of our imposing onto Scripture the preconceived notions we have because of our experiences with others. Also, we need to remember that it is the work of the Holy Spirit, not our unaided intellect, that makes clear the truths of Scripture (John 16:13-15). When we are willing to set aside our prejudices, keep the Cross as our focal point, and ask God to show us himself as we read his Word, he will do exactly that.

In looking to the Bible to understand God's attitude toward me and my struggles, Jesus's interaction with the woman at the well (John 4:4-30) helped me put more confidence in how God accepts me and has mercy on me even though I have sinned. Jesus knew everything about her, right down to the number of husbands who had rejected her and the sinful situation she was then in, but he didn't say a single harsh word to her. In fact, it appears that she was the very first person to whom he revealed that he was the Christ, the Messiah. Throughout his ministry, Jesus gently drew to himself those who were committing very obvious sins. Yes, he had some harsh words for a select few, but it is important that we realize who they were. Only the Pharisees, who were heaping regulations on top of the Mosaic Law and making it harder for people to be in relationship with God, were called "whitewashed tombs" and "vipers." These were stiff-necked, hypocritical leaders who needed to be called to task, not broken people who realized their shortcomings and their need for God's forgiveness and grace. (See Matthew 23:13-36.)

So, looking at Scripture through the lens of the Cross, let's consider some information God reveals in his Word about himself.

- God is our "Abba," which means he is our father. See Romans 8:15-17 and Galatians 4:4-7. Paul uses a term here that was used by small children in talking with their fathers and "denotes childlike intimacy and trust."[5] We can trust God as a small child unreservedly trusts a beloved and respected dad. However, unlike some of our dads, God never changes or fails in his nurturing care for us. (See Hebrews 13:5-6.)
- God loves us unconditionally (Romans 5:8; 1 John 4:19). God's love is not based upon how well we perform for him. His love predates any of our good deeds. His love is due to *his* character, not ours.
- God desires nothing but the best for us (Jeremiah 29:11; Romans 8:28). God does not want you to live in bondage to negative emotions, compulsions, or obsessions of any sort. He is in the process of guiding you into being more and more like Jesus, and he's doing this because that is what will be most fulfilling for *you*.

So often, the harsh tones and impatience we imagine are God's are really the product of our imposing onto Scripture the preconceived notions we have because of our experiences in life and with others.

- God *knows* you intimately (Psalm 139) and delights in you (Psalm 18:19; Zephaniah 3:17). Delighting in someone is not just a "by the way" feeling. It is taking active pleasure in that person. When we feel disgusted with ourselves, it is very hard to accept that God is delighting in us, but God, more than anyone, knows who he created us to be. He knows how truly delightful we are and sees us that way when all we see are our faults.
- Because God is love (1 John 4:8), we can view the "love passage" in 1 Corinthians 13 as a description of God. For a clearer view of God, read 1 Corinthians 13, replacing the word "love" (or "charity") with "God."
- God is not condemning of you (Romans 5:8 and 8:1). He does not condemn you for your emotions or your behaviors. He is at work in you to bring you into line with his purposes (Philippians 2:13). He knows he is able to do this (Philippians 1:6).
- God does not view you in the same way that most people view you (1 Samuel 16:7; 2 Corinthians 5:12b). He does not look at your outward appearance and accomplishments as measurements of your worth. He is looking at your heart, and your heart desires to obey him, even if you have not yet found a way to do that fully.

What the Bible says about God is truer than what you feel or what you experience.

It is likely that you don't yet *feel* all these facts about God's attitude toward you to be true. That is fine. What the Bible says about God is truer than what you feel or what you experience. And, the truth will win out if we keep the truth in mind. (See Philippians 4:8 and Colossians 3:2.) Here's where what I call "prayerful pondering" comes in. Over the next days and weeks, think about and pray about what God is really like. Ask God to reveal himself in special ways to you. My experience was that, when I prayerfully pondered God's character and love, I realized he had been revealing his personal love and care for me all along, but I didn't have the mindset to perceive it. When I started asking God for little reassurances that he really is as good and kind as the Scripture passages referenced above would indicate, he did some pretty interesting things. The one I found most humorous was that every time I'd go for a walk, I'd run across at least one penny. At the time I started finding these pennies (without looking for them at all), my bright red hair had not yet faded with age, and the thought came to my mind that God was telling me, "You are my little copper penny." This was certainly a daddy-like expression of affection, and I secretly (because I felt too silly about it to tell anyone) cherished the childlike feeling I got each time I stumbled onto one of those pennies. Oh, by the way, I take walks several times a week and this penny-finding experience went on for about ten years, followed by finding dimes and nickels (bet you can guess why the coins changed, and it wasn't due to inflation).

The truth about God the Father is that we see him best through God the Son, and that is exactly why Jesus walked the earth, to reveal the Father. When we understand the truth about God's unconditional love, kindness, and mercy, we find the freedom to truly trust him to set us free.

Reflection

1. What people and events influenced your view of God and in what ways was that view affected?

2. To what degree do you "buy into" the fact that God unconditionally loves you? What are the barriers to believing that to be true? (For example, are you using your belief that he is condemning you as a means to keep yourself from sinning?)

What Others Have Experienced

It can be fairly easy to see how what authority figures did or said to us during childhood affected how we expect God to act. For example, a woman told me she knew God thought of her as a "pig." When she thought this through, she realized her dad had called her that many times, trying to motivate her to lose weight. Many people have experienced being yelled at or angrily assaulted by a parent. For them, the expectation that God will get hotly angry with them over even small missteps is a default assumption.

Some of our life experiences may be more subtle and seem relatively innocuous but nevertheless profoundly influence our view of God. When considering how she'd assumed God felt about her, a woman who came from a "good home" told me how her father had frequently praised other children for qualities and characteristics she felt she lacked but very rarely praised her for anything. She realized this was likely at the root of why she had always felt sure God had seen her as less acceptable than others.

For some, it wasn't so much what their parents did as what their parents didn't do that influenced their perceptions about God. Many tell how their fathers just weren't really present at all or that their fathers interacted with them very little. As a result, they believed God was indifferent toward them or that they had to "make a big splash" to get God's attention. For some, parents noticed only negative or outlandish behavior. A small group participant, who suffered from Type II diabetes, blurted out that she ate a quart of ice cream every night just to get God's attention.

Many people who struggle with depression and/or compulsive behaviors hate themselves so much that they cannot imagine God feels any affection for them. They judge themselves harshly or have been judged harshly by parents and assume God is doing likewise. However, Scripture plainly tells us that God's kindness toward us and acceptance of us is what actually leads to godly behavior. See Romans 2:4, Ephesians 2:8-10, and 1 John 4:19. When I see someone deeply struggling with trying to overcome a persistent sinful behavior or painful recurring emotion, I also see God pulling that person toward him and basically saying, "Come over here to me. You keep trying to fix yourself, but you have no power to do that. Come to me and experience my tender care. I do have the power to transform you and want to have a close relationship with you." Over and over again, God has made clear that he designed us to operate out of a loving relationship with him (1 John 4:9). He is not waiting for us to make ourselves better before he'll

God's kindness toward us and acceptance of us is what actually leads to godly behavior.

love us. Instead, he loved us before we ever thought of loving him, and through his love we are gradually becoming who he created us to be. (We'll look at this in more detail in Chapter 4.)

Homework

Read the booklet *FatherCare*, which is reprinted in its entirety, with permission, in Addendum One at the back of this book (beginning on page 141). Take the "Relationship Test" on pages 173 through 176, and complete at least one of the "Characteristics of the Father" studies on pages 178 through 186.

Homework Follow-up

1. What is new in your thinking about what God is like and how he feels about you and your struggles?

2. What old beliefs about God have you now rejected?

Comments on the Homework

What is important here is a willingness to believe differently about God. This involves a willingness to admit to having erroneous beliefs about God. Among the people I've encouraged over the years, many – especially those who are older in their faith – have a difficult time admitting to the possibility that they think anything at all negative about God. They feel this in some way insults God. However, it's really pretty silly to think that we could be born in sin, live in a sin-filled world, and have Satan constantly lying to us about God and still have a 100 percent accurate view of God. Also, God is aware of our doubts and erroneous beliefs, whether we admit them or not, so what's the harm in owning up?

In addition to the fear of insulting God, there can be a fear of God's disapproval – even more disapproval than we already suspect God has for us – if we admit we doubt his character in any way. However, look at the numerous psalms in which people basically told God he was not doing a good job, he was forgetting them, he was being unfair, or he was failing to live up to his promises. Not only did God not strike these people down for writing such sentiments, he included their criticisms in his Word! Also, we see in these psalms a pattern of people admitting to God exactly how they feel about him and then being willing to think through the truth of the matter. Psalm 73 is a good example of this. Here was a guy who was totally put out with God because the wicked had it "made in the shade" and he'd been keeping himself pure only to find his lot in life wasn't all that great. He even said that when he thought about all this, he became a "brute beast" before God. When I read this, I picture an enraged Incredible Hulk-like person.

We see in these psalms a pattern of people admitting to God exactly how they feel about him and then being willing to think through the truth of the matter.

Aaaarrrr! But when this psalmist stopped to think about it – when he went into the house of the Lord and got perspective – he realized God was totally faithful and just. It's important to realize that if we don't admit we're wrong in our thinking about God, we won't ever turn to what's right.

The hardest part about rejecting old beliefs is that we tend to make our emotions our final authority. My emotions constantly tell me that God is going to do something cruel and that it's just around the corner. This is an old emotional habit I developed as a result of some painful childhood experiences and is an attempt to avoid feeling devastating disappointment. My reasoning is: *If I think bad things are just around the corner, I won't be surprised and dejected when they happen; I'll be emotionally prepared.* Even though experience tells me that thinking this way has never really prepared me well for unhappy events and losses, every time I'm especially happy, thoughts about impending God-wrought tragedy flood in like waves.

When I find myself having negative thoughts about God and his character, I have learned to reason in the following way: *Either God is good or he is not good. If he is not good, we are all doomed. If he is not good, why did Christ die on the cross? Okay, God is good and not cruel. So, even if something "bad" happens, God will give me the grace to handle it and it will work out for my ultimate good.* To some, this may seem to be "mental gymnastics," but I believe this is exactly what Paul was talking about when he said to "put off the old self" and "put on the new self" (Ephesians 4:22-24). And, I believe it is the Holy Spirit who reminds me to rethink my beliefs when my old emotional habit of doubting God's goodness and expecting the worst from him kicks in. Instead of going by how I feel, with the help of the Spirit, I turn to what is true, which ultimately changes how I feel.

You too may need to take steps toward making God's Word your final authority instead of relying on how you feel to tell you what's "true." Just like the suggested prayer from *FatherCare*, below, you may need to repeatedly "put off" your wrong ideas about God and "put on" the truth according to Scripture. Ask God to help you in this and to bring the truth to your mind. He is, after all, more interested in you knowing the truth about him than you are!

Instead of going by how I feel, with the help of the Spirit, I turn to what is true, which ultimately changes how I feel.

> My Father, I always considered You an unloving God, but now I know that You are a *loving* Father to me. I choose now in faith to put off my false belief and I choose to believe that You are loving to me. I choose to believe what Your Word has to say about You rather than my feelings or reason or past experiences, and I know that Your Word says that You love me as a person and that your love is not based on my performance or on what I have or achieve. Thank You, my Father, for loving me unconditionally[6]

3   FREEING TRUTH ABOUT GOD THE SPIRIT

"Holy Spirit, breathe on me"[1]
"And I will ask the Father, and he will give you another advocate to help you and be with you forever—the Spirit of truth."[2]
"Praying to the Holy Spirit is wrong. I pray to the Father only."[3]

If you've been in evangelical circles for any length of time, you've probably noticed what I've noticed: There are two prevailing attitudes about the Holy Spirit. I refer to them as "the uncomfortable" and "whoa-ha." Thanks to real and perceived emotionalism and excesses among the whoa-ha folks, there are a number of evangelicals who are very uncomfortable with the topic of the Holy Spirit. And thanks to the dearth of teaching on and reliance upon the Holy Spirit, as well as a lack of passion for God being displayed by the uncomfortable folks, there are a number of people who overdo shows of emotion in worship (whoa-ha!) and call it a work of the Holy Spirit. For the sake of finding freedom through knowing the truth, in this chapter, we will look at some very freeing truths about an often-misunderstood member of the Trinity – misunderstood by the uncomfortable and the whoa-ha and everyone in between.

All the way back in Genesis 1, God started referring to himself as "us" and "we." Genesis 1:1 tells us that God was in the very beginning, and then verse 2 mentions the presence of the Spirit of God. By verse 26, God makes man in "our" image. In light of John 1:1, in which Jesus is called the "Word," we can look back over Genesis 1 and see that "Word" each time God *spoke* something into existence. All three persons of the Trinity have always been present and together. As Deuteronomy 6:4, says, "the LORD is one." But in a way that our finite minds cannot completely understand, God is three in one. We have a pretty decent grasp on who God the Father is, and we see how God shared in our humanity in God the Son, but who is God the Holy Spirit?

We have a pretty decent grasp on who God the Father is, and we see how God shared in our humanity in God the Son, but who is God the Holy Spirit?

Let's look at some ways in which Jesus spoke of the Holy Spirit. With each of these bullet points, think through whether you see the Holy Spirit in the same way Jesus described him. Is the Spirit an individual to you? Do you expect the Spirit to do what Jesus said the Spirit does?

- The Spirit is the "Spirit of your Father" – Matthew 10:20
- The Spirit can and does speak through Jesus's disciples (including you) – Matthew 10:20
- The ministry of Jesus was driven and empowered by the Spirit – Matthew 12:28
- The Spirit spoke through David in the Psalms – Matthew 22:43
- We are to baptize new believers in the names of the Father, Son, *and* Spirit – Matthew 28:19
- The Spirit teaches Jesus's disciples what to say at the proper time – Luke 12:12
- The Spirit is the agent, who brings about new birth in believers – John 3:5-6, 8
- The Spirit gives believers true, eternal life – John 6:63
- Jesus's words were also the words of the Spirit – John 6:63
- When Jesus spoke of "rivers of living water" flowing within his believers, he was referring to the Spirit – John 7:37-39
- People who believe in Jesus receive the Holy Spirit – John 7:39
- The Spirit is "another advocate" (like Jesus), whom the Father gives to true believers in Christ – John 14:16-17

- Jesus referred to the Spirit in a personal way with "he" and "him," so the Spirit is a person (as opposed to a force or power) – John 14:16-17
- If you believe in Jesus, the Holy Spirit lives with you and in you – John 14:17
- The Spirit is how Jesus continues with his believers after his ascension – John 14:16-19
- The Spirit teaches us and reminds us of what Jesus said. (The Spirit reminded the authors of the Gospels about what Jesus had said while on earth.) – John 14:26
- The Spirit testified about Jesus and still does – John 15:26
- The Spirit guides believers into truth, glorifies Jesus, and relays the truths of Jesus to his followers – John 16:12-15

How did this information line up with what you believe about the Holy Spirit? He is as much God as the Father and the Son, and he plays a very important role in the lives of believers. But, why is it important to clearly view the Spirit in order to experience the freedom you already have in Christ? Because it is by the Spirit that you will be led into the very truth that sets you free. When you realize that the Holy Spirit is the means by which Jesus resides in you and guides you (John 14:17; Romans 8:9, 11; 1 Corinthians 6:19), then you can more clearly understand how it's possible for you to live by God's power, rather than through your own power.

In our own strength, we do not have the ability to change ourselves in any truly meaningful or significant way. Jesus made this abundantly clear:

> "Remain in me, as I also remain in you. No branch can bear fruit by itself; it must remain in the vine. Neither can you bear fruit unless you remain in me. I am the vine; you are the branches. If you remain in me and I in you, you will bear much fruit; apart from me you can do nothing." (John 15:4-5)

Apart from Jesus enabling you through his Spirit, change is not possible.

Nothing! Nothing! Apart from Jesus enabling you through his Spirit, change is not possible, fruit is not possible (see Galatians 5:22-23 for what the fruit is), and freedom is not possible. When you know the truth about the Spirit, you know the truth about who enables you to know truth and who empowers you to enjoy freedom from what is crippling you in your day-to-day life. Even your ability to hope is dependent upon the Spirit:

> May the God of hope fill you with all joy and peace as you trust in him, so that you may overflow with hope by the power of the Holy Spirit. (Romans 15:13)

Your ability to turn away from fleshly (unspiritual, ungodly, self-centered) behaviors and emotions is dependent upon the Spirit:

> For if you live according to the flesh, you will die; but if by the Spirit you put to death the misdeeds of the body, you will live. (Romans 8:13)

> So I say, walk by the Spirit, and you will not gratify the desires of the flesh. (Galatians 5:16)

In discussing the Holy Spirit with struggling believers, a question along these lines frequently comes up: "How do I know I'm filled with the Holy Spirit?" Or similarly, "How do I walk/live in the Spirit?" These questions arise because of teachings on Ephesians 5:18, which appear to indicate that one can be filled or not filled with the Spirit. First, it is important to understand that you would not even believe in Jesus if the Holy Spirit hadn't opened your eyes to the truth of the

Gospel. When you believe in Jesus, you are "born of the Spirit" (John 3:6-8), and the Holy Spirit takes up residence within you (1 Corinthians 6:19). Second, the context of Ephesians 5:18 needs to be taken into account when interpreting the concept of being "filled with the Spirit." The context is drunkenness. Paul is exhorting believers to see that drunkenness does not fill us in a truly meaningful way and can even preclude the work of the Spirit in and through us. He wants believers to see that our "intoxication" should be in the power and presence of the Spirit. Intoxication with alcohol is an example of how we can grieve the Holy Spirit (Ephesians 4:30) and "quench" his work within us (1 Thessalonians 5:19). The issue is not whether we are filled with the Spirit or whether we are more filled or less filled, but whether we are acknowledging and yielding to the Spirit who is already within us.

When we insist on doing things our way rather than relying upon the truth provided by God in his Word and on the enabling power provided by his Spirit, we are not walking in step with the Spirit (Galatians 5:25); and therefore, we are hindering the work of the Spirit in us and through us. Knowing the truth about the Spirit – that he is Jesus within us, enabling us to see, remember, and apply truth – is freeing because then we realize our freedom is God's doing. We need only cooperate with the Spirit who is guiding us into that freedom.

A Word about Faith

Once you know the truth – about God the Father, about the Son, about the indwelling Spirit – it takes faith to believe that truth. Many people tend to think *they* are responsible for having enough faith to live out what they believe. However, Scripture makes clear that even your faith is given by God (Ephesians 2:8-9). Our reliance on God includes looking to him to supply the faith we need.

There is no shame in admitting to faltering faith. Sometimes it can be difficult to believe what God says about himself and what God promises in the Bible. Different people have different areas in which their faith is weaker, usually because of their experiences and how they've interpreted those experiences. If you've experienced physical or sexual abuse, it can be quite difficult to understand, let alone have faith in, all the Bible passages that promise God will protect you or that God is mindful of you and your welfare (for example, Psalm 91). If you've repeatedly engaged in immoral acts even after you believed in Jesus, it's difficult to believe that God will enable you to behave in godly ways when sorely tempted (1 Corinthians 10:13).

Our difficulties with having the faith to believe the truth that sets us free is one more evidence of what Jesus said in John 15:5: "apart from me, you can do nothing." Nothing means nothing. We are deeply humbled by this reality, and yet we can also be deeply relieved. I don't have enough faith to believe God's freeing truths, but Jesus in me does! The Holy Spirit is so close that he's in us, enabling us to believe as we rely on him, not on ourselves.

If you believe Jesus is the Son of God who atoned for your sin, then God has already given you faith or you wouldn't believe even that. Now that you do believe, you can say with the desperate man in Mark 9, "I do believe; help me overcome my unbelief!" (v. 24). Oh, what a relief it is to know it has never really been *my* faith; it is given to me by God!

Over and over again I hear myself telling people that faith is *not* easy. It *is* difficult to believe in someone you can't see or audibly hear. It is difficult to reject the beliefs you've formed because of your experiences. But you can go to God and ask for the faith to believe and trust in him and

There is no shame in admitting to faltering faith.

The more we know God as revealed in Jesus and as attested to by his Spirit, the more we will trust him over our own understanding.

the truth in his Word. The need to understand God and his character is the first truth covered in this book because your understanding of God is the foundation for every aspect of your Christian life and growth. The counselor who most influenced me in living in freedom often said, "You won't trust someone you don't know." The more we know God as revealed in Jesus and as attested to by his Spirit, the more we will trust him over our own understanding.

> Trust in the LORD with all your heart and lean not on your own understanding; in all your ways submit to him, and he will make your paths straight. Do not be wise in your own eyes; fear the LORD and shun evil. (Proverbs 3:5-7)

It really is impossible for us to be wise apart from "the only wise God" (Romans 16:27). God has given us a way to access his wisdom – in his Word, with our understanding of his Word enabled by his Spirit, the Counselor, who guides us into truth (John 16:13). God has revealed his empathy and compassion for us in Jesus, who opened the way for us to fearlessly approach God for all we need, even for faith (Hebrews 4:14-16).

A Word about *Feeling* the Spirit

A much-repeated complaint I've heard is, "I'm never moved by the Spirit." A similar objection is, "I can't tell if I'm in the Spirit or in the flesh." These statements indicate a misunderstanding about living a life of faith in Christ. Most people get things backward by validating what they believe by how they feel. If they feel moved to extend love to a difficult person, then they are reassured that the Spirit is at work in them. This line of thinking also shows up in how people talk about their "worship experiences." For example, "The Spirit really showed up at church this morning" is said when many in attendance became tearful or raised their hands during the musical portion of the worship service. The mostly-unconscious thinking behind that sort of statement is, "If I feel emotionally moved to adore God and love others, then I know the Spirit is working in and through me." The inference is that if you don't feel these emotions, the Spirit is not at work. This would mean that the work and presence of the Holy Spirit is like a spigot that gets turned on and off – and that we have some sort of control over, or at least an accurate gauge for measuring, the presence of the Spirit.

Jesus promised his followers that he would be in them, and that happens through Jesus sending his Holy Spirit to live inside each believer.

> And I will ask the Father, and he will give you another advocate to help you and be with you forever—the Spirit of truth. … I will not leave you as orphans; I will come to you. Before long, the world will not see me anymore, but you will see me. Because I live, you also will live. On that day you will realize that I am in my Father, and you are in me, and I am in you. (John 14:16-20)

Whether or not we feel as though the Spirit is present in no way determines his presence.

This means that whether or not we *feel* as though the Spirit is present in no way determines his presence. Jesus's promise and his follow-through on that promise determines that the Spirit is present in each believer at all times.

> And I will put my Spirit in you and move you to follow my decrees and be careful to keep my laws. (Ezekiel 36:27)

> But very truly I tell you, it is for your good that I am going away. Unless I go away, the Advocate will not come to you; but if I go, I will send him to you. (John 16:7)

Each person who is "born again" (John 3:3) is the dwelling place of the Holy Spirit (1 Corinthians 6:19). This means our feelings of joy and tearful gratitude are not the evidence that the Spirit "showed up," but evidence of our greater awareness of his presence. Whether we *feel* the Spirit or not, we can rely fully on his power and presence in us.

The "Just Do It Gospel"

If you're like me and most of the tired Christians I've known, you've heard a number of sermons and read a number of articles that tell you what you should be doing because you're a believer – be kind to one another, show hospitality, be grateful, repent of every sin before you pray, love strangers, honor your parents, give more, etc. – you know, just do it! And the Scriptures associated with each of these to-do's are plainly cited. But you've lived your life long enough that you've discovered you can't *do* any of this at all well! (I've found that young people often feel as though they can – give 'em a little time...)

An oft-repeated assertion made in many evangelical writings can be paraphrased as, "You're saved by grace and now you live a life of obedience in gratitude for so great a salvation." But, wait, what if my gratitude ebbs and flows? Yes, there are a number of Scripture passages indicating that gratitude is a motivation for obedience; however, *my* gratitude will never be powerful enough to enable me to "be perfect as your heavenly Father is prefect" (Matthew 5:48). Only one person ever lived a perfect life, and that person has come to live within me, by his Spirit, empowering me to love and obey – even empowering my gratitude!

I recently read a short article about being kind to one another. The author pointed out many New Testament passages that exhort believers to be kind, as well as many benefits of being kind, both to believers and to those around them. The conclusion of the article was along the lines of "God is love, kindness is commanded and beneficial, so 'be ye kind one to another' (Ephesians 4:32, KJV)." In other words, just do it! I found that article to be very discouraging, even exhausting. I wanted to scream, "Have you met these people?!" Then I remembered what the author left out – John 15:5. Apart from Jesus, who dwells within me by his Spirit, I can do nothing! But, "I can do all things through him who strengthens me" (Philippians 4:13, ESV). The presence and power of God's Spirit within us enables us to experience the freedom God has already given, because "where the Spirit of the Lord is, there is freedom" (2 Corinthians 3:17).

Apart from Jesus, who dwells within me by his Spirit, I can do nothing!

Reflection

1. What is new in your thinking about who the Holy Spirit is and the role he plays in your path to experiencing freedom?

2. What old beliefs about the Holy Spirit have you now rejected?

What Others Have Experienced

So many lights go off when people realize the very personal presence of the Holy Spirit within them.

So many lights go off when people realize the very personal presence of the Holy Spirit within them and that they can rely on him to empower their choices and behaviors. They start asking the Spirit to guide them as they read Scripture, often realizing they have previously read into the Scripture negatives that simply are not there. The seemingly impossible to-dos of the New Testament become much less daunting when you realize God is interested in giving you the power to do what is needed in each situation.

The erroneous beliefs people frequently report having rejected in light of the scriptural truth about the Holy Spirit are:

- The Spirit is only active in people who heal others or pray in tongues.
- The Spirit is like the Force in "Star Wars."
- The Spirit leaves me when I sin.
- The Spirit guides me through my feelings.
- It's all up to me to figure out what God is saying through Scripture.
- Some people are more spiritual than others.

What a freeing revelation to know that God, by his Spirit, is at home, dwelling in each of his children, empowering transformation and freedom (2 Corinthians 3:17-18).

Homework

1. Fill in the blanks in the following study of New Testament verses regarding the person and work of the Holy Spirit. (An answer key is provided in Addendum Five on page 223.)

    a. Romans 5:5 _____

    b. Romans 8:6 _____

    c. Romans 8:11 _____

    d. Romans 8:15-16 and Galatians 4:6 _____

    e. Romans 8:26 _____

    f. 1 Corinthians 3:16 and Ephesians 2:22 _____

    g. 1 Corinthians 6:19 _____

    h. 1 Corinthians 12:4, 11 _____

    i. 2 Corinthians 1:22 and Ephesians 1:13-14 _____

    j. 2 Corinthians 3:17 _____

k. Galatians 5:16 _____

l. Galatians 5:22-23 _____

m. Ephesians 3:16 _____

n. Ephesians 6:17 _____

o. Philippians 3:3 _____

p. 1 Thessalonians 1:6 _____

q. 2 Thessalonians 2:13 _____

r. 2 Timothy 1:14 _____

s. Titus 3:5 _____

2. Read John 14:16-20, 26-27 and 16:13-15 and write who the Holy Spirit is to you as a believer.

Homework Follow-up

1. Share with another person an example of how the Spirit worked in your life this week. Would you have noticed the Spirit at work in this way if you had not changed your mind about the person and work of the Holy Spirit?

2. In what areas of your life would you like the Spirit's powerful help?

Comments on the Homework

A deeper understanding of the character and work of the Holy Spirit within the life of the believer causes people to feel a much greater intimacy with God. They'd had this intimacy all along, but they had not truly realized it. Knowing that the Spirit empowers and motivates believers highlights the many ways in which God is at work in and through us. We see God's inspiration in reminding us of a Bible passage when it was really needed at a particular moment.

A deeper understanding of the Holy Spirit causes people to feel a much greater intimacy with God.

We feel God's presence (which was always there but not always felt) when we find we are able to offer very loving and touching words to a friend or relative in distress. We realize that when we love, God is giving us that love through his Spirit within us. We rejoice that "God's love has been poured out into our hearts through the Holy Spirit" (Romans 5:5). Because the power is not from us, but from God, we know that we have the power to experience greater and greater freedom.

4 FREEING TRUTH ABOUT WHO YOU'VE BECOME AND WHY YOU STILL SIN ANYWAY

"I once was lost, but now I am found"[1]

"...God, who is rich in mercy, made us alive with Christ even when we were dead in transgressions..."[2]

"I'm just a dirty, rotten sinner saved by grace."[3]

According to 2 Corinthians 5:17, when we put our trust in Christ as Savior – when we become Christians – a dramatic change takes place. We become "new creations in Christ." For many Christians, however, it is very difficult to reconcile this verse with their day-to-day behaviors. "Old things are passed away; behold, all things are become new" (2 Corinthians 5:17b, KJV). Well, one of my "old things," which was quite an issue before I was a Christian, did not appear to "pass away" at all after my conversion! In fact, after I became a Christian, my compulsive overeating became worse, not better. I gained about 25 pounds during the first three months after I, at age 19, believed in Christ as my Savior.

It was not until I had some fairly extreme emotional problems during my mid-twenties that I was exposed to an explanation of what it truly means to be a "new creation." Up to that point, I had worked very hard to make myself into what I believed a "new creation" should be. I faithfully kept many "rules" regarding work, church participation, evangelism, daily Bible study, and prayer. To many I appeared to be a really good Christian, but my good works were largely powered by self-effort, and it was extremely exhausting. Eventually I ran out of steam. This sort of experience has occurred in the lives of many of the people I've had the opportunity to encourage in their Christian growth. For many, "being a Christian" ends up being very, very tiring and eventually impossible. They either bail out of "the Christian walk" altogether or go through cycles of trying harder to do better, followed by various levels of failure, and then trying even harder, followed by failure, etc., etc.

The way in which being a "new creation in Christ" was presented to me brought great freedom, as it has to many others. It involves, however, a view regarding the basic nature of human beings that causes debate among some Christians. The debate centers on whether human nature is seen through the lens of "dichotomy" (two parts: body and soul) or "trichotomy" (three parts: body, soul, and spirit). Although I can see the value in both camps, for our purposes here, and because it is my best understanding of Scripture, I'll be discussing a three-part ("trichotomous") nature of people, as mentioned in 1 Thessalonians 5:23 and Hebrews 4:12. The terms I'll be using, such as "body," "soul," and "spirit," have numerous and varying uses in Scripture, depending on context. The definitions I'm using in this chapter are:

> **Body**=whatever is material or has physical substance in a person. For example, the brain is physical but the mind is not, so the brain belongs to the body.
>
> **Soul**=the personality of an individual comprising thoughts, beliefs, decisions, and emotions. These immaterial aspects of a person (the mind, will, and

I appeared to be a really good Christian, but my many good works were largely powered by self-effort and it was extremely exhausting.

emotions) are not visible to the naked eye, although they can be discerned sometimes by what the body does, such as smile or make a snide remark.

Spirit=the innermost aspect of a person that is either alive or dead to God. If one is spiritually dead, there is a sense in which the spirit is still alive, but only to evil and its author, Satan. When a person is "born again," the human spirit is enlivened and awakened to God and becomes the very dwelling place of God through his Holy Spirit.

These definitions of "body," "soul," and "spirit" are not all-inclusive, but rather provide a somewhat simplified outline of human nature in order to better understand the concept of "new creation" and how being a "new creation" affects our experience of the freedom we already have in Christ.

When Adam ate of the forbidden fruit, God's pronouncement that Adam would "surely die" came to pass both instantly and eventually. Instantly, Adam's intimacy with God was lost – Adam hid from God. Adam spiritually died. Eventually Adam physically died, the process of dying having begun the at the moment he disobeyed God. What didn't die was the personality of Adam. Adam was still Adam – feeling, thinking, deciding. His personality persisted, even though it was devastatingly marred by sin and his separation from God. Everyone born since Adam and Eve – with one stunning and infinitely important exception – has been born into the condition that Adam was in after he bit into that forbidden fruit. We are born separated from God, spiritually dead and hurtling toward physical death.

Being "spiritually dead" has always seemed an inadequate term, since prior to being born again in Christ, we are actually quite spiritually alive, but alive to the wrong spirit! Here's how Paul puts it in Ephesians 2:1-2:

> As for you, you were dead in your transgressions and sins, in which you used to live when you followed the ways of this world and of the ruler of the kingdom of the air, the spirit who is now at work in those who are disobedient.

When we are not in Christ, we are actually ruled by Satan, who is at work in us to make us follow him and his ways!

When we are not in Christ, we are actually ruled by Satan, who is at work in us to make us follow him and his ways! This is downright alarming! Thank God for his grace in Jesus! Paul goes on to say in Ephesians 2:4-5:

> But because of his great love for us, God, who is rich in mercy, made us alive with Christ even when we were dead in transgressions—it is by grace you have been saved.

And when God made us alive with Christ, that really changed us! We went from being ruled by Satan and his ways to being a "new creation' in Christ (2 Corinthians 5:17) and "created to be like God in true righteousness and holiness" (Ephesians 4:24). In fact, we moved from being "slaves to sin" to being "slaves to righteousness."

> But thanks be to God that, though you used to be slaves to sin, you have come to obey from your heart the pattern of teaching that has now claimed your allegiance. You have been set free from sin and have become slaves to righteousness. (Romans 6:17-18)

Let's look at two diagrams that can help in understanding these three aspects of who we are – body, soul, and spirit. The diagram on page 38 shows that our "outer layer" is the body – or as the late biblical counselor Bill Gillham called it, our "earthsuit."[4] Within the body are the soul and spirit, with the spirit at our very core. Prior to becoming Christians, we are spiritually dead to God and alive to sin and Satan (as we've seen in Ephesians 2:1-2). This permeates our entire lives and imprints our souls (mind, will, and emotions) and bodies with ungodly thoughts, beliefs, and habits.

The diagram on page 39 shows how we change after we receive Christ. God takes up residence within us – in our spirit. We become spiritually 100 percent brand new. This is what 2 Corinthians 5:17 references. Because of our identification with the death of Christ on the cross, at the core of our being, all the bondage to Satan is broken. (See Romans 6:6-7.) Then, because of our identification with Christ's resurrection, we begin a new life with a transformed spirit, which has become a holy place where God actually dwells. (See Romans 8:9-11.) For the rest of our lives, we are participants in a process of the indwelling Holy Spirit transforming the rest of us – transforming our souls and our bodies – changing our false beliefs, erroneous thinking, and negative habits. Theologians refer to this process as "sanctification." When we put our trust in Christ's death and resurrection as the means for our eternal salvation, we are instantly spiritually "reborn." (See John 3:7.) From then on, we gradually become more and more Christ-like as we cooperate with the work of the indwelling Holy Spirit. (See 2 Corinthians 3:17-18.)

Because of our identification with the death of Christ on the cross, at the core of our being, all the bondage to Satan is broken.

This is not to say that our bodies won't continue to age and eventually die. Thank God that we will someday receive new, imperishable bodies (1 Corinthians 15:42). This does mean, however, that God helps us to overcome the physical dependencies – such as on drugs – that we developed while trying to maneuver through life without depending on him. It appears that some people are instantly delivered from dependencies at conversion, and for some, it is more gradual or comes later in their Christian experience. But, for every bondage, God is in the business of working it out of our lives and heading us toward freedom. (See John 8:36.)

In the diagram on page 39, I refer to our erroneous or sinful beliefs and thoughts and our negative emotional and physical habits as "sin measles." This is in order to address an unfortunate tendency people have to define themselves by their negative behaviors or emotions or by their sins. When someone has the measles, we do not say, "You are one big, red measle." In the same way, when a person becomes a "new creation in Christ" and continues to struggle with sin, we are mistaken when we say, "You are a dirty, rotten sinner." Rather, the person is a saint ("someone who is set apart for God's special purposes"[5]), a holy dwelling place of God, who still has sin in his or her soul and body. The Corinthians were engaging in sinful behaviors when Paul wrote to them and called them "sanctified in Christ Jesus" (1 Corinthians 1:2). They were "new creations," but they were still being influenced by the sin that remained within them and around them. Because we are "new creations," it is inappropriate for us to refer to ourselves with labels such as "compulsive eater," "liar," or "anger-aholic." At worst, we are saints who still behave at times in ways that are not totally in line with who we are spiritually and who we will be eternally. (See 1 John 3:2.)

WHAT YOU WERE LIKE BEFORE TRUSTING CHRIST

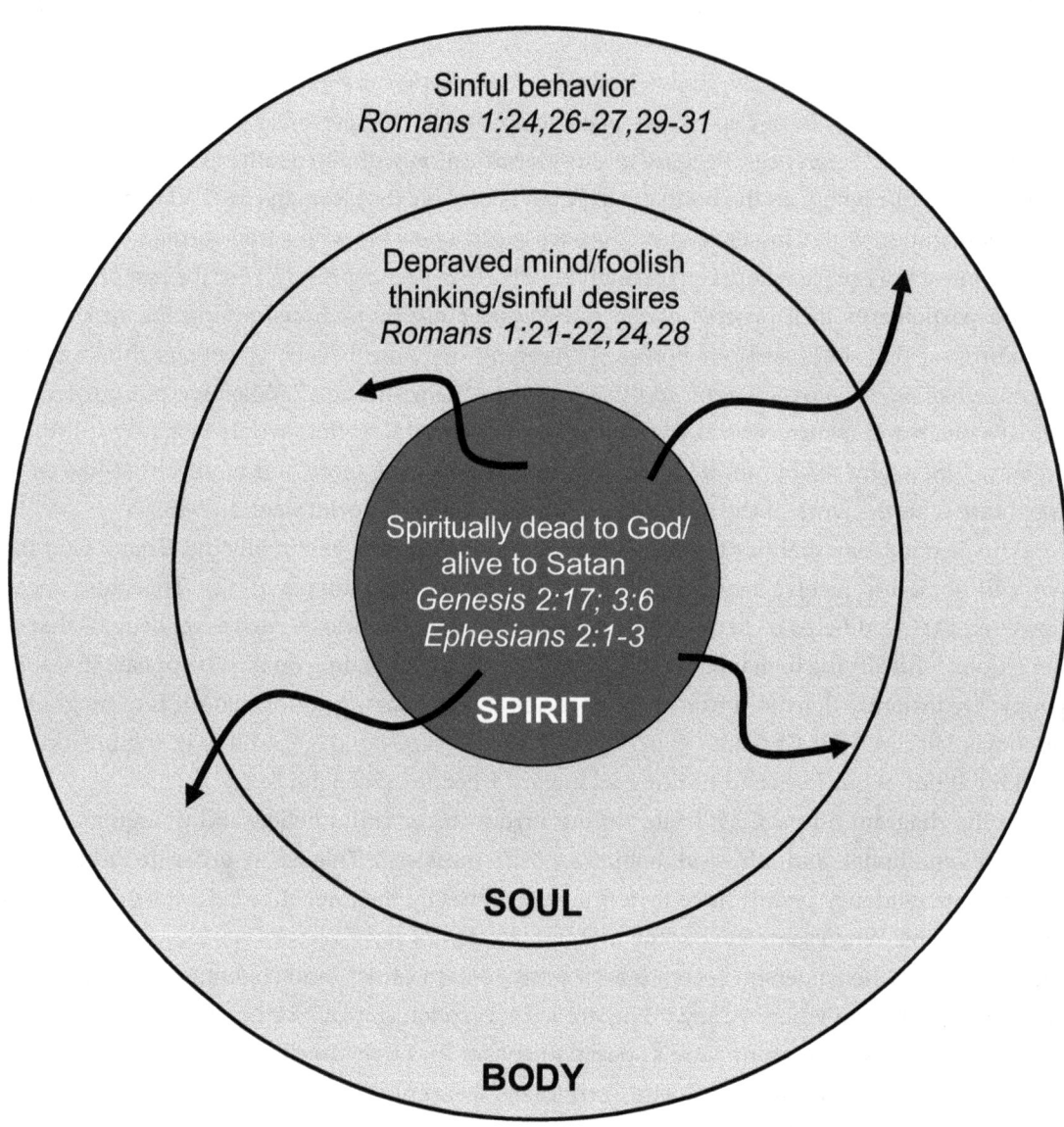

WHAT YOU ARE LIKE AFTER TRUSTING CHRIST
2 Corinthians 5:17

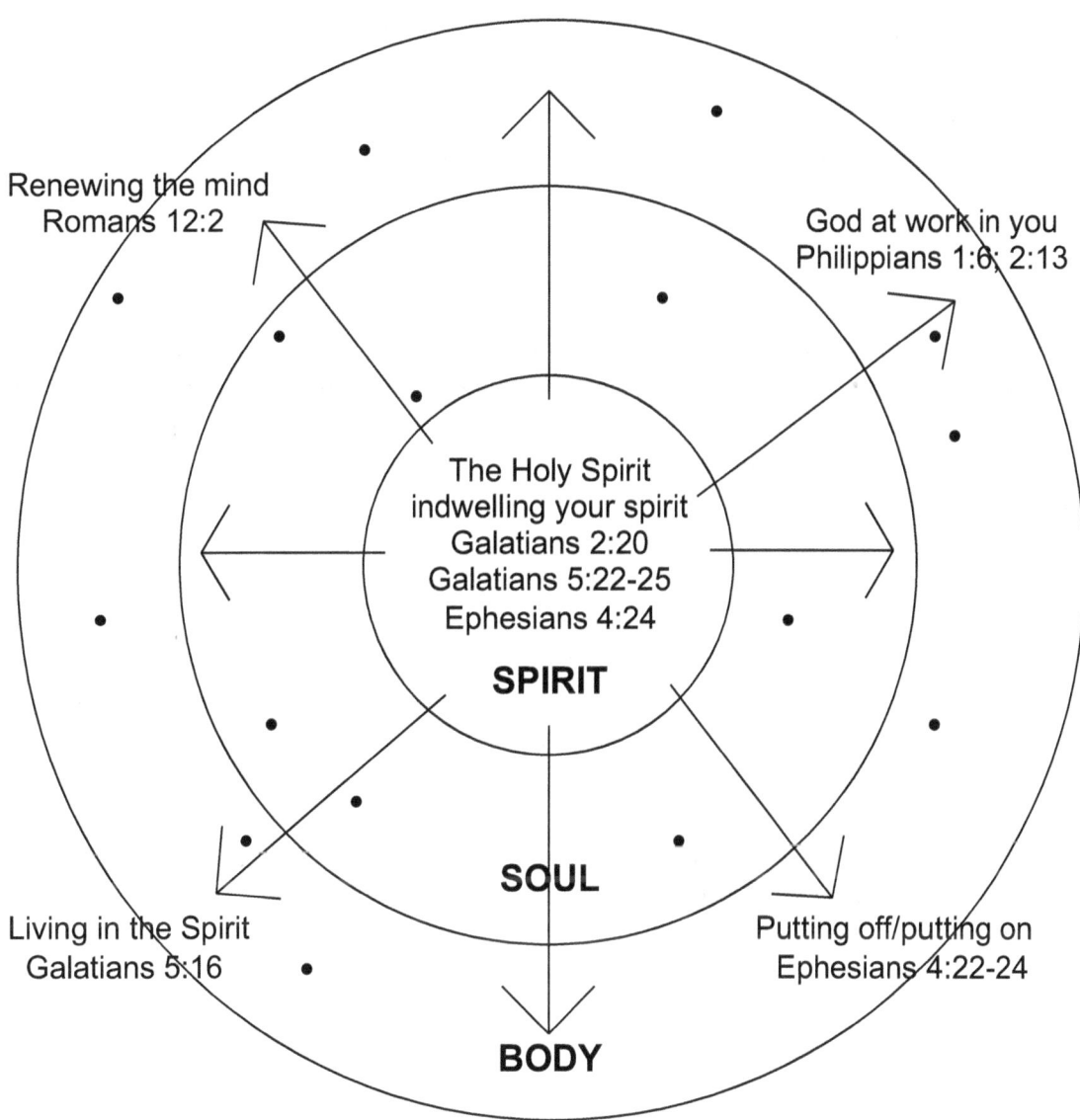

- Sin measle – Romans 7:21-23
  Examples: physical and emotional habits, wrong beliefs, erroneous thinking

Throughout your life, the Holy Spirit is gradually curing you of the "sin measles," making you in your soul and body more and more like who you already are in your spirit.

The Bible has a lot of amazing things to say about what we are like as "new creations" in Christ. We are holy (1 Peter 2:9), perfect (Hebrews 10:14), complete (Colossians 2:10), and competent (2 Corinthians 3:5). We possess the "fruit" of the Spirit; therefore, we are loving, joyful, peaceful, patient, kind, good, faithful, gentle, and self-controlled (Galatians 5:22-23).

"Oh, right!" you might say. "I'm not like that!" When confronted with "new creation truths," the question immediately arises, "If I'm a new creation and all these things are supposed to be true about me, why don't I behave, think, and feel like it?!" The answer lies in those "sin measles." Although we have a 100 percent new spirit in which God's Spirit dwells, the influence of having been born separated from God and having functioned under the influence of Satan remains with us. In Romans 7:21-25, this is referred to as "the law of sin." Sin is at work within our "members" (Romans 7:23, ESV).

There are a number of erroneous beliefs about which we become convinced as a result of sin's and Satan's influence.

There are a number of erroneous beliefs about which we became convinced as a result of sin's and Satan's influence. There are a number of negative emotional and physical habits that we developed apart from God's guidance and in response to our painful (and erroneous) beliefs and thoughts. These do not totally vanish the moment we become Christians (although some of them do for most people). What totally vanishes is Satan's grip on us. (See Romans 6:6-18.) As Christians, because we are vitally linked with God – for he has taken up residence within us – we now have the freedom and power to choose whether we sin or not (although the ravages of our former bondage to Satan sometimes cloud our perceptions so that we don't always see our choices clearly). Despite all the negative influence of sin and Satan and the corrupted world in which we live, as new creations in Christ, we are on the mend! The indwelling Holy Spirit is guiding us into all truth (John 16:13); God is at work in us to enable us to obey him (Philippians 2:13); and we are being transformed into the likeness of Christ (Romans 8:29; 2 Corinthians 3:18). The Spirit is gradually curing us of the "sin measles."

Another way I like to look at "sin measles" is based on a very old cartoon featuring a Dalmatian. The dog is walking along, spotted all over, and then he encounters something he wants to run from. He shoots away so quickly that his white body travels faster than his black spots. The spots linger momentarily in the air before all falling, kerplunk, to the ground. We are like that dog. We are walking along through life with a number of spots. When we reach the end of our lives and pass over into eternity, all the spots will drop off! Who we are is the white dog. The spots are not part of our eternal "new creation" nature. In this life, any behavior that is not commensurate with our new nature in Christ is not part of our *eternal* self. God sees who he has made us to be forever. He knows who we are, but we don't have that clear picture yet.

> Dear friends, now we are children of God, and what we will be has not yet been made known. But we know that when Christ appears, we shall be like him, for we shall see him as he is. (1 John 3:2)

Being a new creation in Christ does not mean we can just sit back and watch our maturity in Christ take place. There are a number of imperatives in the New Testament that indicate we have a role to play in our own transformation. Romans 12:2 tells us to "be transformed by the renewing of your mind." Ephesians 4:22-24 tells us to "put off" the "old self" and "put on" the new. Galatians 5:16 tells us to "walk [live] by the Spirit." Colossians 3:15 says to "let the peace of Christ rule in your hearts." And, there are many, many verses along these lines. These passages indicate that the process of becoming more and more on the "outside" (in our souls and bodies) like our "inside" (spirit) requires our participation. This process can be compared to a ballroom dance, where God and the believer are "dance partners."[6] God leads and the believer follows. God has made you a new creation and given you the power to live a godly life through the indwelling Holy Spirit, but you won't live like a new creation until you respond to his lead by believing you are a new creation and acting in light of this truth.

When we believe we are new creations in Christ, then we can see ourselves in a freeing light. Despite evidence in our behavior and emotions to the contrary, we can start believing that what God says about us is truer than what we feel and think about ourselves. If God says that he has given us "self-control" (Galatians 5:23), then we know when we behave in ways that are "out of control," we are not "being ourselves." The real you, even though none of us has fully experienced that yet, is a person who is free of the compulsion to cope in ungodly ways. There are just a few "sin measles" (mostly well-suppressed false beliefs) getting in the way of you experiencing the freedom you already have – and you'll likely recognize and address many of those "measles" in the course of working through the principles presented in this book. (Just look at the title of the next chapter.)

We can start believing that what God says about us is truer than what we feel and think about ourselves.

A Word about "the Flesh"

A more biblical term for "sin measles" is "the flesh." In *Lifetime Guarantee*, Bill Gillham provides an excellent discussion of the flesh – what it is and how it manifests itself in different people. The definition he uses for "the flesh" is "the old ways or patterns by which you have attempted to get all your needs supplied instead of seeking Christ first and trusting Him to meet your needs."[7] Before we were aware of the ways in which God has planned for our needs to be met, we worked out ways to try to meet them ourselves. Many times, compulsive behaviors result from the ways we seek to meet our emotional needs. They are a "work of the flesh."

Sadly, when we do not understand "the flesh," we can think that our negative emotions and behaviors define who we really are. However, God knows who we really are and tells us that we are spiritually alive and "slaves to righteousness" (Romans 6:18). I've heard many people say they need "heart change" when they feel unspiritual or act in an unspiritual way. No, it is clear in Scripture that those who are in Christ have a brand new heart and are indwelt by the Holy Spirit. (See Jeremiah 31:33 and Ezekiel 36: 26.) What we're really observing when we act in ways contrary to our new nature in Christ is *the flesh*. The flesh is not an eternal part of you. It is not the *real* you! Satan wants you to believe that's who you are so you won't find the freedom you already have as a new creation in Christ.

Before we were aware of the ways in which God has planned for our needs to be met, we worked out ways to meet them ourselves.

When it comes to distinguishing "walking in the Spirit" from "walking in the flesh," there is a problem that arises, particularly for highly conscientious people. It is possible to act in very Christian ways while relying on one's own willpower, determination, or some other personal ability, such as intellect, intuition, or verbal acuity, rather than turning to God and relying upon his guidance and power. Paul certainly knew about this when he described what Bill Gillham calls "USDA Choice Flesh"[8] in Philippians 3:4b-6:

> ...If someone else thinks they have reasons to put confidence in the flesh, I have more: circumcised on the eighth day, of the people of Israel, of the tribe of

Benjamin, a Hebrew of Hebrews; in regard to the law, a Pharisee; as for zeal, persecuting the church; as for righteousness based on the law, faultless.

Paul really looked good! He was doing it all for God, too. I know this sort of flesh all too well. In my mid-twenties, I taught at a private Christian school, earning far less than teachers in the public school system of that city. I sponsored the junior and senior high cheerleading squads and pep clubs, as well as the ninth-grade class. I also provided at-home lessons to students who had to miss school due to prolonged injury. I was a very active church member and regularly attended two Bible studies, one of which worked during weekends within an inner-city neighborhood, seeking to assist residents in obtaining aid and education while witnessing to them about Jesus. I had no idea that I was doing what a counselor referred to as "gluing fruit onto your tree." The fruit of the Spirit comes naturally from relying on the power of God within us. (See John 15:5!) My "good works" were not a result of "walking in the Spirit," because I had no idea how to do that. My works were my way of meeting my need to feel justified before God and others. "My way of meeting my need" is another way of describing "the flesh."

"My way of meeting my need" is another way of describing "the flesh."

So, how do you know if you are walking in "USDA Choice Flesh" or in the Spirit? This can be a terrible mind game I've seen torment people who tend to be hyper-conscientious. But it can be rather easy to resolve by considering just a few questions that make it clear whether or not you're operating out of your flesh:

- Are you attempting to **prove** something?
- Are you trying to **protect** yourself?
- Are you **providing** for yourself in some way?
- Are you **punishing** yourself or someone else?[9]

We can be pretty sure we're operating in the flesh when we are seeking self-serving results. When we walk in the Spirit, we are concentrating on God's will and God's glory, as well as the benefit of others, sometimes to our own detriment. If you're still not sure if you're "walking in the Spirit," simply turn to God for him to give you discernment and trust he will direct you if you are willing to do what *he* wants, giving up your rights to have what *you* want.

Reflection

1. What are some of the negative things you have believed to be true about yourself, either because society or your parents – or even you – have convinced you of them?

2. Can you see specific ways in which what you've believed about yourself has affected your behavior and/or emotions?

3. As you think through your unwanted behaviors and emotions, how does it make a difference to consider those as "sin measles" that are *not* part of your new and eternal self?

What Others Have Experienced

There is a trend in our culture, even in the evangelical Christian subculture, to view ourselves in terms of what we do, especially what we do wrong, rather than in terms of who God made us to be. We say we are "compulsive gamblers," "alcoholics," "compulsive overeaters," or "addicts." We've been told that using such labels takes us out of denial and makes us more able to address these struggles. Certainly, denial is not good, but people who are seeking freedom are not in denial about the fact that they're struggling with a "besetting sin." The use of behavior-centered labels usually is accompanied by a belief that the label suggests at least a lifelong struggle, if not a lifelong incurable disease, and that the best we can hope for is to control the struggle day-by-day or to go into "recovery" for a time.

When a professional editor from a respected Christian publishing house read the first few chapters of my book *The Weight of Grace*, he asked me, "Really, how much do you still struggle with overeating every day?" I answered that, just as I'd made clear in my book, I do not struggle with overeating at all anymore. After he made some observations about how to change my writing style, he asked me, "No, really, isn't overeating a daily temptation?" When I told him it was not at all a temptation any longer, his face clearly indicated he thought I was lying, and he pressed the point. "Don't you have to deal with this for the rest of your life?" Part of me wanted to slap my forehead with the palm of my hand out of frustration, but then I realized something and asked him if he had ever struggled with overeating. He said it was indeed a daily issue for him, having gained about 30 pounds since he graduated from college. As he told me more of his story, it became clear that he had been convinced by a support group that he was a "compulsive overeater" with an incurable "disease." I told him that I'd moved away from that way of thinking, but he seemed to feel as sorry for me as I felt for him!

No, I did not have the incurable disease of "compulsive overeating." I had a very curable case of the "sin measles," which were the thoughts, beliefs, and habits of coping that I'd developed apart from God's influence and truth. Because of what I believed to be true about myself, thanks to having been separated from my father by divorce and then sexually molested by a stepfather, who told me that I'd brought it on myself, I had a terrible inner conflict between 1) wanting to be attractive to men so I could get the male attention I craved, and 2) wanting to shun sexual advances because I was afraid I'd be unable to resist them. I developed two ways of coping with this conflict. I felt a little nauseated whenever I was alone with a man, and I compulsively ate so that I'd stay just "fat" enough to feel no one would "hit on" me. This was how my "flesh" dealt with my inner conflict. Once I realized that because I am a new creation in Christ, the Holy Spirit would empower me to say no to sexual advances, I stopped feeling nauseated while alone with a man, and I started binge-eating less and less. Instead of acting in accordance with my "flesh" –

The use of behavior-centered labels usually is accompanied by a belief that the label suggests at least a lifelong struggle, if not a lifelong incurable disease.

my old ways of dealing with life apart from the Holy Spirit – I started living in the truth of who I am in Christ and in the power of the Spirit more and more.

I did not have an incurable, lifelong ailment; I had some erroneous beliefs and I was ignorant about how God works in people's lives. The "cure" to compulsion ("besetting sins" or "coping mechanisms") is found ultimately in a Spirit-led life. Ephesians 5:18 points to this, as does Galatians 5:16.

Many people seek to control themselves through what ends up controlling them.

Because of what they've surmised about themselves – based on what authority figures or peers have told them, on their own past behaviors, or on past negative events – many people seek to control themselves through what ends up controlling them. The overwhelmed pastor, believing he cannot tell anyone about his unbearable anxiety because it's not "manly," secretly distracts himself from that anxiety by watching pornography online. The woman, believing herself to be prideful and thinking that pride has the potential to separate her from God eternally, eats herself into chubbiness to keep her pride at bay. The young woman, remembering that the only attention she received as a child was sexual, now cannot seem to stop seeking the affection she craves except through offering herself to each boyfriend. Such people, once they realize God truly cares and has freed them from sin, as well as has re-created them with godly motivations, can learn to rely on the forgiveness of Jesus and power of the Spirit to enable them to see themselves in new ways and experience life in a new way. The pastor can realize he is not "addicted" to pornography and admit to his anxiety, since manliness as exemplified by Jesus is tender and vulnerable. The woman can see that her pride is not part of her true self; therefore, should she feel or act proud, she can recognize it as a "sin measle" and ask for the help of the Spirit to "count others more significant" than herself (Philippians 2:3, ESV). The affection-starved young woman can start to see herself as someone who was not created to get her needs met through sexual immorality and that God is providing her with attention and affection in legitimate, moral ways through fellow believers.

Putting faith in God's desire to work in and through who you now are as a new creation in Christ gives you the freedom to be yourself, your true self that God created you to be.

Homework

In the following "Becoming Who You Already Are" chart, find some statements in the first column with which you identify and put a check mark by each of them. Read the contrasting statements in the second column and look up the Bible verses in the third column. Ask God to make these truths more and more real to you.

Becoming Who You Already Are[10]

What I Feel or Think about Myself	What Is True about Me According to Scripture	Scripture
I am unworthy/unacceptable.	I am accepted/worthy/welcomed.	Ps. 139; Rom. 15:7
I am alone.	I am never alone.	Rom. 8:38-39; Heb. 13:5b
I feel like a failure/inadequate.	I am adequate/competent.	2 Cor. 3:5-6; Phil. 4:13
I have no confidence.	I have all the confidence I need.	Prov. 3:26; 14:26; Eph. 3:12; Heb. 10:19
I feel responsible for my life.	God is responsible for/faithful to me.	Ps. 138:8; Phil. 1:6; 2:13; 2 Thes. 3:3
I am confused/think I'm going crazy.	I have the mind of Christ.	1 Cor. 2:16; Eph. 1:17; 2 Tim. 1:7
I am depressed/hopeless.	I have all the hope I need.	Ps. 27:13; Rom. 5:5; 15:13; Heb. 6:19
I am not good enough/imperfect.	I am perfect in Christ.	Eph. 2:10; Col. 2:10; Heb. 10:14
There is nothing special about me.	I have been chosen/set apart by God.	Ps. 139; 1 Cor. 1:30; 2 Thes. 2:13
I don't have enough.	I have no lack.	Phil. 4:19
I am a fearful/anxious person.	I am free from fear.	Ps. 34:4; 2 Tim. 1:7; 1 Pet. 5:7
I lack faith.	I have all the faith I need.	Rom. 10:17; 12:3; Heb. 12:2
I am a weak person.	I am strong in Christ.	Is. 58:11; Dan. 11:32; Phil 4:13
I am defeated.	I am victorious.	Rom. 8:37; 2 Cor. 2:14; 1 Jn. 5:4
I am not very smart.	I have God's wisdom.	Prov. 2:6-7; 1 Cor. 1:30; Eph. 1:17
I am in bondage.	I am free in Christ.	Ps. 32:7; Jn. 8:36; 2 Cor. 3:17
I am miserable.	I have God's comfort.	Is. 51:12; 2 Cor. 1:3-4
I have no one to take care of me.	I am protected/safe.	Ps. 91; Ps. 121
I am unloved.	I am very loved.	Jn. 15:9; Rom. 8:38-39; Eph. 2:4; 5:1
I am unwanted/don't belong to anyone.	I have been adopted by God. I am His child.	Rom. 8:16-17; Gal. 4:5; Eph. 1:5; 1 Jn. 3:1-2
I feel guilty.	I am totally forgiven/redeemed.	Ps. 103:12; Eph. 1:7; Col. 1:14, 20
I am a sinner.	I have been declared holy, righteous, and justified.	Rom. 3:24; 1 Cor. 1:30; 6:11; 2 Cor. 5:21
I have no strength.	I have God's power. I am indwelt by the Holy Spirit.	Acts 1:8; Rom. 8:9-11; Eph. 1:19; 3:16
I can't reach God.	As a believer, I have direct access to God.	Eph. 2:6; Heb. 4:15-16, 10:19-20; 1 Pet. 2:9
I feel condemned.	I am not condemned/am blameless.	Jn. 3:18; Rom. 8:1; Col. 1:22
I have no direction/plan.	God directs me/has a plan for me.	Ps. 37:23; Jer. 29:11; Eph. 2:10
Nothing will ever change.	I've been given a brand new life.	2 Cor. 5:17; Eph. 4:22-24
I am afraid of Satan.	I have authority over Satan.	Col. 1:13; 1 Jn. 4:4; Rev. 12:11
Sin overpowers me.	I am dead to sin.	Rom. 6:6, 11, 17-18

Homework Follow-up

1. What was a striking lie that the Holy Spirit revealed you have believed about yourself? Where did it come from? What is the truth?

2. Of the statements in the first column of the "Becoming Who You Already Are" chart that stood out to you, do you believe the contrasting truths? Why or why not?

Comments on the Homework

Here are examples of some of the "striking lies" small group participants have mentioned when discussing the "Becoming Who You Already Are" chart. (As you might expect, most of the people I have the opportunity to encourage are female.) I've paraphrased their statements and provided the choices they decided to make in light of "new creation" thinking.

- *My grandmother always told me, "You can't do anything right," and "You'll never amount to anything."* This small group member realized that she had believed her grandmother's pronouncements to be true and that she had engaged in many behaviors to either fulfill them (didn't even try to make good grades) or overcompensate for them (perfectionistic work performance that crowded out a social life). In light of Scripture, she chose to believe that God does indeed adequately equip her for any circumstance to which he calls her (Philippians 2:13; 4:13). She started to expect to succeed or, if her efforts did not turn out as she hoped, she chose to believe that God had a purpose in that also.

- *Throughout my adulthood, I married mainly because I was tired of supporting myself. I couldn't seem to stop myself from marrying the wrong kinds of men. So, I started believing that the only way to keep from marrying again was to stay so fat that no one would come around and tempt me to marry him.* This woman had had four unhappy marriages and had started to truly trust in Christ after her fourth husband died. Ironically, shortly after she realized she held this false belief and even though she was quite large, a man she was seeing and who appeared to her to be a "nice man" (but apparently not a vital Christian) asked her to move in with him. Being "fat" hadn't succeeded in fending off opportunities to be supported by a man! However, as a result of believing God would direct her to do what was right and what was best for her, even though the man presented her with a more convenient financial circumstance, she turned him down. She credited this to the work of the Holy Spirit in her life.

- *In reaction to my father molesting me, I tried to be perfect so no one would know how weird I really was. When the truth came out about Dad, I gave up on being perfect because everyone knew I wasn't. Now I mess up a lot so I won't have to be "perfect."* It's a horrible strain to be perfect, and this young woman obviously believed she was terribly imperfect. However, in light of her new understanding about her nature as a new creation in Christ, she stopped viewing herself as "weird" because she'd been molested. She also saw that there had never really been a need to be perfect, because God does not insist on our perfection in order for us to be acceptable to him. Jesus has met the standard of perfection for us (2 Corinthians 5:21). Therefore, she no longer had to do anything (such as work at doing poorly) to combat the pressure to be "perfect."

In light of her new understanding about her nature as a new creation in Christ, she stopped viewing herself as "weird" because she'd been molested.

The most difficult part about believing the truth about ourselves lies in what we decide to be our authority on that matter. One woman told me she "believes her lying eyes." In other words, she's seen what a messed-up person she's been for years, so that's what she believes herself to be. She has come to a conclusion about herself based on "sin measles," not on God's Word. It's understandable, but it's not believing in the truth, and it's the truth that sets us free. Her lying eyes have lied to her and kept her chained to behaviors she assumes are natural for her when, as a new creation in Christ, they're not natural, just familiar.

Another common issue is making feelings the final authority in our lives. In the back of a popular evangelistic pamphlet, there's a diagram of a little train. The engine is "Fact." The first car behind the engine is "Faith," and the caboose is "Feeling."[11] This illustration is a reminder that the *feeling* that we are "created to be like God in true righteousness and holiness" (Ephesians 4:24) and in possession of all the fruit of the Spirit may not come right away. What's important is to be willing to "be transformed by the renewing of your mind" (Romans 12:2).

When I do what I call "prayerful pondering," I ask God to help me think through his truth and how it applies to my life. I often do this while I'm on a walk or driving. I think through the scriptural principles that tell me what I'm really like, pondering how they are true even though my behavior or feelings don't always line up. I remind myself – and I believe the Holy Spirit prompts me to do this – that at the very core of my being, in my true nature, I am a person who wants to live according to truth, who loves unconditionally, who is patient toward people, and who deeply desires to be in total dependence upon God to live a holy life. I ask God to do whatever it takes to eliminate whatever is in me that results in my behaving in ways contrary to my true nature. While pondering, I sometimes realize I'm trying to meet a need through a "fleshly" behavior. Then Scripture passages come to mind that show how *God* meets that need. This thinking is evidence of God at work in me (Philippians 2:13). This is engaging in an intimate relationship with God – thinking his truth through, talking it over with him, and allowing him to bring issues and pertinent Scripture to light. Ultimately, this leads to my *feeling* that what God says about me as a "new creation in Christ" is really the truth. Sometimes my feelings have changed in just a moment and sometimes it has taken several years. What's important is to realize that the truth doesn't always *feel* like the truth to us, but that doesn't change how true it really is! And it doesn't change how that truth is what brings the freedom we so desire.

This is engaging in an intimate relationship with God: thinking his truth through, talking it over with him, and allowing him to bring issues and pertinent Scripture to light.

5 FREEING TRUTH ABOUT HOW YOUR BELIEFS MOTIVATE YOUR BEHAVIOR

"I did it my way!"[1]
"There is a way that seems right to a man..."[2]
"I just do it because I like to."[3]

The "ways" that seem right to us are our beliefs. And our beliefs influence absolutely everything we do. For example, when you sit down on a chair, you do so because you believe it is sturdy enough to support your weight. You don't think through this basic belief. You just make an assumption (an assumption is a type of belief) based on experience. From repeatedly sitting on chairs and having your weight supported, you formed a belief that most chairs, which have certain recognizable characteristics, are sturdy enough to hold you.

Christians have many beliefs that are accurate, but because we still suffer from the "sin measles" (i.e., the "flesh"), we are swayed by ungodly aspects of our culture and the institutions of this world. Additionally, Christians are even directly tempted by Satan and his minions, resulting in a number of inaccurate beliefs. These are the "ways" that *seem* right to us – but lead to our destruction. (Look at what the second half of Proverbs 14:12 says.) When it comes to continuous struggles with unwanted emotions and behaviors, the beliefs that we hold – the ways that seem right to us – are what keep us in defeat no matter how many times we try to change how we feel or act. As long as certain beliefs are present, they will affect how we behave and feel. For example, as long as I believed that I would automatically succumb to the temptation to engage in sex outside of marriage, I also believed I needed to stay "fat" in order to ward off being faced with that temptation. No diet plan or program could change that basic belief. Being "thin" just didn't feel right to me, and I repeatedly sabotaged my efforts to lose weight. Also, as long as I believed that overeating was a lifelong addiction, I saw myself as someone who was either "on the wagon" or who had totally fallen off of it. I didn't believe I was capable of moderation. I either rigidly dieted or ate like a fiend. My beliefs *seemed* right to me. They were totally wrong. But they totally influenced my behavior.

We have formed beliefs about every aspect of life, and they are the basis upon which we make decisions and take action (or take no action). Also, our beliefs are the grid through which we perceive everything. For example, if you hold the belief that you are not good at public speaking, when you are put in the position to give a public address and then receive a compliment for it, you will very likely say to yourself, *Oh, he just said that to be nice.* It wouldn't matter if the compliment had been truly deserved; your belief would lead you to interpret the compliment as insincere (albeit "nice").

Time and time again, I have heard husbands complain about how their wives do not accept their compliments, especially regarding their appearance. Given the many images in magazines and movies to which women compare themselves, it is very easy for them to believe they are "ugly." Similarly, I hear wives decry how their husbands feel inadequate to participate in, let alone lead, family Bible study and prayer. An erroneous belief about what constitutes "success" in this area holds many men back from even trying.

When it comes to continuous struggles with unwanted emotions and behaviors, the beliefs that we hold – the ways that seem right to us – are what keep us in defeat.

We were not born with the beliefs we have. They were formed as a result of our experiences. Some of our beliefs were taught to us, directly or indirectly, by family, teachers, and churches. Some of what we were taught was positive and based upon biblical truth, but if you're like just about every "stuck Christian" I've met, most wasn't. We also pick up beliefs from our peers, the media, literature, and our culture. And so much of our media, literature, and culture is not influenced by God and is, in fact, antagonistic toward God and his Word. Many Christians have a belief that "if I love this person, then God must have put him or her in my life and it's okay that I'm living with/sleeping with him or her." This is not based upon Scripture. It opposes many verses about avoiding sexual immorality and reserving sexual intimacy for marriage. This belief, however, does jibe with a pervasive *cultural* standard that it is acceptable to live with or have sex with someone as long as you love that person. In fact, recently an acquaintance told me it would be foolish not to live with someone before marriage because a "trial run" is only wise! (Hmm… Proverbs 14:12!)

Most of the time the errors in our beliefs are not obvious.

Most of the time the errors in our beliefs are not obvious. An example of a subtle erroneous belief is the person who, when he was a small child, was told by his parents that he was clumsy.[4] The parents did not realize that what they called clumsy was really a display of normal motor skills for a toddler. To them, how clumsy "Junior" was, was their little family joke. However, Junior formed the belief that he really was clumsy. He then went through life perceiving all of his behaviors as either evidence of his clumsiness (when he'd knock something over as most of us do from time to time) or as an amazing departure from his "norm" of clumsiness (when he didn't bump into anything or drop anything as the opportunities arose). A person having a belief such as this will either actually act clumsily because he believes that he is clumsy or become overly careful in order to avoid acting as clumsy as he fears himself to be. Remember, the "clumsy" person was never actually clumsy in the first place! And, he's probably totally unaware of the erroneous belief that's motivating his behaviors.

The belief that was a big motivator for my unending binge-eating and remaining "fat" is one common to many victims of incest. My stepfather made comments and behaved toward me in ways that inferred I had brought his advances upon myself. Also, since this was the only male attention available to me, I had on occasion actually put myself in his way with the hope he would molest me. These factors led me to believe that I was the type of person who, given half a chance, would behave in sexually inappropriate ways and that the resulting guilt would be unbearable. Because of this belief, I developed a "flesh pattern," a way of coping using my own devices. (Remember, "the flesh" is our attempt to get needs met in our own way instead of allowing God to meet our needs his way.) I kept myself just "fat" enough to feel sure that no one would be attracted enough to me to make any advances and, therefore, tempt me to become sexually involved. My reaction to the belief that I was a "slut," as I used to hear myself say in my head, was to be overly careful not to act like or look like the slut I knew myself to be.

I know a woman whose childhood experiences were very similar to mine. She, too, had the belief that she was a "slut," but she reacted in a very different way as a result of that belief. Her thinking was, *Since I am this way, there's no use in fighting it.* So, she became sexually active at an early age and "slept around." What was sad about both of us was that, especially as Christians, neither of us was a slut! I was overcompensating for how promiscuous I believed myself to be on the inside, and she was living out what she believed herself to be.

It really should be no surprise to us that we hold inaccurate, twisted beliefs. Romans 1:21-22 tells us that our "thinking became futile" and we "became fools" as a result of our separation from God. Also, Romans 12:2 refers to how the "world" – our media, culture, and institutions – tries to "conform" us, tries to "press us into its mold."[5] Jesus told us that, for now, Satan is the prince of this world (John 12:31). Satan uses the world to pressure us into thinking we should all act as he desires. Movies, advertisements, books, magazines, podcasts, and television shows can pressure us to believe we should be sexy, strong, self-reliant, and wealthy while also pushing us to be asexual, vulnerable, needing and deserving assistance, and living a Spartan lifestyle. Satan loves the confusion and inner conflict that result from these contradictory beliefs.

What is really scary about our inaccurate beliefs is that what we hold to be true controls the decisions we make, how we feel, and how we behave. Most people around my age (I was born in 1953) remember the singer, Karen Carpenter. She got the idea that she was "chubby," and she spent most of her adult life overcompensating for her chubbiness by starving herself – until she died as a result.[6] That appears to be an obvious and easily identified false belief. But it wasn't obvious to her, just as the beliefs that control us aren't obvious to us.

So, if our beliefs are oftentimes erroneous and have a controlling influence over us, is there any hope for us? Read Romans 12:2 and Ephesians 4:22-23. Now that we are new creations in Christ and are no longer controlled by sin, we have the power to change our beliefs. Thanks to the indwelling Holy Spirit and the inspired Word of God, we have the ability to identify false beliefs, turn from them, and start accepting beliefs that are based upon God's truth. In Romans 12:2, this is called "renewing of your mind." In Ephesians 4:23, it's called being "made new in the attitude your minds." Second Corinthians 10:4-5 refers to "strongholds," "arguments," and "pretension" that try to block our knowing the truth. In response to them, we are directed to enter into the process of "taking every thought captive to the obedience of Christ" (NASB). When we become aware that a belief is erroneous, we can exchange it for the truth. But, *how* do we do this? How do we renew our minds?

To begin with, we must realize that the Holy Spirit is our guide. As the one who leads us into all truth (John 16:13), he will show us what specifically needs to be renewed, when it needs to be renewed, and then will provide us with the power to do so. This is an integral part of our relationship with God. We are not engaged in a "religion" of only rituals and dogma, but in a vital *relationship* with the living God, who desires to interact with us, to personally communicate with us, and to transform us. This means we can expect to "hear" from the Holy Spirit.

Hearing the Spirit can happen in a number of ways. It is said that Scripture is the vocabulary of the Holy Spirit. When we read Scripture, no matter what passage we may be reading at the time, God speaks to us through his Word. An example in my life is my persistent temptation to worry about becoming elderly and having no one to help me in my old age because I have no children. Just as persistently, the Spirit reminds me of Matthew 6:25-34 and Psalm 68:6a. Through these passages, the Lord very personally speaks to me. He redirects my thinking, reassures me, and confronts me with my need to reinvest trust in him and his promise of provision for every stage of my life.

Not only does the Holy Spirit speak to us through the Scripture we're reading, but also he brings passages of Scripture to our minds at appropriate times. My feelings toward God have not always been of the warm, fuzzy, affectionate variety. As a result, I used to berate myself for not

What is really scary about our inaccurate beliefs is that what we hold to be true controls the decisions we make, how we feel, and how we behave.

Now that we are new creations in Christ and are no longer controlled by sin, we have the power to change our beliefs.

loving God. Believing myself to be a second-class Christian, I would use Deuteronomy 6:5 (and those passages in which Jesus quoted that verse) as the club with which I beat myself up because I didn't *feel* affectionate toward God. However, an experience when a verse popped into my head at just the right moment cured me of the false belief that I was a disappointment to God because of my lack of affectionate feelings for him. I was very much in love with the man I was dating, and although we were not having sex, I believed we were too physically involved. The morning after an evening of particularly heavy "necking," I called my boyfriend and told him I could not date him any longer. Given how much I craved affection and how much affection I felt for this man, I could hardly believe I was doing this. This was the first man I had dated in quite a long while and I greatly feared it would be the last. Nevertheless, I truly felt giving the relationship up was what God was asking me to do in order to be obedient to him. After I hung up the phone, I heard a verse in my head: "This is love for God: to obey his commands" (1 John 5:3). Then I also heard, "And you say you don't love me." I realized that my love for God did not have to be a "mushy" feeling. As the old chorus goes, "Love is something you do; it's not always something you can feel, but it's real."7 In a very personal and caring manner, God communicated with me by bringing to my mind a specific verse related to my false belief. As a result, I changed my beliefs about myself and God's acceptance of me.

God communicated with me by bringing to my mind a specific verse related to my false belief.

Although the Holy Spirit would never contradict Scripture, the Spirit is not limited to only Scripture in speaking to us. Nearly every day I hear the "still, small voice" of God. (See 1 Kings 19:12 in the King James Version.) I hear that voice in thoughts such as, *It's all okay; things will work out for the best*, or *Just do the best you can; I'll take care of your reputation*, or *No, you're not an irritating person; that's an old belief that's untrue*. Yes, these could just be my own thoughts, but I believe if you're seeking to be in humble submission to God, he puts thoughts into your mind to encourage and direct you. (See Daniel 10:12.) In contrast, you know a thought is really from Satan or from one of your false beliefs if it's contrary to Scripture or evokes condemnation (Romans 8:1).

Other ways in which the Spirit speaks to us about our false beliefs are through fellow believers (Ephesians 4:15 and Colossians 3:16), Christian music (Ephesians 5:19 and Colossians 3:16), and even in dreams and visions (Acts 2:17). Of course, you can't base important life decisions on impressions or dreams. It is necessary to carefully test them against Scripture and to seek the feedback of mature Christians with whom you're in fellowship (1 Thessalonians 5:21-22). However, even though it is possible to be led astray by Satan or by our own desires, this does not discount how God can and does communicate to us in unusual ways. I have many times been greatly encouraged by visions I have had or by those that others have had about me. Still, our most reliable source for direction is in the Scriptures with the Holy Spirit as our guide and interpreter.

Let's go through another example to better understand how beliefs can influence behaviors and can be changed by the renewing of the mind. As I've mentioned, I struggled for years with going on horrendous eating binges. I always considered them to be caused by a profound lack of self-discipline. However, when I started considering that my eating was motivated by beliefs rather than the result of a lack of self-discipline, I began to ask God to show me the thinking and beliefs behind these wild binges. Initially God used my roommate, Karen, to show me the main issue. She noticed that I would frantically eat and eat but seemed to feel no emotions. When I was binge-eating, she would ask, "Are you upset about something? Do you feel stressed?" I'd always say, "No, I just want to eat the world. I don't feel anything." But Karen noticed on several occasions that when I'd gotten to the point of having eaten so much I felt ill, I'd start crying and telling her about some incident in which I'd had a negative interaction with a friend or co-worker.

After we realized the pattern, the next time I started to binge, instead of asking if I was upset about something, Karen asked me, "What happened today?" She already knew I didn't *feel* anything, so she just asked me to tell her the events of my day. When I did, she commented regarding an exchange I'd had with a co-worker, "If he had talked to me like that, I would have felt really mad!" I said, "No, I don't feel angry about it at all," and continued on my binge. As usual, though, when I could eat no more and felt terribly ill, I started to cry and realized how hurt I felt because of the incident that day with my co-worker, who was also a friend. Later, I mentioned this pattern to a trusted counselor, who said that it seemed pretty obvious to him that I was suppressing anger by eating. Once I ate as much as I possibly could, I wasn't able to hold down the anger and hurt any longer. He also suggested that I was punishing myself for feeling angry toward someone I believed I should never feel anger toward.

I started praying about what Karen and my counselor friend were seeing as one of the underlying beliefs motivating my binge-eating. Then I heard that "still, small voice" saying, "You believe anger is so horribly threatening that you are trying to punish yourself enough so that you will be motivated by that punishment to avoid ever getting angry again. You think that, if you feel angry with someone, you will lose your relationship with that person." Then I remembered a lesson I'd heard on Ephesians 4:26 and how anger, in and of itself, is not necessarily sin. I realized that I could feel the anger but didn't have to express it inappropriately; therefore, I need not alienate a dear friend just because I felt anger toward him or her. God used two friends, prayer, a Bible lesson I'd heard, and his Word to change my wrong belief of "If I get angry at someone, I'm a horrible person and I'll lose that friendship." As a result, the painful, bulimic-like binges tapered off. However, anger was not the only motivator for my binge-eating. Other beliefs needed to be addressed before the binge-eating stopped altogether.

Hopefully, you noticed there was no formula involved in how God revealed to me my erroneous belief about anger. Formulas are not the same as relationship. God desires a relationship with each of us. Each of my false beliefs that have been changed to align with the truth have been changed through a different means, but each time God's Spirit and God's Word have been at the core of the process. My role was a willingness to enter into and participate in the process.

Let's Dive Deep with God

Each painful or alarming emotion we feel and all of our ungodly "coping mechanism" behaviors have a starting point in our thinking – how we see ourselves, how we interpret events, what we think God is doing, etc. Emotions and behaviors do not just happen or come out of nowhere. They are the outward evidence of beliefs we have about God, ourselves, and how life works. Getting down to the beliefs we have and changing our minds to align with the truth leads to freedom from the negative emotions and behaviors that spring from erroneous beliefs. Then we are free to enjoy the positive emotions and behaviors that spring from believing in the truth. But how do we get to the bottom of what we actually believe?

On the next page is a modified version of an exercise used at the biblical counseling ministry where I was helped and where I later worked for many years.[8] This is a guide for prayerfully

Each of my false beliefs that have been changed to align with the truth have been changed through a different means, but each time God's Spirit and God's Word have been at the core of the process.

addressing a pattern of negative emotions and/or behaviors that particularly plague you (such as overeating, binge-shopping, losing your temper with loved ones, or viewing pornography). Or it can be a resource if something has flared up but you don't understand why (such as a seemingly unreasonable fear, a feeling of rage toward a relative, or a sudden wave of shame).

At the top of the diagram is the surface of a pond. As you work your way down the diagram, you are asking God to help you dive down into "deeper water"; that is, the thinking and beliefs below the surface that are motivating what you're experiencing at the surface level of your emotions and behavior. Finally, you dive down to the bedrock issue of who you believe God to be. Once you dive down, then you have the opportunity to renew your mind (aka "repent") and start thinking in line with God's truth, rising back to a surface that is calm and free.

This exercise is totally useless if it's seen as a four-step process in which you analyze yourself and determine to gut out a personal reformation. That would be completely contrary to what Jesus lovingly told us in John 15:5 – "apart from me you can do nothing." As we contend with the struggles of life, as new creations in Christ, God is guiding us back into the intimate relationship we lost in the Garden of Eden. We are actually hardwired for dependence upon our loving heavenly Father. We can turn to the indwelling Spirit to guide us as we seek to discover and change the beliefs that are motivating and enslaving us. God certainly knows what you believe much better than you do, so be sure to earnestly request his input and insight.

We can turn to the indwelling Spirit to guide us as we seek to discover and change the beliefs that are motivating us and enslaving us.

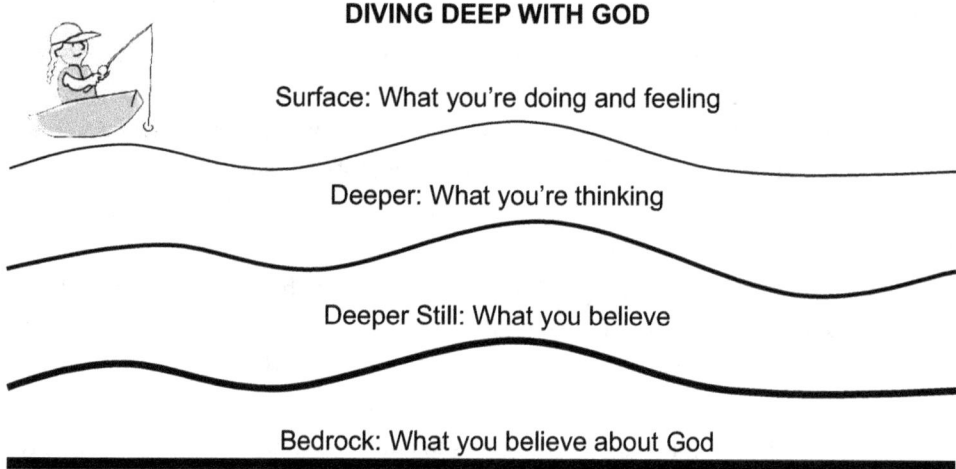

DIVING DEEP WITH GOD

Surface: What you're doing and feeling

Deeper: What you're thinking

Deeper Still: What you believe

Bedrock: What you believe about God

On the following page is an example of prayerfully working through this exercise by going down deep and then resurfacing, layer by layer. Other than asking God to guide you through the layers, the most important aspect of this exercise is making a decision to agree with God's truth and reject what you've been believing to be true (this is what true repentance really is – a change of mind according to God's truth). That decision enables you to rise up to the surface and experience freedom.

Freeing Truth about How Your Beliefs Motivate Your Behavior ▶ 55

DIVING DEEP WITH GOD

Surface: What you're doing and feeling
Snacking on sweets and carbs at bedtime even though I'm not hungry. Feeling depressed, lonely, and frustrated.

Deeper: What you're thinking
*I need to be married. I'm all alone and get no affection.
God is withholding marriage from me.*

Deeper Still: What you believe
*Marriage/sex=only way to get affection needs met.
Married people have more worth than singles.*

Bedrock: What you believe about God
*God is mean and doesn't care about me and my needs.
God only cares about my "spiritual growth" and serving him.*

RESURFACING FROM THE DEEP WITH GOD
START AT THE BOTTOM OF THE DIAGRAM!!

Surface: What you're doing and feeling
*Contented and grateful. Feel loved.
No longer feel the need to snack at bedtime.*

Rising up some more: What you're thinking
*All my friends show affection in various ways. I'm not lonely.
I am unique and special and do not need to be married to be happy and fulfilled.*

Rising up: What you believe
*There are many sources of affection in life – God has provided friends and spiritual family.
My worth is not determined by my marital status – Jesus and Paul never married.*

Bedrock: What you believe about God
*God does care about me and is actively meeting my needs.
Matthew 6:25-34; 7:9-11*

Sadly, ever since the Garden of Eden, we all tend to rely on our own ideas of what will make us happy. We actually believe we know best. Is that because we can see all of time stretched out before us and every possible consequence of each decision we make? If there is someone who not only made us but also loves us and really can see every outcome, why wouldn't we seek that person's guidance, follow that person's advice, and be confident that advice is what's best for us, way better than what we dream up for ourselves? That's not a rhetorical question. There is an obvious answer that most people would admit if they were truly honest with themselves. We do not trust that what God clearly tells us is best and will indeed result in our happiness. We see God as different than he actually is. We see him as stingy or mean or wanting us to suffer to prove our loyalty. We know just enough of the Bible to be scared about how God may treat us, but not enough of the Bible to have the real, accurate picture. That is why the topic of getting a new perspective on the character of God was addressed near the beginning of this book.

To grow in our trust in God's goodness and loving guidance, the best place to begin is with understanding that everything in Scripture must be viewed through the lens of the Cross.

To grow in our trust in God's goodness and loving guidance, the best place to begin is with understanding that everything in Scripture must be viewed through the lens of the Cross. If Jesus is the ultimate manifestation of God's character, if God wanted us to see to what lengths he'd go to transform us from alienated rebels to deeply beloved children of God, then when we think God's goal is to be the cosmic killjoy, we can look to the Cross and renew our minds – repent of our wrong beliefs – about God. When we see ourselves doing what we hate or feeling emotions that crush us, we can ask, "Lord God, what do I believe about you that has led to what's going on with me right now?" His answers will lead us to the truth that sets us free.

It's Not Just You and God

There is a danger in providing any hurting person with exercises to do, even if those exercises direct the person to seek God's guidance. Although new creations in Christ are "hardwired" to desire a relationship with God, God's design for his children is to enjoy him one-on-one *and* in relationships with his people. In Chapter 3, we looked at how each of us is the temple of the Holy Spirit (1 Corinthian 6:19). That verse is indicating that each individual is the temple of the Spirit. In the same epistle, the apostle Paul tells the whole church that they are, as a group, the temple of God's Spirit (1 Corinthians 3:16). This means that to "go it alone" in the Christian life – just you and God – is to miss one of the chief ways in which God ministers to us and grows us more and more into the image of Christ. (See Romans 12:3-8, Ephesians 4:11-16, and Colossians 3:16.)

Many struggling Christians have felt wounded by events or relationships within a church body and have given up on church participation. You've heard it many times or you've said it yourself: "I believe in Jesus, but I don't believe in organized religion." Witnessing hypocrisy, experiencing harsh judgments when seeking compassion, and being on the receiving end of abuse of authority is truly off-putting! At the same time, having those negative experiences doesn't change the fact that we were created for relationships, and growth in Christian maturity depends in large part on being in fellowship with other believers. (See Hebrews 10:25.)

The need to find fellowship in which you can contribute and by which you can receive encouragement and edification is yet one more opportunity to turn humbly to God for direction. Sometimes God provides a group of people that isn't a full-blown congregation but provides Christian family until we can more comfortably become involved in a church. For five years after my emotional collapse, my nerves were so shot that I could not go into a setting of more than a few people, especially if singing and musical instruments were involved, without needing assistance to find my way out of the sanctuary and having to find a ride home. A typical church service was just too overwhelming and overstimulating for me at that time. Also, the church I had been attending was not understanding of my situation and "called me on the carpet" for failure to attend regularly, so I withdrew my membership. During that time, I was, however, surrounded by friends and co-workers who provided small group Bible study opportunities, caring accountability, and prayer. Despite negative experiences with churches and knowing no church is ever perfect (especially since people like me go there!), I greatly benefit from the inspiration of church worship, the edification of solid biblical preaching, and the warmth and accountability of friendships formed within the church.

One of the main reasons this book's format is geared for small groups is that Christian fellowship is so vital to spiritual growth. Discussing struggles and the ways in which God is ministering to each group member brings a multiplication of insight as compared to simply reading a book, even if the reader does all the homework and answers all the question.

Despite negative experiences with churches and knowing no church is ever perfect (especially since people like me go there!), I greatly benefit from the inspiration of church.

Reflection

1. What are some behaviors you've observed among others that are clearly motivated by misunderstandings about God and how he has designed life to operate?

2. When you think about something you do or feel that you hate, why do you hate it?

3. When you think about something you do or feel that you hate, what are some things that it's actually doing *for* you?

What Others Have Experienced

It is much easier to see what is motivating bad behavior in others than in ourselves. However, when we see others doing what we hate, our tendency is to be very critical of the person and expect them to change or to think they ought to know better. How we view the behaviors of others can reflect how we think we should change our own behaviors.

The parents of a woman I know – I'll call her Daisy – are very openly disdainful of what they think of as "ugly" women. Their constant negative comments about television personalities, various relatives, and even strangers they see in the grocery store or on the street indicate an elaborate set of rules regarding what constitutes attractiveness in women. Without even thinking about it, Daisy adopted this way of thinking, and in her thirties, she realized that she did not adhere well to the family's guidelines! She hated to go to family functions, knowing that every negative pronouncement about the flaws in this TV reporter or that cashier was also an indictment against her. Other women in the family were doing better than Daisy at falling within the very tight parameters of the family standards of beauty, and there were many compliments paid to these women, but none to Daisy. Not only that, but Daisy felt deep disgust and disdain for women who were not "pretty," and she was most disdainful of those who had "failed" in the same ways she had. She not only hated herself for her "ugly" appearance, but she also hated herself for her inability to show grace to others who were "ugly."

In talking with Daisy about her critical attitude toward herself and others, I asked her to study some passages of Scripture about how God evaluates the worth of people – 1 Samuel 16:7, John 7:24, 2 Corinthians 5:12 and 16, and 1 Peter 3:3-4. I also told her how much pity I felt for her parents, who obviously didn't know Jesus very personally if they were qualifying and disqualifying women primarily on the basis of their outward appearance. Daisy did the Bible study I suggested, but it just didn't sink in. I continued to challenge her to agree with how God evaluates her, but she continued to be horribly judgmental about herself and others. Finally, I asked her what would happen if she gave up on judging herself and others on the basis of their appearance. She blurted out that she'd never be motivated to change into what her parents wanted her to be! After all, she had done this (become "ugly") to herself, so there really was nothing God was going to do for her in regard to getting better looking. It was all up to her to fix her "ugliness."

Facing what the unwanted behavior is doing for us is the most difficult thing about getting free from what enslaves us.

Facing what the unwanted behavior is doing *for* us is the most difficult thing about getting free from what enslaves us. Most people just do not want to accept that what they hate doing is actually what they believe deep down is doing something good *for* them. Daisy finally realized that she wanted her parents' approval more than even God's approval, and she knew the only way to get her parents' approval was by being "pretty." So, in order to make sure she would stay motivated to become "pretty," she was extra hard on herself (and others). She realized she believed that God would never allow her to be as pretty as she needed to be, partly because she'd done things that "ruined" her looks and partly because she knew deep down that her being pretty was not a goal God had for her. I asked her if being hard on herself was working, and she had to admit she'd been really hard on herself for years with no permanent results – her hair was not thick enough, her body was not slim enough, and her budget didn't allow her clothes to be "in" enough. I asked her to keep prayerfully pondering how God felt about "ugly" women.

A few weeks later, Daisy told me that she'd seen a woman she would have normally felt critical about, but instead of thinking critical thoughts and feeling disgusted, Daisy felt empathy. She also realized that this woman might be perfectly happy and not even thinking about judging herself and others by their appearance. She wondered what sort of woman this was and what sorts of things she'd gone through in her life. Obviously, Daisy had turned a corner, deciding to believe in God's value system instead of her parents'. She still dreads the next family function, but she feels she can honestly say that her worth is in Christ, not in her parents' approval.

Homework

1. Prayerfully choose a recent painful emotion or a time when you engaged in ungodly behavior. Then prayerfully go down through each level and then back up again using the following charts.

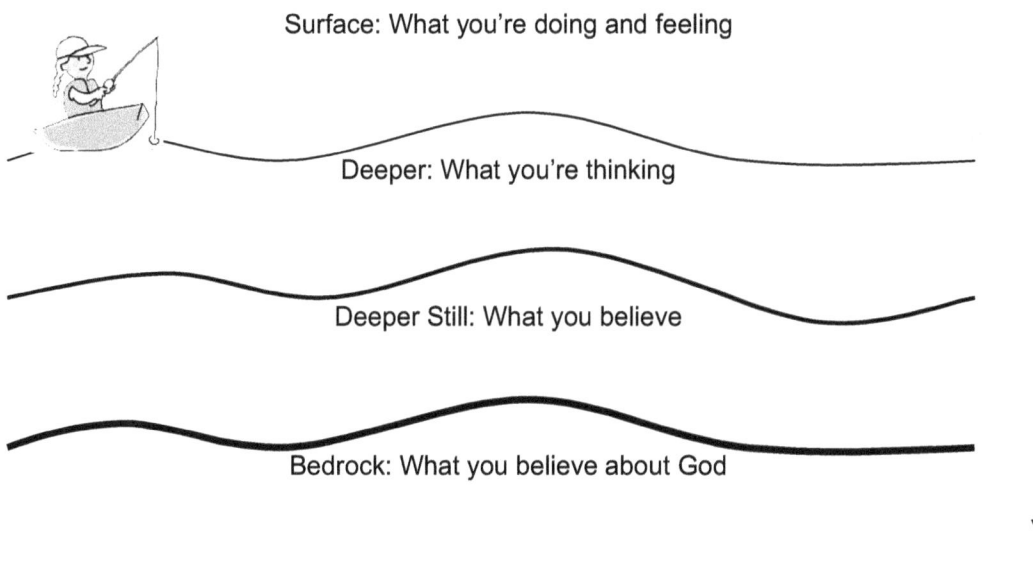

DIVING DEEP WITH GOD

Surface: What you're doing and feeling

Deeper: What you're thinking

Deeper Still: What you believe

Bedrock: What you believe about God

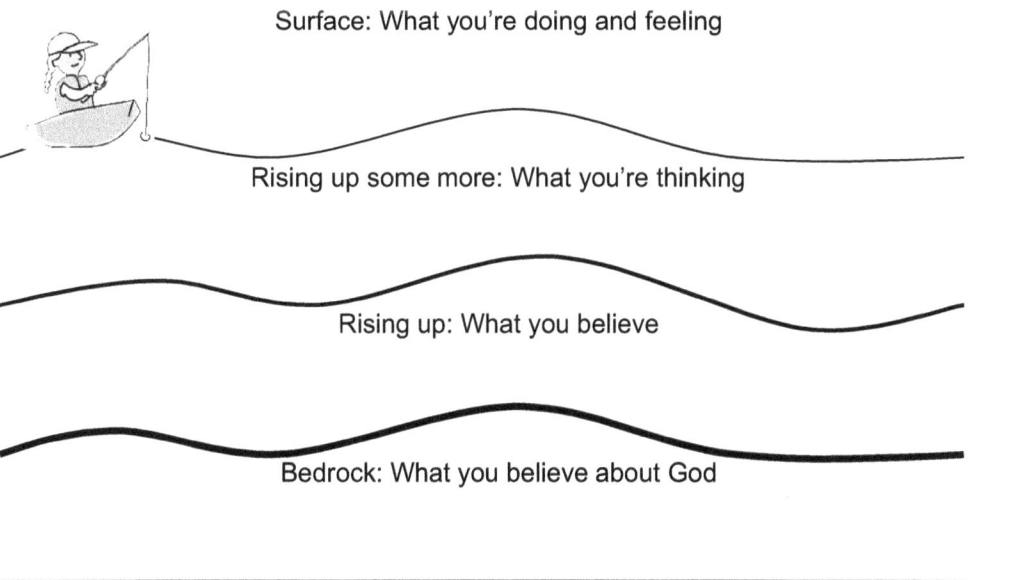

RESURFACING FROM THE DEEP WITH GOD
START AT THE BOTTOM OF THE DIAGRAM!!

Surface: What you're doing and feeling

Rising up some more: What you're thinking

Rising up: What you believe

Bedrock: What you believe about God

2. Ask a Christian friend to provide feedback on your charts, above. What does your friend see as beliefs you have about God, yourself, and how life works that would motivate your uncomfortable emotions and/or unwanted behaviors?

Homework Follow-up

1. In what ways did a friend's input change the way you viewed your beliefs and thinking that underlie your emotions and behaviors?

2. What are the scariest aspects of "diving deep" into beliefs that motivate your feelings and behaviors?

3. As a result of doing the "Diving Deep" exercise, what decisions have you made about beliefs you need to change? How do you plan to remind yourself of any new beliefs you've adopted?

Comments on the Homework

For many, going through an exercise such as "Diving Deep" can seem artificial and tedious. Comments I've heard in small groups include: "I just didn't have time this week to think about all of this." "You don't understand how chaotic my life is." "I really don't think this way." "I don't understand what you mean by 'prayerfully' doing an exercise." Such comments remind me of how engaging in "prayerful pondering" is similar to learning a foreign language. When I took Beginning Spanish in college, I managed to totally avoid ever actually speaking a single word of Spanish! I was so sure I'd never pronounce the language well that I didn't even try to do so. Unlike my unwillingness to speak Spanish, although it felt awkward, I did try out prayerfully completing homework provided by counselors and exercises in books I was reading. The result was that after about two years, I experienced complete freedom from chronic binge-eating, compulsive exercising, and painful self-loathing and shame. Apparently, my desire to overcome emotional pain and embarrassing behaviors was greater than my desire to speak Spanish!

Really, what do you have to lose? Sitting down for a little bit of quiet time (maybe in a library or in an empty church sanctuary) and asking God to guide you may feel weird, but it could turn out to be worth the discomfort and awkwardness. Apparently, what you've been doing isn't getting you where you want to go. Turning to God is what you're actually created to do. Jesus could not have been clearer when he said, "Apart from me you can do nothing" (John 15:5). He didn't say this to prove how important he is. He said it to help you realize you need him and that he very personally cares for you and wants to guide and empower you. Diving deep with God is one of the ways in which you have an opportunity to experience closeness to God.

Turning to God is what you're actually created to do.

This chapter is placed after chapters about the nature and character of God and what it means to be a new creation in Christ. This is because once you start to understand the truth about the loving, redemptive, in-there-for-the-long-haul character of God and once you start to see that, in Christ, you are no longer a "dirty rotten sinner" with a "deceitfully wicked" heart but a reborn child of God with new motivations, you are then freer to explore how your past influenced your view of everything – and how it no longer needs to do that anymore!

Including input from a friend is another opportunity for God to speak to you through his body. Diving deep with God is also aided by your own regular personal study of the Bible, participation in Bible study groups, and hearing God's word preached and sung. The Spirit uses what you've read and heard to remind you of truths that correct your erroneous beliefs and thoughts.

Once thoughts and beliefs are uncovered and seen as not in line with God's truth about his character, your nature as a new creation in Christ, or what God has plainly revealed about how life works best, you have a choice. You can continue to believe what you believe and operate based on those beliefs. Or you can decide that what you have believed is not really the truth and agree with God about the actual truth. But it can be easy to slip back into beliefs you've held onto for many years.

An example of slipping back into old beliefs occurred in my life about a year after I started experiencing ongoing freedom from chronic overeating and binge-eating. A long-time friend who had become a co-worker stopped spending time with me, and a rumor started circulating at work that the friendship had ended because I was "emotionally dependent" on my friend. Unfortunately, several who heard this rumor believed "emotionally dependent" was Christian code for "homosexual." Co-workers started avoiding me or giving me advice about how to get over my "dependence." This was all very jarring and certainly cause for personal evaluation, which led to self-doubt. I also felt betrayed and angry – and I started to engage in a form of overeating many refer to as "grazing." As my clothes became tighter, I turned to God and prayerfully "dove deep." I had reverted to thinking that I had very little worth and should never feel angry with the significant people in my life. My "grazing" was my way to avoid the painful thoughts about my worth and the intense negative emotions about friends and co-workers believing the worst about me. And my bedrock belief about God was that he had hung me out to dry with no defense, since defensiveness only increased everyone's suspicions about me.

That experience and my reactions to it motivated me to turn again to review God's truth about me, and I was greatly helped by one of the older women at the office. She stopped me in the hall one day and handed me a note with a Scripture reference written on it, 1 Peter 2:23. God used this little note to encourage me to keep entrusting myself to "him who judges justly." There was one person, the Lord, who knew the truth about me, even if no one else believed it. I made the decision that God knew I didn't have homosexual feelings and knew that I really didn't understand why the long-term friendship had so drastically changed. I also reviewed "new identity in Christ" passages, as well as verses about the role of the Holy Spirit in my life. Even if I had unwittingly made terrible mistakes that had resulted in the loss of that friendship, I could trust that I was forgiven by God and that he would reveal whatever needed to change within me in his timing. As a result, I no longer felt anger toward those who were spreading rumors about me. I felt sorry for them that they were not more compassionate. I no longer felt angry with the friend who had dropped our friendship. I felt sorry for her that she had not believed she could tell me what had gone wrong. And I completely stopped grazing.

I also learned the importance of keeping what I call "pocket verses" at the ready. There are a number of Bible passages that I have either memorized, recorded in the Notes app in my cell phone, or written on sticky notes positioned here and there in my home that serve as constant reminders of the truth I seem to find easy to forget. In other words, I keep them figuratively in my back pocket, hence "pocket verses," so they can be whipped out whenever I need to apply them when a doubt or lie assails me. Your "pocket verses" will probably differ from mine, so just begin your list as you come across Scriptures that specifically speak to you in addressing your struggles. God uses such passages to remind you about who you really are in Christ and the freedom you already have.

> *I reviewed "new identity in Christ" passages, as well as verses about the role of the Holy Spirit in my life. I no longer felt angry and I completely stopped grazing.*

6   FREEING TRUTH ABOUT YOUR EMOTIONS

"Feelings, wo-o-o feelings"[1]
"When I was in distress, I sought the Lord."[2]
"I'm not upset."[3]

What do you do when you get angry? When you're lonely? When you're bored? What do you do when you feel sad or anxious or stressed out? If you're like I was for many years, whenever you have any uncomfortable emotion, you turn to a "coping mechanism" (or you at least think about doing so). For me, it was eating and eating and eating. For you, it might be zoning out with a video game or binge-watching television shows. Or it might be much more dangerous – looking at online pornography, purchasing way more things than you need, misusing legal or illegal drugs, gambling, or drinking enough alcohol to pass out or stay intoxicated for hours. So far in this book, we've looked at how our beliefs – about God, ourselves, and other aspects of life – influence our behavior. Now, we'll turn to another big contributor to persistent unwanted behaviors – how we respond to and manage our emotions.

Everyone has quite a few feelings about their feelings, ranging from total denial that they feel anything at all to "letting it all hang out." Most conservative evangelical Christians have some degree of guilt over their negative emotions and inability to control them in the manner they feel they "ought." Because of this, many see their emotions as their enemy. They try to eliminate them and suppress them, often through behaviors that distract them from the discomfort of what they're feeling.

There are many emotions worth welcoming – joy, love, contentment – and even some that don't feel good but help us out, such as the fear that causes our adrenaline to pump when we see a big black bear approaching and we need to run, fast! However, emotions can be very unwelcome, not only because they feel bad, but also because of how we respond to them.[4]

Without even realizing it, most people live their lives primarily in response to their emotions. They make how they feel their ultimate authority for deciding what they do and don't do. An example of making emotions the authority in one's life is when a person is sure he has lost his salvation because he *feels* guilty and doesn't *feel* forgiven. This usually leads to a great deal of repeat professions of faith in Christ and "walking down the aisle" to pray the "sinner's prayer." It is the *feeling* of guilt, rather than the truth about the atoning death of Christ, that motivates this behavior. Even when people deny their emotions, they still make them their authority, dictating their behavior. When I used to binge-eat, it was because I *felt* as if I *had* to eat. I didn't realize I was suppressing anger. It was my fear of feeling angry that was controlling my decision to binge-eat.

Without even realizing it, most people live their lives primarily in response to their emotions.

Not only are people unaware that they're letting emotions run their lives, but also their beliefs about their emotions create even more emotional havoc. Many people believe that there are emotions that are, in and of themselves, sinful. For conservative Christians, this is especially true regarding anger. As a result, they experience constant guilt over every angry feeling and/or they suppress their anger through unhealthy behaviors, such as compulsive shopping, excessive screen watching, or overeating.

Given all of the negatives about our emotions, how is it possible to gain a positive perspective on them, even the ones that feel really horrible?

To begin with, it is important to recognize that emotions are a God-given part of our nature. There are numerous references in Scripture to God's emotions, such as grieving, joy, affection, anger, and indignation. Since we are created in God's image, it is natural that we also have a full array of emotions. (See the Homework section of this chapter for many Scripture references regarding God's emotions.)

Even if emotions are a natural part of our makeup, it's difficult to accept them when we find them to be very painful and more in control of us than we are of them. It's certainly understandable that many people try to suppress their emotions through distracting themselves with what are often referred to as "compulsive behaviors." However, when people distract themselves from feeling their emotions, they are squelching what has the potential of being one of their best friends. You've heard the expression, "Don't shoot the messenger." Well, that's exactly what people do when they deny, suppress, and despise their emotions. What they don't realize is that their emotions are serving as messengers, telling them to check out what is going on inside of them. When we have painful emotions, *they* are not the "problem." They can be likened to a red light that shows up on a car's dashboard when the oil level is low. The light isn't what needs fixing. It's telling you there's an unseen problem that needs attention. In a similar manner, our emotions can and do tell us that something needs attention "under the hood," in our thinking and beliefs.

Emotions are serving as messengers, telling us to check out what is going on in our thinking and beliefs.

An example of emotions as messengers in my life is the anxiety I used to feel at my workplace when I was a legal secretary. When work stacked up on my desk, I got worried that my boss would disapprove of me for not working quickly enough. I knew I was working as efficiently as I was able, but I still feared that I was failing to meet my boss's expectations. Then my anxiety made it even more difficult for me to concentrate and get my work finished. This resulted in more anxiety, creating a vicious cycle. Before I remembered that emotions are messengers, I tried to address the anxiety directly by browbeating myself with thoughts such as, *Stop worrying! You know worry is a sin. After all, we are to 'be anxious for nothing.'* And, following through on the rest of Philippians 4:6, I prayed about everything, but the prayers were all the same: "God, help me get this all done really fast!"

When I paused and remembered that my emotions are serving as messengers, I realized my anxiety was telling me something was wrong "under the hood." I turned to God, asking him to show me what I was thinking that resulted in feeling anxious. God brought to my mind that I was returning to an old belief about needing constant approval from people in order to feel I'm okay. Then, instead of asking God to help me work more quickly, my form of "praying about everything" was more along these lines: "God, I know you are really the one I'm working for and you know I'm trying my hardest, so help me relax and accept that you will protect my reputation with my boss if it needs protecting." I also had the thought, *If my boss really does disapprove, that is his problem, not mine. If he fires me because I can't do this volume of work, God will provide me with a more suitable job.* The anxiety itself was not my problem. The problem was with my belief that I would be a worthless person if my boss disapproved of me or fired me. Once I prayerfully thought through the belief underlying my anxiety (which only took a minute or so), I no longer felt anxious. Do you see how different this process was than praying for God to help me try harder or to just remove my anxiety?

But what about the big one, anger? Is it also a messenger, not a sin? People who believe feeling anger is a sin usually point to the Sermon on the Mount, where being angry is equated with murder (Matthew 5:21-22). However, by contrast, Ephesians 4:26 can be paraphrased: "You may be angry, only do not sin."[5] The inference here is that you can feel anger and yet not commit any sin. The dividing line has to do with allowing anger to be harbored and to turn into bitterness or acting on anger by verbally or physically lashing out or taking revenge. What is done with anger is what Jesus was condemning. It has been said, tongue in cheek, that anger is not a sin until it travels to the end of your fist and punches someone in the nose. The *feeling* is not the sin; it's what you do with it that may be sin.

Even if you are not persuaded by this line of thinking and are convinced that anger is almost always a sin (of course, God's anger never is), sin or not, it still serves as a messenger. Just because it's a sin doesn't mean you'll never feel it. We are not, after all, fully regenerate yet. We still suffer from the "sin measles" (the "flesh"). Simply calling sin "sin" will not cure us of it. When we are willing to see anger as a "red light on the dashboard," we are then able to ask God to show us what needs addressing "under the hood" and thereby address the beliefs and thinking underlying the anger. We will look much more thoroughly at anger and other specific emotions in the next chapter.

Recognizing that our emotions are messengers can free us to accept and feel our emotions rather than "stuff" them or distract ourselves from them through unwanted or ungodly behaviors. But, simply recognizing them as messengers is really the first step in experiencing them in a healthy way. And, as with everything that has to do with "life and godliness" (2 Peter 1:3-4, ESV), the Bible is what gives us the best pattern for how we are to respond to our emotions. In looking at the psalms, we certainly see a lot of emotions expressed, many of them negative. Psalms 55, 73, and 77 provide very clear examples of how godly people expressed and resolved their emotions in a godly way, sometimes referred to as "biblical lament." For ease in remembering this process, I'm borrowing an acronym, "REED."[6] But, please note that this is *not* a formula by which *you* can take "four easy steps" to overcoming your every difficult emotion. Rather, it is an aid for remembering to include God in your emotional struggles, to help you enter more fully into an intimate relationship with him that will transform you and your emotions.

The "**R**" in "REED" stands for "**recognize**." Before you can respond appropriately to an emotion, you have to acknowledge that you're feeling it. This isn't always easy if you've developed the habit of automatically suppressing your "unacceptable" feelings, such as depression, anxiety, and anger. Rather than actually feel an emotion, you might just feel that you need to eat or shop or watch TV or play a video game. This is what I did when I got angry with close friends. I didn't *feel* angry; I just felt ravenous!

If you're feeling as though you have no choice but to turn to a "coping mechanism" behavior, this is very likely a sign that there's an emotion you're trying to avoid feeling. When this happens, you can turn to God and ask him to help you recognize what you're feeling. Prayerfully look back over what has happened recently and ask yourself, *If this had happened to someone else, what would I assume he or she would feel in the same situation?* You may also want to try talking with a friend about your day to see what he thinks is likely bothering you. Remember that God uses fellow

Recognizing that our emotions are messengers can free us to accept and feel our emotions rather than "stuff" them or distract ourselves from them through unwanted or ungodly behaviors.

believers as one means by which he communicates with us. Another way to identify emotions is to read through some psalms and see if you find yourself identifying with any of them. Ask yourself, *What was this person feeling when he wrote this psalm?* You might want to prayerfully "test out" a list of emotions to see if one or more fit.[7]

What is most important about the "R" in "REED" is to realize that you can call upon the Holy Spirit to enable you to recognize what exactly it is that you're feeling.

Once you've recognized that you're feeling something – and even if you can't quite put a name to it yet – move to the next part of "REED," the first "E," which stands for "**express** to God." Time and time again, we see in the psalms how the writers openly expressed to God exactly what they were feeling. Here are a few examples:

- Psalm 10:1: Questioning God about whether he really cares
- Psalm 22:1-2: Expressing doubts to God about his goodness
- Psalm 38:1, 4: Guilt and fear of reprisals
- Psalm 51:1-3: Remorse and confession of sin
- Psalm 64:1-6: Complaining to God about other people
- Psalm 70:1: Fear
- Psalm 74:9, 11: Anger at God

Not only was God willing to listen to these expressions of peoples' emotions, but also he recorded them in the Bible. (This is a list of "negative" emotions. The psalms also contain a great number of "positive" emotions people expressed to God, such as praise, joy, zeal, and affection.)

When you really think about it, who is best equipped to handle what you're feeling? There is nothing you can say to God that threatens him (unlike how many people might respond). Many "good Christians" are terrified of offending God. This is certainly understandable, but not very logical. God already knows what we're thinking. He understands our thoughts and feelings better than we do (Psalm 139:4). Whether or not we talk with him about our feelings, he is fully aware of them. We might as well go ahead and be honest with him, keeping in mind verses such as Psalm 62:8; Romans 8:1, 31-39; and Hebrews 4:15-16, which assure us that, thanks to Christ, it's okay to boldly approach God and that we are secure in his love.

There are many people with emotional and relationship problems because they do not know they are supposed to turn to God with their emotions. Typically, people respond to their emotions in one of two ways: 1) lashing out and dumping their emotions on others, which burdens or breaks their relationships, or 2) stuffing and suppressing their emotions, which lead to their emotions "coming out sideways" through ulcers, nervous breakdowns, high blood pressure, chronic depression, self-loathing, and compulsive behaviors.

God has demonstrated throughout Scripture that he is willing and able to listen to us when we need to express how we're feeling. So, once we've recognized that we are feeling something ("R"), we need to express what we're feeling to God (the first "E").

The second "E" in "REED" stands for "**evaluate**." Look at Psalm 73. Here was a man who nearly "lost it" with God. He said that when his "heart was grieved" and his "spirit embittered," he was a "brute beast" before God (vv. 21-22). He did the "R" and knew he was grieved and angry, and he did the first "E" and "let it all hang out" before God. *Then* he came to a turning point and did an about-face when he "entered the sanctuary of God" (v. 17). This psalmist was

God has demonstrated throughout Scripture that he is willing and able to listen to us when we need to express how we're feeling.

willing to listen to God, willing to check out what he had believed against what God had to say and what he knew was true about God's character. And God revealed to this man where his thinking was off and gave him an accurate perspective of the situation. He had envied others who, for a time only, appeared better off than he, but God showed him how all would be resolved in eternity.

Similarly, we too can invite God to show us what's going on "under the hood"; i.e., what we're thinking and believing that is resulting in our feeling upset. An example of an underlying issue would be if you flare and feel automatically defensive when criticized. This may be a sign that you are not secure in your beliefs about God's unconditional approval for you regardless of your performance. Or, if you're anxious, is this revealing that you're not all that sure God will come through for you in your situation? God has demonstrated in Scripture that he is interested in pointing out to us our "heart issues," the beliefs that underlie our emotions and behaviors. (See Psalm 25:8-9, 32:8, and 139:23-24.)

The "E" for "evaluate" is not intended to encourage you to psychoanalyze yourself! Allow the Holy Spirit to be who he is – the Counselor. If you're willing to hear him, he will reveal to you what underlies the emotions you're feeling. He will enable you to evaluate, in light of truth of Scripture, the thoughts and beliefs you hold that result in the troubling emotions you feel.

Finally, the "**D**" in "REED" stands for "**decide**." It's not enough to give intellectual assent to the fact that what you've been thinking and believing is in error; you must decide to replace those thoughts and beliefs with God's truth. This is probably the most difficult part of responding to our "messenger" emotions. Many people are convinced they cannot believe in something until they *feel* that it's really true for them. But those feelings can be liars, programmed by years of erroneous messages from others or oneself. The fact of the matter is that, whether you feel it's true or not, what's true is true! Whether you feel God's Word is true or not, it's true! So, how do you make the decision to replace your wrong thinking and beliefs with God's truth?

As with everything we are called upon by God to do in life, the Holy Spirit is our power source. Ask him to help you take the steps necessary to believe in the truth and act upon it. Then be willing to thoroughly and prayerfully think through the truth and how that can positively affect you. For example, here's a "decide" line of thinking: *Even though I feel like a failure and feel I should conform to society's standard of "success," I'm not going to keep dwelling on these "things of the earth." I am going to continue to believe I'm a new creation in Christ, acceptable by God's standards, and that my "success" is found in knowing and surrendering to him and his will.* The result should be less panic over being a "failure" and no longer worrying about criticisms from anyone, including parents and peers. Then you will no longer need to alleviate that anxiety through behaviors, such as workaholism or buying things you really can't afford and probably don't need.

"REED" is *not* a four-step process that you follow and then feel you've "handled" your emotions. That would be responding to your emotions in "the flesh." Instead, "REED" is a reminder of how you need to turn to God with your emotions and allow him to lead you in working out the messages they're sending, as well as guiding you into the truth that sets you free.

The "REED" pattern is another way we're reminded to "dive deep with God." In fact, if you look more closely at the example of "diving deep" on page 55, "REED" came into play as I worked my way down the layers and back up again.

> *We can invite God to show us what's going on "under the hood"; i.e., what we're thinking and believing that is resulting in our feeling so upset.*

> *It's not enough to give intellectual assent to the fact that what you've been thinking and believing is in error; you must decide to replace those thoughts and beliefs with God's truth.*

When my clothes started to feel tighter than they had for a few years, I realized that for several weeks I'd felt a need to snack at bedtime, but I didn't actually feel any emotional upset. I knew I wasn't physically hungry, so I prayerfully thought through what emotions I was trying to avoid by eating those bedtime snacks. It came to me in that "still, small voice" that I was avoiding feeling lonely and depressed. I recognized that, at bedtime, I was most aware of being unmarried, and this was very painful to me. God helped me recognize ("R" of "REED") that I was feeling lonely, depressed, and frustrated about being single, complaining about what was clearly God's plan for my life at that time.

But recognizing what I was feeling wasn't enough. Once I knew what I was feeling, I needed to express (the first "E" in "REED") those feelings to God – to be honest about my emotions, getting them out instead of stuffing them down with food. It was at this time that I started writing a series of journal entries, passionately expressing the pain I felt over being single during my thirties and forties. (I married a couple of months before I turned 45.) Such feelings aren't necessarily resolved by thinking them through just once. They recur at different times and for different reasons. Each time is an opportunity to turn to God with our pain and invite him into our struggles. I poured out my heart to God in my journal.

Once I was perfectly honest with God about how I felt, I then gave him a chance to provide me with his input.

Once I was perfectly honest with God about how I felt, I then gave him a chance to provide me with his input. This is the next "E" of "REED," evaluate. Asking God to lead me, I evaluated my thinking in light of God's truth. I realized I believed that I needed to be married to be happy and thought God was cruel to withhold marriage from someone who craved companionship and affection as much as I did. I believed that marriage was the only means by which I could get my affection needs met and that my worth would be greater if I were married. I had "bought into" some of the cultural standards prevalent in the conservative evangelical subculture – that marriage was a sign of greater maturity and value. I had also "bought into" what the current Western culture dishes out regarding sex being the primary means by which adults get their affection needs met. In addition, I believed that God was not interested in my emotional well-being, but was cruelly withholding what I wanted most in order to make me into a "better Christian." I was back to my "God is mean" belief.

In contrast to these erroneous beliefs, God brought to my mind Scripture passages that assured me that he really did care about me and was interested in providing for my needs – even my need for affection. And I remembered that my worth was not dependent upon my marital status but on what Christ did for me on the cross.

Now it was up to me to make a decision, the "D" of "REED." In light of God's assurance that he meets my needs, I started purposely looking for how God was providing me with affection. Suddenly I realized how much affection I was receiving from my friends, co-workers, and fellow church members through their hugs, attentive listening and eye contact, thoughtful cards and notes, and small gestures such as a touch on the arm or a pat on the back. I also decided to agree with God about my worth and started having thoughts such as: *It is perfectly fine to be single – it's people, not God, who might judge me according to whether I'm married or not*, and *The combination of my age and marital status makes me unique*.

Soon the need to have a snack at bedtime went away. I never had to consciously concentrate on not snacking at bedtime. I just noticed one day that I wasn't doing it anymore. From time to time, I still found myself wanting to eat a bedtime snack even though I didn't feel physically hungry. Having already thoroughly prayed and thought through this behavior in the past made it much easier to recognize it for what it was when it cropped up again, although the reasons changed after I married. (My husband worked a night shift and I worked days.) I continued to invite God to speak to me about what was going on in my thinking and beliefs.

To the degree we realize that God provides us with a means to respond in a healthy, godly way to our emotions by turning to him and his truth – thus deepening our intimacy with him – we are freed from the need to turn to ungodly or unwanted "coping mechanism" behaviors in the face of painful emotions.

Reflection

1. What are some of the emotions you suspect you are trying to avoid when you turn to behaviors you wish you weren't doing?

2. What are some emotional needs you might be trying to meet through the behaviors you wish you weren't doing?

3. What would happen if you felt your emotions rather than avoiding them?

4. What are some ways in which God may be meeting your needs but you just didn't previously recognize he was doing so?

What Others Have Experienced

Nearly every "stuck Christian" I've talked with has seen what they're doing that they wish they weren't doing as *the* problem. They want badly to address that problem directly, not realizing that it is a symptom of the *real* problem. Most say something along the lines of "If I just had more faith, I wouldn't do this anymore," or "If I just had more will power…," or "If I just saw my sin as truly sinful…" But, that's exactly what they've been working on for years without experiencing freedom for any length of time. When challenged to ask God what emotion is being avoided by engaging in a compulsive behavior, many have a knee-jerk reaction: "I'm not feeling anything." And, of course, that's the point of the behavior. Emotions are scary stuff; it seems safer to avoid them. But the behavior used to avoid certain emotions leads to actually feeling some other emotions very intensely – embarrassment, guilt, shame, and self-loathing because of overeating, over-spending, sneaking porn, or spending excessive time playing video games. So, it's either continue doing what you're doing, or start asking God to show you what emotions you're avoiding by doing what you're doing. Which is most beneficial for you?

At the same time that emotions are avoided by engaging in distracting behaviors, other emotional needs are also being met. Feelings of success and accomplishment can result from workaholism and even video game victories. Overeating can feel soothing and comforting for a while. Being seen as having an "addiction" can allow for the avoidance of unwanted responsibilities. Watching porn, pulling out one's hair, or engaging in petty shoplifting can all provide a little surge of excitement that more acceptable behaviors don't seem to offer. When attempts to meet emotional needs are through illicit or ungodly behaviors, this is usually a symptom of the person seeing God as not caring enough to give what is really needed and/or not seeing how God is already providing for those needs in unexpected ways. When you are accustomed to getting needs met your way, it can be difficult to see the alternate ways in which God is providing for those needs. Your loving heavenly Father is, however, interested in showing you how he is providing for you through his exhilarating Word, his caring personal attention, his people that are spiritual family, and his vast resources in his creation.

I have encountered in others – and have personally felt – a great deal of fear regarding strong emotions. There is a dread of losing control. This is where building trust in God is crucial. If you see God as someone who is not only capable of handling your feelings, but also willing to listen and provide you with the strength and means to move through them, you will venture forth and start expressing how you feel to him. It often feels like walking on seemingly thin ice and taking some baby steps in order to test just how solidly you're supported. But look who's been out there skating before us! In the psalms, many of the writers virtually hollered at God regarding their fears and frustrations. And God helped them through it all. Almost every psalm that starts out with despair or railing against God ends with hope and praise for him.

Actually feeling and expressing your emotions to God need not result in meltdown. Even spending time engaged in hysterical crying won't kill you. Many people feel that, once they start feeling an emotion – or start crying – they'll never stop. But you do stop. There's always some task that comes up that you have to do. Also, you just get tired of crying or it comes to its natural end, especially if you're letting God in. His desire is to lead you into hope and light (Jeremiah 29:11; Ephesians 5:13-14). If you let yourself feel your emotions and express them fully to God, the worst that will happen is you'll feel bad for a while, but then you'll feel much, much better and the "need" to engage in distracting behaviors will diminish and eventually disappear, because it was really a need to avoid or cope with emotions, not to actually do the behavior. Working through negative emotions with God's power and presence frees you from them.

If you see God as someone who is not only capable of handling your feelings, but also willing to listen and provide you with the strength and means to move through them, you will venture forth and start expressing how you feel to him.

Homework

1. At least one time this week, make use of the following "REED"[8] outline when you feel negative emotions or find yourself engaging in an unwanted or ungodly behavior.

> **RECOGNIZE:** Acknowledge your emotions; don't suppress them. Ask God to help you identify what emotions you are feeling.
>
> _____
>
> _____
>
> **EXPRESS:** Write to God how you feel.
>
> _____
>
> _____
>
> _____
>
> **EVALUATE:** Consider, and ask God to reveal to you, what your emotions say about your thinking on the issue at hand. How do your behavior and feelings reflect what you are thinking and believing? What false beliefs about yourself and God are your emotions indicating? How does what you think and believe compare with God's Word?
>
> _____
>
> _____
>
> _____
>
> _____
>
> _____
>
> _____
>
> **DECIDE:** Choose to agree with God's truth concerning the issue at hand. Then, choose to act on that truth, knowing that the Holy Spirit will empower you. For example: "Father, I feel anxious about my husband possibly losing his job. It's hard for me to trust you in this area when I think of our family's needs. Thank you for listening and caring about how I feel. I know you promise to meet all our needs (Philippians 4:19), so I am casting all my cares on you (1 Peter 5:7). Therefore, I choose to go about my life, not focusing on the potential problem, but trusting you to work this out for the good and to meet our needs in your way and in your timing."
>
> _____
>
> _____
>
> _____
>
> _____
>
> _____
>
> _____

2. Complete the following Bible study.

EMOTIONAL INTIMACY WITH GOD

Is God emotional? When you think about how emotional God is, what do you usually think?

After you are clear about your thinking regarding how emotional God is, look up each of the following passages and jot notes about what each says concerning God's emotions.

Genesis 6:5-6 _____

Exodus 32:10 _____

Psalm 25:6 _____

Psalm 145:8 _____

Isaiah 62:5 _____

Jeremiah 31:20 _____

Mark 10:21 _____

Luke 13:34 _____

Luke 22:44 _____

John 11:35 _____

2 Corinthians 1:3-4 _____

Hebrews 5:7 _____

How do these passages compare or contrast with your sense of God's emotions?

How does God feel about your emotions? What do you think his opinion is about how you feel?

Once you've thought through how God feels about your emotions, look up the following passages and make notes about how God responded to and/or accepted people's emotions.

1 Samuel 1:12-20 _____

Psalm 51:17 _____

Psalm 55:16-17, 22 _____

Psalm 56:8 _____

Matthew 11:28 _____

Matthew 12:20 _____

John 20:24-28 _____

Hebrews 4:15-16 _____

1 Peter 5:7 _____

How do these passages compare or contrast with how you usually think God feels about your emotions?

Homework Follow-up

1. As a result of completing the "Emotional Intimacy with God" Bible study, in what ways have your beliefs about God's emotions and his attitude toward your emotions changed?

2. In going through the "REED" worksheet, what did God reveal to you about underlying thoughts and beliefs when you wanted to engage in a behavior you wish you could stop doing?

Comments on the Homework

The overwhelming majority of people I've heard answer the question about God's emotions and God's attitude toward their emotions had not previously thought of God as particularly emotional at all. Most assume God is rather unemotional and stoic. For others, only God's "wrath" came to mind. However, their ideas about God's emotionality came from sources other than Scripture – such as how their parents acted or what they'd heard in a scary sermon. The Bible reveals that God's emotional palette consists of many colors and hues. God is passionate, feeling deeply such emotions as grief, joy, elation, anger, and delight. It is no wonder that we, who are created in his image, also experience a broad array of emotions.

Most assume God is rather unemotional and stoic.

Not only does God feel emotions, but also he accepts that we feel emotions too. When Hannah cried out for a son, God didn't say, "Get over it, woman. Be grateful for what you do have!" although that is what her husband basically said to her! No, God took pity on her and granted her the desire of her heart (1 Samuel 1:15-18). When Thomas doubted and wouldn't believe Jesus had risen from the grave unless he had concrete proof, Jesus didn't rebuke him or turn him away. He took the initiative in allowing Thomas to obtain the tangible proof he wanted (John 20:24-27). We have a Savior who is able to "sympathize with our weaknesses"! (See Hebrews 4:15-16.)

Many people believe God feels fed up with their emotions and lack of emotional control. Most of these have experienced parents, a spouse, or other significant people in their lives losing patience with them or being very rejecting of them when they had "emotional displays." It is easy to transfer to God what we have experienced with significant people, but it is not accurate. God understands why we feel the way we do better than even we can. He accepts how we feel and can handle our expressions of emotion better than anyone else. And he knows that he has the truth that will bring us peace in the midst of even the most intensely troubling feelings.

Often, emotion-avoiding behavior is never analyzed and certainly never analyzed with the help and guidance of the Holy Spirit. Realizing what we're really feeling and why we want to engage in troubling behavior definitely brings us at least halfway to no longer using our behaviors to avoid or allay emotions. This is the "R," "E," and "E" of "REED." But, the most important part is the "D." Once we start deciding that God is indeed interested in meeting our needs; once we start looking for how he *is* meeting them; and once we start communicating with God about our feelings, believing he wants to hear and wants to comfort and change our perspective, we are set free from the felt need to engage in distracting "fleshly" behaviors. The behavior isn't the real problem. What's necessary is to lift the hood and let God play master mechanic – exchanging our old, worn-out, damaged thinking and beliefs for his freeing truth.

7 FREEING TRUTH ABOUT SOME SPECIFIC, ESPECIALLY TROUBLING EMOTIONS

"Everybody hurts sometimes."[1]
"Be angry and sin not."[2]
"You make me so mad."[3]

My colossal eating binges almost always started at Dunkin' Donuts® with a baker's dozen that I carefully chose – fat and greasy pastries that were cream-filled and chocolate covered. The next stop was usually Long John Silver's™ for some fried fish to go, along with a dozen or more hushpuppies. Then I continued up – and then back down – the five-mile stretch of Northwest Expressway where nearly every fast-food chain had a franchise. I'd stop and buy cookies, ice cream, shakes, burgers – constantly munching along the way – but making sure to buy enough food so I'd still have plenty left by the time I got home. Having already busted my budget, I then proceeded to bust my gut. But usually, the food I'd bought wasn't enough. So, once the good stuff was eaten up, I'd start making "rough cookies," a concoction of whatever was on hand – chopped up corn flakes if there was no flour, pink packets of sweetener if there was no sugar, extra baking soda if I had no eggs. Whipped all together and cooked till golden brown. Then I'd gobble them up without even really tasting them. I ate and ate until I felt physically ill. I ate and ate until I lay on my back on my bed and started crying, crying because I was sooooo ANGRY!

In the last chapter, we looked at emotions in general. In this chapter, we'll concentrate more specifically on the most common emotions with which people cope through unwanted, compulsive-feeling behaviors: anger, frustration, depression, anxiety, loneliness, and boredom. You can probably immediately think of times when you've gone to a coping mechanism because you were feeling one or more of these emotions – or because you were trying to avoid feeling one or more of these emotions. In the small groups that I've led, I've found that most of the participants take it for granted that they *will* engage in a coping behavior if they feel any of these common emotions. We have been conditioned by television shows and movies to think that we can "medicate" ourselves by engaging in eating junk food, zoning out while binge-watching streamed series, going shopping, or playing video games in just about the same way one might take aspirin or Xanax®. But, the positive effects of this "medicine" are minimal and short-lived. And the side effects are worse than what we were "treating," because not only do our coping behaviors result in guilt, self-condemnation, shame, and self-loathing, but also they don't help resolve the underlying issues that brought about the feelings of anger or anxiety or boredom that we're trying to avoid.

It was always the same on the day after one of my monumental binges. I told myself I'd never do it again and I'd always stick to my diet. I worked out a schedule that included more exercise. I planned low-calorie meals for the next several weeks. But mostly, I hated myself. And, of course, within a week or so, I binged again. There came a point in my life, however, when I realized that, rather than directly attacking the binge-eating with self-recriminations or attempts to crack down on myself with more discipline, the long-term and truly effective solution is to learn godly ways to think through and pray through difficult emotions. In general, as discussed in the last chapter,

In this chapter, we'll concentrate more specifically on the most common emotions with which people cope by engaging in compulsive-feeling behaviors: anger, frustration, depression, anxiety, loneliness, and boredom.

the reminder of "REED" is appropriate for addressing any negative emotion, but more specifically, let's look in detail at some emotions that seem to most frequently trigger ungodly coping behaviors.

Anger and Bitterness

Anger is probably the most powerful and uncomfortable emotion many people feel. There is an abundance of overt, as well as subtle, messages within our culture, and especially within the evangelical Christian subculture, that condemn especially women – much more than men, but also men – for feeling, let alone displaying, anger. Because of the guilt associated with feeling angry and the belief many hold that feeling anger is sinful, it is an emotion people frequently try to "stuff" by doing something intense to distract them from the anger. For years, I unconsciously believed anger to be so totally unacceptable that I didn't even feel my anger, but in response to any incident in which someone offended me, I bypassed feeling angry altogether and went straight to "eating the world."

Because of the guilt associated with feeling angry and the belief many hold that feeling anger is sinful, it is an emotion people frequently try to "stuff."

As I started to look into a new way of thinking about my coping behaviors, I found in my own life – and in the lives of many struggling Christians I know – that a better understanding of what motivates anger brings about a greater acceptance of the emotion and a decreased desire to suppress it through "coping mechanisms." The following is a helpful diagram regarding the usual progression involved in feeling and harboring anger, which results in bitterness, which leads to a downward spiral of negative attitudes and emotions.

EXPECTATIONS, ANGER, AND BITTERNESS[4]

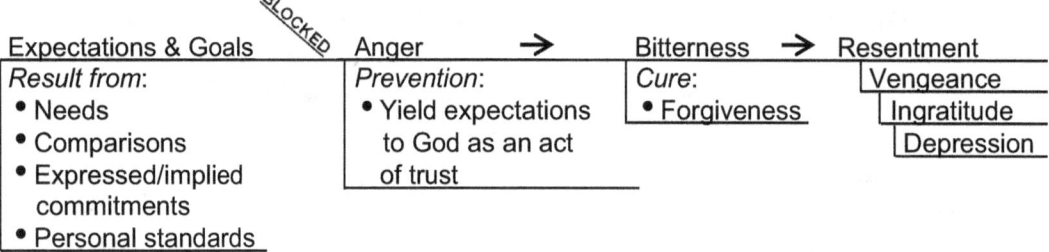

Anger has its roots in the expectations we have, and we form our expectations through various means. Our own sense of need for love, appreciation, worth, affection, comfort, etc., leads to developing expectations about how these needs should be met and by whom. For example, if I feel a need for affirmation, I may have an expectation that my husband should commend me for my accomplishments.

Also, we look around and see how life is for others and, through comparison, formulate expectations. Just about anyone who grew up during the early 1960s and watched television developed certain expectations about parents – that they should in some way resemble Andy Griffith of Mayberry or the Beaver's mother, June. I used to feel terribly disappointed that my father hadn't come up with a nickname for me similar to the ones that Robert Young of "Father Knows Best" used for his daughters, "Kitten" and "Princess."

Another way expectations are developed is in response to the commitments people really do make or make by implication. When a husband vows in a public ceremony to be faithful until "death do us part," the wife's understanding of faithfulness may result in an expectation that he won't look approvingly at other women. When parents have (or adopt) a child, the implication is that the parents are making a commitment to faithfully care for that child. Family members and the child himself would naturally expect consistently kind and loving treatment to be extended to him.

As natural as it is for us to have expectations about the people in our lives, it is just as common for us to run into occasions when those expectations are sadly disappointed, when they just are not met. The usual knee-jerk emotional reaction to unmet expectations is anger.

In addition to expectations, experiencing blocked goals often results in feeling anger. Each of us has a set of personal standards, which provide the basis for all our goals, large and small. An example of a goal is the desire to have the house cleaned up before guests arrive. When there is an impediment to reaching that goal, such as two active toddlers dragging all of their toys out of the closet into the living room, a common reaction is anger. What young mother hasn't screamed at her children – or worse – when they've foiled her personal goals by just being kids?

All our expectations of people and all the goals we have for ourselves set us up for experiencing anger from time to time (or maybe most of the time!). Wouldn't it be nice if there were a way to prevent even getting to that point of feeling angry? Well, there is a way to cut off anger at the pass, at least some of the time. The best preventative for anger is to relinquish our expectations and goals to God. Often, as we grow older, we begin to realize that many of our expectations and goals developed in youth were unrealistic and overly idealistic. These are pretty easy to give to God. But just as often, goals and expectations are extremely hard to relinquish. Many times, we don't even realize we have expectations, or the perceived "rightness" of an expectation or goal is taken so for granted that it is not even open to question. Examples of hidden expectations might be believing it's only right that your husband praise you when you dress up for an evening out, feeling your parents should unconditionally accept you, or being sure your children should consistently obey. In order to uncover the goals and expectations we are not even aware we have, we can turn to a wonderful Counselor, calling upon the Holy Spirit to reveal to us the expectations and goals to which we cling and to provide us with the grace to surrender them to God, trusting he will enable us to meet his goals in his timing.

When it comes to yielding our goals and expectations to God, it's important to remember that "there is a way that appears to be right, but in the end it leads to death"! (Proverbs 14:12) Yes, a certain goal may seem very right, but insisting upon its achievement can sometimes be the death of us. Demanding that things go the way we want sets us up for a tremendous amount of anger when they don't. However, when we shift our focus to "all things work together for good" (Romans 8:28, KJV) for God's children, we can more easily relinquish our demand that "it really ought to be this way" and trust that, whatever happens, God will ultimately make it a plus in our lives. In fact, when circumstances don't "go right" for us, this is an excellent opportunity to seek God and put trust in him, to experience a deeper personal intimacy with him. This is in part why an emphasis early on in this book is the need to have an accurate view of our loving heavenly Father. The more you are able to trust God, the less difficult it is to give up on expectations and to be willing to see even the most well-intentioned and godly goals sidetracked or delayed.

But, let's face it, we don't always perfectly trust God and we don't always know we have expectations or goals until we've already come face to face with a whopping dose of anger. You just can't anticipate or prayerfully discover ahead of time every single expectation and goal. So,

All our expectations of people and all the goals we have for ourselves set us up for experiencing anger.

what do you do when preventative measures weren't taken and you find yourself experiencing feelings of anger? Well, there's a cure! It's two-fold: forgiveness and trust. If you're angry at a person, forgiveness is the cure – and true forgiveness involves trust in God. If you're angry over circumstances or unrealized goals, trust in God is the cure.

Let's look at forgiveness first. It is very important to make clear what forgiveness is *not* before most people can find extending forgiveness possible and even natural. Forgiving is *not* the same as condoning. Some people think, *If I forgive her for criticizing me, it's the same thing as saying it's okay that she does it.* But, actually, forgiving implies that the act for which you're extending forgiveness was *wrong*. If the person had done nothing to offend, he or she would need no forgiveness! If you believed what the person did to be right, if you condoned his or her behavior, you would not then need to forgive.

Forgiving is not the same as condoning.

Also, forgiveness does *not* mean you automatically feel good about what has happened. Love does not delight in evil (1 Corinthians 13:6). Evil deeds are very sad indeed. We can rejoice in how God makes everything work to the good (Romans 8:28), but we can still know and feel that the offense was a sad, even horrible event. There is a powerful story of a man who forgave the woman who murdered his sister and became friends with her while she was on death row. His forgiveness of the murderess in no way diminished his sense of loss or mourning over his sister's gruesome death. It was sad; it was wrong; it was a terrible loss. He did not have to think, *I'm fine with it now*, in order to forgive the offender.

Forgiveness does not mean you auto-matically feel good about what has happened.

Forgiveness does *not* mean you must trust the offender. If someone embezzles from your company, you need to forgive him, but it would be foolish to turn around and entrust him with handling your company's funds again! I forgave my stepfather for molesting me, but should I then have suggested he babysit a five-year-old girl? No, forgiveness is not the same as trust. But forgiveness does leave the door open to trust should the offender repent and show convincing evidence of significant change.

Forgiveness does not mean you must trust the offender.

So, if forgiveness is *not* condoning, changing your feelings, or trusting, what *is* it? I personally find it difficult to define – especially succinctly. I've heard forgiveness described as breaking the chains that bind you to your offender. I like to look at forgiveness as entrusting God with the offender and the offense, believing that God will work out your injury to your ultimate good. Excellent examples of people's ill deeds working toward God's ultimate goals for them and others are found in the life of Joseph (Genesis 37 and 39-50).

Forgiveness is a decision and not an emotion. I remember when I was 25 years old, I chose to forgive my parents and stepparents for the many ways in which I felt they had hurt me during the course of my upbringing. I had to admit that I really didn't *feel* like forgiving them. However, I was the one suffering emotionally – not them – because of my bitterness and resentment and resulting depression. At the time, I told God that, as much as I didn't feel like it, I was choosing to forgive them because I believed he was directing me to do so. As half-hearted as that sounds, the results were amazing. Within a few days of making that decision to forgive, I went from feeling deeply depressed and being almost totally withdrawn to feeling hopeful and eager to be with people.

Forgiveness goes back to one's beliefs about God and his character. To the degree that we trust that God will work all things together for our ultimate good, no matter how horrible the offense, we will find it easier to forgive. And forgiveness does become a little easier with "practice." Seeing what God does with our forgiveness makes us more eager to forgive the next time the occasion presents itself.

Even when you make a choice to forgive and to be a person who is willing to forgive, there are still a few times when it appears forgiveness isn't "working." We sometimes think that, because we've forgiven someone once, we should never feel angry with him or her again. However, it is not possible to anticipate future offenses or their impact ahead of time, even when you've had long experience with forgiving someone repeatedly. This seems to come up often with people in regard to their parents. "I forgave her for saying that the last time, so why am I angry now that she said it again?" The issue here is that Mom has indeed offended *again*. You cannot forgive someone for a future offense, even if it's a familiar one. For each new offense, forgiveness is again necessary. It is sometimes helpful, however, to think through why you take it so hard when there is a repeated offense. It seems that, especially with our parents and spouses, we have difficulty giving up the "they should be [fill in the blank]." Our thoughts tend to be along the lines of, *She should be accepting and not criticize me*, or *He should be loving and pay attention when I talk*.

We have little power to make people what we feel they "should be." The "Serenity Prayer"[5] provides a good reminder for us in this regard. We need God to grant us the wisdom to know what is beyond our control and to give us the courage to put our lives, relationships, and circumstances into *his* hands. So it is with the people who are repeat offenders. We need to acknowledge the expectations we have about such people that are better left with God and rely on Christ in us (Galatians 2:20) for the grace to repeatedly forgive *as each offense occurs*.

It is also good to bear in mind that it is possible to forgive someone for an offense and then, later in life, have to forgive again for the same offense when it becomes apparent that it is affecting you in a new way. An example of this would be the teenage incest victim who forgives her father for molesting her, but after getting married, finds she struggles with enjoying sexual intimacy because of flashbacks to incestuous events. She may need to forgive her father for this new effect of the offense she'd previously forgiven.

Finally, in regard to forgiveness, the question often arises, "What if I'm angry with someone who really didn't do anything wrong?" Rather than go into detail about what types of offenses may or may not be "wrong," the answer is quite simple. Whether the person truly wronged you or you just perceive the offensive act to be wrong, treat it as though it is a real offense – and forgive. In addition, ask God to reveal to you, not the rightness or wrongness of the offense, but if you are being overly sensitive and need to change your beliefs regarding that type of perceived offense. For example, I tend to take umbrage when a young person calls me "dear." This reveals my insecurity and fear of being looked down upon because of my age. Usually, our personal sensitivities are born out of erroneous beliefs about ourselves as "new creations," God's acceptance of us, or his power within us.

Whereas anger with people is usually resolved through forgiveness, anger over circumstances and blocked goals is addressed through turning to God in trust, trusting that God is taking care of us despite our circumstances and is accepting us despite the fact that we haven't reached our goals. Often, the anger we feel in the face of difficult circumstances is directed toward God. At these times, stepping back and asking God to help us see the "big picture" restores our faith that circumstances don't determine contentment or success – God does. Remember Psalm

73 – that guy was a "brute beast" before God until he allowed God to show him an eternal perspective. When we put our trust in God – that he does indeed care for us, no matter how circumstances may look at the moment – we stop railing at our circumstances and start looking for how God is blessing us in the midst of them.

Blocked goals may not only lead to anger with God, but also they can result in anger at one's self. After my monumental eating binges, there were many times when I realized the only person I was mad at was me – usually for not doing as well in my work or relationships as I thought I should. This type of anger is a result of believing one's worth is tied to achieving certain goals. Prayerfully pondering what goals we have and whether they are in line with God's value system can lead to renewing the mind, adopting God's goals, and experiencing freedom from self-loathing in the face of frustrated personal goals.

A goal many women share is in regard to their appearance, and they get very, very angry with themselves for failing to look the way they think they should look. A great deal of my own self-loathing and anger was over how "fat" and "ugly" I perceived myself to be and how great a failure I was at achieving the goal of becoming thinner and prettier. When I realized and adopted God's standards for evaluating people – looking at the heart (1 Samuel 16:7) – I changed my mind (repented) about how to evaluate myself. As soon as I agreed with the truth that God has given me a new heart that longs for what God desires, the self-loathing was pretty much over. Yes, there is still temptation to judge myself by worldly values, but I know that road is the road to destruction, so I repeatedly cling to the truth and experience freedom. In Chapter 9, we will look more closely at why our personal standards backfire when it comes to experiencing true freedom.

Yielding expectations and goals and deciding to forgive must be practiced in the context of relying upon the power of the Holy Spirit.

Understanding what causes anger and how to prevent and address it is a big step toward eliminating the need to engage in unwanted behaviors to suppress that anger. However, understanding is not enough. Yielding expectations and goals and deciding to forgive must be practiced in the context of relying upon the power of the Holy Spirit. It is ineffectual to turn "dealing with anger" into a mental exercise of checking for expectations and goals and then deciding to forgive. Because God created us to require *him* as our Counselor, his participation in the process is absolutely necessary. When you start binge-watching TV shows, eating when not hungry, pulling out your hair, gaming for hours on end, or engaging in any ungodly or unwanted behavior, that is your cue to *turn to God* and ask him for guidance and insight into what is going on "under the hood." If he reveals you're angry, that is another trigger – to turn to him for understanding about your unmet expectations and blocked goals and for the grace to forgive the offender and to put more trust in God. It is only the empowering grace of God that enables us to overcome such a painful and difficult emotion as anger.

Frustration

It is much more acceptable to admit to feeling frustration than to admit to feeling anger.

Whereas anger is often associated with blowout, bingeing behaviors, frustration is what many people associate with "grazing" or repeatedly turning to a behavior in small ways throughout the day. "When I get frustrated, I eat chocolate." "I get so frustrated I just have to do something, and that something is usually picking my face." We're so used to frustration in our culture that we see it as a totally separate issue from what it really is – another form of anger. Also, for most people, it is much more acceptable to admit to feeling frustration than to admit to feeling anger, which is seen as a more serious and negative emotion. However, even though it may not be felt as intensely, frustration is just a mild, or perhaps chronic, form of anger. Frustration almost always has to do with blocked goals, either goals for ourselves or goals we have for others, especially family members, friends, and co-workers.

Most of the frustration I hear expressed is with spouses. It is much less threatening to admit to being frustrated with one's spouse than to admit to out-and-out anger. It is scary to think of being angry with someone you're supposed to love more than any other person and with whom you plan to live the rest of your life. Also, as I previously mentioned was the case for me, many people believe feeling anger will destroy relationships. We usually don't think of frustration as being quite that "dangerous." However, frustration has just as much potential for hurting relationships as does anger, because it *is* anger and leads to bitterness and resentment if not addressed.

I find it's difficult to convince people that frustration needs to be addressed in just the same way as anger. They tend to feel that frustration is rather trivial and, therefore, can be "brushed off." However, as long as that attitude is taken, the chronic coping behaviors continue because it is through those behaviors many people keep their anger at the "only frustrated" level. Once a person admits his or her frustration is indeed anger and that God-empowered yielding of expectations or goals followed by forgiveness needs to take place, the frustration dissipates and so do the chronic unwanted behaviors.

Frustration needs to be addressed in just the same way as anger.

Depression

Now that we've looked at anger and "anger lite," when we turn our attention to depression, the emotion usually associated with eating "comfort foods" or zoning out on television programs or video games, you might think this is a totally different emotion from the ones we've discussed so far in this chapter. However, whether it's just "the blues" or debilitating hopelessness, depression is very often an emotional alternative to feeling angry. As with anger, expectations have been disappointed, and as a result, the person feels hopeless about getting what he or she feels is needed. Sweets and starches or mind-numbing video gaming become the "medication" people take in order to soothe the sadness or to get a little pick-me-up from an increased blood sugar level or the small victories of gaming. Also, these comforting and distracting behaviors are seen as what can be relied upon in contrast to circumstances and people. Of course, none of the medication-like, comforting, or distracting behaviors alleviate depression. Though there may be a temporary distraction from depression, the guilt over wasted time, wasted calories, and procrastination adds to one's depression.

Depression is very often an emotional alternative to feeling angry.

With the sense of disapproval people feel regarding their anger, it's no wonder they would instead express their disappointment, frustration, and even rage through sadness and hopelessness rather than through the more guilt-producing anger. Forms of anger-based depression are expressed in phrases such as "I feel hurt" and "I guess I don't deserve good things to happen to me." When we acknowledge that we feel depressed and turn to God for insight into the root issues, it almost always boils down to unmet expectations and blocked goals. Getting God's perspective on which expectations and goals are unrealistic and how he is meeting our needs his way enables us to turn away from the disappointment we feel and find hope in the reality of how good God is to us. Also, since God is our Comforter and Counselor (John 14:16-17, 26, AMP; 2 Corinthians 1:3-4), there is no better one to whom we can turn when we are feeling depressed. And, when we get more and more into the habit of turning to God with our disappointments and asking him for his perspective, we have less and less of a desire to find comfort, such as it is, in behaviors we regret as soon as we've engaged in them.

One of the most common areas of anger-turned-to-depression that I've witnessed is in response to dashed hopes and plans regarding family. Our culture sets us up to expect a "happily ever after" romantic marriage that includes rearing godly, respectful children. We are constantly confronted with images of lovely, well-furnished homes filled with happy memory-making celebrations. Not only is this very far from reality in a sin-sick world, but also these are not what God considers most valuable in life. There is nothing wrong with being married, loving your children, having nice furniture, or enjoying family gatherings. However, when any of those things are valued more than knowing and following Christ, even if it means never having what our culture (run by the "father of lies") tells us we "deserve," then we have missed the beauty and desirability of the one and only perfectly loving God. In Chapter 10, we will look more closely at relationships. Admitting to God your belief that life cannot be enjoyed unless you have [put your personal wishes and dreams here], and seeking his truth about what truly satisfies enables you to experience the freedom and joy God has already given to you in Christ.

Anxiety

Now we *are* switching gears when we consider another common emotion that triggers unwanted coping behaviors: anxiety. Anxiety is such an uncomfortable feeling that people try to distract themselves from feeling it by turning to any number of behaviors that run from the mundane to the bizarre. Hair-pulling, excessive shopping, obsessive gambling or online gaming, viewing pornography, face-picking, overeating, shoplifting, constantly tattooing and/or piercing, cutting, and binge-watching television shows are all something to *do* when it seems there is nothing that can be done to address whatever is causing the anxiety. "Coping mechanism" behaviors are an attempt to apply a soothing "tranquilizer" to one's jangled nerves and to calm that alarming sense of tension in the throat, chest, and stomach. Even physical pain can be preferred over the stress of anxiety.

Many people reproach themselves for failing to "be anxious for nothing."

Many people try to attack their anxiety with what I call "club verses" (as in "hitting yourself over the head with a club"). They reproach themselves for failing to "be anxious for nothing" (Philippians 4:6, NASB), but this is not helpful, because telling yourself it's a sin to be anxious will not stop you from feeling the anxiety. In fact, it just adds a new anxiety about how much you're sinning! Instead, we need to look more closely at the two most commonly quoted verses about anxiety because they reveal its root issue, which is the degree to which we do not trust God to take care of us.

First Peter 5:7 says, "Cast all your anxiety on [God] because he cares for you." The reason we have anxiety, which is really a form of fear, is that we believe something horrible or unbearable is about to happen. What's difficult about anxiety is that it's not always easy to put a finger on what exactly is causing it. As was emphasized in the last chapter with "REED," it is vital to engage in dialog with God, to seek his input regarding what is feared, to ask him for insight and perspective – to cast all anxiety on him. Even if you do not determine the exact cause of your anxiety, you can decide to trust that God will work things out and get you through the uncomfortable sense of panic you're experiencing. You can count on him to do this because *he cares for you* – he cares about you and takes care of you. Even when it does not look as if he is doing so, he is. He sees eternity and we see only this one moment in time, and that not too clearly! He knows what will work out best for us in the long run and is carefully weaving together all the messy looking threads of our lives to form an incredibly beautiful tapestry.[6]

Now, let's go back to the verse many people use as a "club" to try to make themselves stop feeling anxious, Philippians 4:6, but let's add verse 7 also.

> Do not be anxious about anything, but in every situation, by prayer and petition, with thanksgiving, present your requests to God. And the peace of God, which transcends all understanding, will guard your hearts and your minds in Christ Jesus.

Many people will say, "I already know that passage," but what they mean is that they just know it rather than *do* it. As was mentioned in the last chapter, the psalms give us a model for presenting requests to God in a really honest, heartfelt way. We want to get rid of our anxiety instantly, but instead of pushing the emotion away, we need to see anxiety as an alarm sounding. It is telling us to express our fears to God – to tell him all about it – to be willing to hear from him and to decide to believe him, instead of trusting in our own perceptions and negative projections into the future. When we allow ourselves to feel the anxiety and talk with God about it, rather than try to avoid it through various distracting behaviors, we actually get through it and over it because God's desire is to become intimately involved in our concerns and to show us his love, which casts out fear (1 John 4:18). In fact, Philippians 4:6-7 should always be read in light of Philippians 4:5b, which tells us, "The Lord is near." He is as available as the air we breathe and is truly interested in hearing all about whatever is causing us anxiety. (See Hebrews 4:15-16 regarding the availability of God when we need help.)

Be willing to hear from God and to decide to believe him, instead of trusting in your own perceptions and negative projections into the future.

Loneliness and Boredom

The last two emotions we'll address in this chapter are related: loneliness and boredom. Both have to do with wanting circumstances to be different to the point of not appreciating all the good that there is in one's life, and both have to do with a discomfort with one's own thoughts. Loneliness leans a little more toward the former and boredom more to the latter.

I have never met a person who is truly alone in life. I have met a great many people who so long for a "certain someone" or for their certain someone to act in a particular way that they do not even see all the special people God has placed in their lives for them to love and be loved by. A wonderful message that was directed primarily toward married couples but applies to everyone is "The Principle of Receiving" by Jack Taylor.[7] The title says it all. When we're willing to receive the people God has placed in our lives, we can then see the ways in which God is so wisely meeting our needs through them. When we stop insisting that people be the way we want them to be and when we are willing to appreciate the way that they actually are, we can accept what they are able to give. We not only receive who they are, but also we start receiving from them, receiving their unique ways of loving us.

Many people so long for a "certain someone" or for their certain someone to act in a particular way that they do not even see all the special people God has placed in their lives for them to love and be loved by.

Various "busy-making" behaviors can distract you temporarily from feeling lonely – from the uncomfortable thoughts you have about yourself when your perception is that you are "alone" – but loneliness can be relieved permanently when you allow God to show you how much love he has placed in your life through your relationships with him and with the people he has placed all around you.

Boredom is also about wishing one's circumstances were different. But, instead of wanting people to be more to one's liking, boredom is a result of wanting more interesting activities in which to engage. But that desire for something "better" to do – with the "something better" often ending up being a refrigerator raid or mindless Facebook scrolling – is usually a "red flag" that can alert you to the need to ask God, "What am I trying to avoid thinking about?" When you say you're bored, you may really mean that you're afraid of "down time" when you might start to think thoughts you'd rather not think. People who say they can't stand being bored are often people who feel the need to stay distracted from their own thoughts.

A college friend of mine used to sit at his kitchen table for about half an hour nearly every morning, doing nothing. When I'd hear him talk about this, it made me horribly uncomfortable. I'd ask him, "Aren't you bored doing that?!" And he'd say, "No, I'm thinking." But many of us are not comfortable with what comes to our minds when we're just thinking. When I was in my teens and twenties and my binge-eating was at its peak, I was constantly distracting myself from my own thoughts, which were dominated by self-loathing, my nearly unbearable desire to have a boyfriend, and my horrible fear of having one.

It took me years to become truly comfortable with having time – when stopped at red lights or waiting in lines – when thinking is all there is to do. But I did not have to become totally comfortable with my own thoughts to stop binge-eating rather than think them. In fact, being honest with God about what I was thinking and being willing to feel the negative emotions that accompanied those thoughts made it almost impossible for me to eat. Emotions "choke you up" and make it hard to swallow. In fact, once you are willing to feel your emotions, it's difficult to actually engage in any of the behaviors that typically enable you to suppress the emotions. The hardest part of getting comfortable with my own thoughts was just getting started down the path. Once I'd tried feeling the feelings and mentally screaming about them to God, this became easier and more and more my habit rather than turning to distracting myself by binge-eating.

Not only was my just-sit-and-think friend comfortable with his own thoughts, he also was comfortable with the idea of not actually *doing* anything for several minutes, even as long as an hour! In our culture – and this seems to be especially true for Christians – there is a prevalent message that one must be *doing* something at all times except when asleep. When you're supposed to be doing something at all times, but you don't want to do all the things that you are "supposed" to do, it's boring, and an alternative is to eat or watch TV or play video games or pick your face. After all, that's *doing* something. And those behaviors can be a way of procrastinating, putting off what you feel you *should* be doing but don't really want to do.

The answer to boredom is *not* to crack down on yourself and get busy doing all those dreaded chores. The answer is, instead, to avoid letting yourself be "pressed into the mold"[8] of this culture (Romans 12:2) that insists on constant activity. "Redeeming the time" (Ephesians 5:16, KJV) may mean taking the time to think – to *do* nothing in terms of outward activity – to "be still and know that" God is God (Psalm 46:10). After all, the most important activity we "do" – prayer – does not appear to accomplish anything at the time we're doing it. Scripture encourages thinking about "things above" (Philippians 4:8; Colossians 3:2). And, certainly, we cannot discuss our concerns with God nor hear from him about those concerns unless we take time to pray and prayerfully

When you say you're bored, you may really mean that you're afraid of "down time" when you might start to think thoughts you'd rather not think.

think them through. Addressing boredom without using "compulsive behavior" as a distraction usually means accepting the fact that, even when there is much to be accomplished, it is still important to spend time that has absolutely no structure, if only to give yourself a chance to think, even if those thoughts are not always perfectly pleasant. When God is invited into the thinking, he has the opportunity to help us think through and get past our negative thoughts.

Identity and Persistent Emotional "Themes"

Many people who struggle with persistent, troubling emotions appear to have developed what I think of as an "emotional theme." This is when "always feeling that way" has become intertwined with their perceived identity. More than with other emotions, people can see depression as inextricably part of who they are. If you consider your very personality to be someone who sees everything as a dark cloud where there's never a silver lining, it can be threatening to your sense of self to consider letting the depression go. This can also be true for anger or even anxiety. My observation is that women are more likely to say of themselves, "I'm just a melancholy person" or "I'm anxiety-prone," and men are more likely to resign themselves to "I'm just an angry guy" or "I need to get angry to get motivated" or "This is how I roll." To some extent, we all identify ourselves by our feelings. We view how we feel, even if the feelings are painful, as part of our personalities. The underlying question is, *Would I still be me if I didn't feel this way most of the time?*

The truth is that feeling angry, anxious, or depressed is not the same as being an angry person or an anxious person or a melancholy person, especially if you are a "new creation in Christ." If you identify yourself in this way, I hope you take the challenge to ask God if *he* sees you this way. Is the new person God created you to be and who will live for eternity someone who will always feel angry or depressed or anxious? If you won't be that way in heaven, you really aren't that way now. These feelings are arising from beliefs about life, God, or yourself that are not in line with God's truth. The feelings are part of your flesh, those "sin measles" that are actually foreign to who you've been re-created to be. Can you go to God and ask for his help in experiencing who you really are even if it may be scary to give up what you've always thought you were?

Sometimes it helps to look around at people who live their day-to-day lives without whatever your particular "emotional theme" is. My theme used to be depression, but I started to notice some people around me who had experienced difficulties but remained truly joyous. Did I want to remain down all the time? Or did I want to enjoy my life? Part of the problem is that if you stay depressed, you think you'll have a softer fall from disappointments. You're already depressed; how much worse can it get? This seems right, but it really doesn't work that way. Happier people recover more quickly from disappointment, and people who are already depressed just go deeper into that depression. There is no way to prepare yourself for future heartache by trying to feel it now. The only preparation for any future disappointment is to immerse yourself in the love of God, knowing there is no disappointment that he won't ultimately work into what's best for you (Romans 8:28).

A Common Theme in Addressing Emotions

Hopefully, you've seen that the constant theme in lessening your desire to cope with emotions through regrettable behaviors is to increase your willingness to acknowledge your

The truth is that feeling angry, anxious, or depressed is not the same as being an angry person or an anxious person or a melancholy person, especially if you are a "new creation in Christ."

feelings, feel them, and turn to God with them. People who do not turn to "coping mechanisms" in the face of emotions are usually people who take feeling a wide range of emotions for granted. For those of us who have tried to avoid our emotions through seemingly compulsive behaviors, we need to realize that we can turn to God to help us learn how to feel emotions, as scary as that may seem. And that learning process is also the opportunity for us to learn the truth about just how very intimately involved and caring God is, as well as how much freedom he has given us from the unwanted behaviors, emotions, and thoughts that plague us.

Reflection

1. What do you think and feel about being angry? How did your parents handle anger – yours and their own?

2. How have you believed you were supposed to address anger and how successful have you been at that?

3. What are some expectations and hopes you've had that have been disappointed? Have you responded with anger, depression, or both? How have you avoided experiencing those feelings?

4. What alternatives do you see to using "coping mechanism" behaviors as "medication" for or distraction from your emotions?

What Others Have Experienced

Of all the emotions people feel, by far the one that stands out most often as the one to be shunned is anger, especially by women. Whereas it is taken for granted that men and boys get angry – even to the point of fist fights – girls and women are expected to be gentle and "quiet in spirit." Girls are even told that "little girls don't get angry." But, of course, little girls do. For many people who struggle with suppressing anger through overeating or other bingeing behaviors, their parents forbade displays of anger and never addressed their child's reasons for feeling angry or frustrated. If you were angry, you were already wrong, regardless of the precipitating factors.

As an adult observing friends and their children, I have seen parents respond to their children's anger in constructive ways that address both inappropriate behavior and the child's reasons for frustration. But the parents of struggling adults I've met were not so emotionally mature when rearing their children. The child's expressions of anger or frustration were cause for defensiveness, harsh punishment, the "silent treatment," threats of abandonment, and worse. When we are reared to believe anger is forbidden, it makes sense that we would find ways to totally avoid feeling it, let alone expressing it. This is where the input of the Holy Spirit is so needed. He is willing and able to point out to us what is really going on inside us when all we want to do is engage in some sort of unwanted behavior. He is also able to comfort our disappointment and frustration once we allow ourselves to start feeling them.

The scariest part is that first time of letting yourself feel really angry. It feels so bad. You think you'll explode and scatter into a thousand pieces or that you'll inappropriately express your anger toward a friend or family member. However, is it better to stay locked in a pattern of negative behaviors – thereby avoiding feeling your anger – or to ask God to bring you to emotional healing, able to feel your emotions, to present them to him, and to get his perspective so that you can resolve the anger and move past the feelings? After all, you are only avoiding *feeling* your anger. You're not avoiding the anger itself. It's still there, but it is under the surface, eating away at you – and it's coming out "sideways" in some form of behavior that you hate doing!

The scariest part is that first time of letting yourself feel really angry.

People who feel depressed rarely believe their own choices resulted in how bad they feel. They usually point to negative circumstances or to people who disappointed them as the causes for their depression. "If I were married, I wouldn't be so depressed all the time." "If my husband appreciated me more..." "If I could move to a warmer climate..." "If I could change jobs..." "If I could find more friends..." These are statements that indicate a focus on what is believed to be "wrong" about one's life and not on what is "right." These are statements that indicate unmet expectations and the need to express those expectations to God, entrust them to him, and ask him how he *is* meeting needs. When I feel depressed, I now see that as a "red light" that alerts me to ask God, "What have I wanted that I didn't get?" And the next question is, "Do I need it and how are you providing for me in ways that I haven't perceived?"

What about physiological factors that can contribute to depression? Sometimes this is a chicken-or-the-egg issue. Did one's disappointment lead to an imbalance in brain chemistry that resulted in depression, or did an imbalance in brain chemistry lead to the depression? My own experience is that there *are* factors that can lead to depression apart from just "wrong beliefs," a failure to forgive, or unmet expectations. As I was growing up, I experienced several traumatic events. At age 25, I exhibited many symptoms associated with "post-traumatic stress disorder." One of those symptoms was depression. Over the course of about five years, I gradually recovered, with all of my symptoms lessening and most of them disappearing totally. Yes, the stresses of my childhood did contribute to my having what I believe are physiological brain-chemistry deficits that leave me, for example, more susceptible to depression, especially when

I'm infected by a virus, such as influenza. However, I've found the ultimate resolution in applying the principles I would apply if the depression were completely the result of erroneous thinking about God and my circumstances. No matter what the reason for the depression, turning to God and expressing my feelings and thoughts to him, being willing to feel my sadness, and having friends with whom I can discuss my struggles all contribute to overcoming the depression and ultimately the need to "medicate" it with any sort of unwanted behaviors.

Hopefully, you're starting to believe that the most important alternative to compulsive behaviors and getting stuck with painful emotions is turning to God with – and feeling – your emotions. Sometimes it is just not possible to feel feelings all alone. I, like many others, sometimes need a friend with whom I can air my frustrations and disappointments. Talking with a friend does not automatically mean you're turning to a person rather than to God. You can turn to God and ask him to use your friend to help you hear from him. However, it is not only possible, but also gratifying, to hear directly from God, either through that "still, small voice," through a passage of Scripture, or even through a spiritual song, in regard to what's wrong "under the hood." When it comes to our emotions, there's no better Master Mechanic!

Hopefully, you're starting to believe that the most important alternative to compulsive behaviors and painful emotions is turning to God with – and feeling – your emotions.

Homework

1. List any incidents in your past that cause you continual hurt. List each person who has contributed to your hurts.

2. Ask God to make you willing to forgive these people – and even yourself – and to trust him to work all things together for the good.

3. By faith, choose to forgive the offenders by an act of your will, apart from what your emotions or reason are telling you. Put this choice in writing. Trust God to change your feelings of anger and hurt in his timing. Read Matthew 6:25-34 and Matthew 18:21-35.

4. Is there a negative emotion you see as an integral part of your personality? Does God see this emotion as part of who you are as a "new creation in Christ"?

5. Sometime in the next few days, when you experience a negative emotion or when you start to engage in a behavior that you know is a "coping mechanism," prayerfully fill out the following "REED" pattern.

   Recognize

   Express to God

   Evaluate

   Decide

Homework Follow-up

1. Did God reveal any forgiveness that you needed to extend? What did you do as a result?

2. What would happen if you stopped persistently feeling the emotion you consider to be an integral part of your personality?

3. What did you experience in going through the "REED" exercise? How did your perspective change and how did that affect your emotions and behavior?

Comments on the Homework

It is not unusual to find it difficult to forgive certain people, especially those who are unrepentant or prone to repeat their offenses. But who is this really hurting? Are *they* suffering from your refusal to forgive? Are they changing because you won't forgive? No, but you are – you're growing more entrenched in coping behaviors as you suppress that anger and bitterness. Prayerfully look to the root issue. Do you trust that God will take care of you even though you've been sinned against? If you don't, tell God why you don't and ask him to help you see your circumstances from his point of view. Even if you're not sure about God providing for you, it is wise to forgive anyway. God has commanded it (Matthew 18:21-22; Ephesians 4:32), not because he makes the rules and demands we obey them, but because he knows how we are made and what will work best for us. We were created – especially as new creations in Christ – to forgive. It is part of our very nature, because Jesus is part of our very nature (John 14:20; Galatians 2:20). Going against our nature only throws us out of whack, and one symptom of being out of whack is being enslaved to debilitating emotions and ungodly behaviors.

We were created – especially as new creations in Christ – to forgive. It is part of our very nature, because Jesus is part of our very nature (Galatians 2:20).

Hopefully, if you do consider your personality to include a particular painful recurring emotion, such as anxiety, depression (maybe referred to as "melancholy"), or anger, you are willing to take this to God in prayer, knowing that he loves you and wants what's best for you. The truth about who you really are and always will be – for eternity – can free you from that "old friend" emotional theme that is actually an enemy keeping you in bondage.

I'll be honest, I've known only a handful of people who have completely let go of an emotional theme, even when it was frequently debilitating. Usually feeling the persistent emotion was doing something significant *for* the person feeling it – reducing the expectations of others, curtailing personal responsibilities, keeping pride at bay, providing a reason for avoiding uncomfortable socializing. In a sense, the emotional theme was helping them in ways they thought God would not help. In fact, they feared God would require much more of them if they didn't have a "chronic problem" with anxiety or depression. In these cases, renewing one's mind in regard to being a new creation in Christ and seeing the "sin measles" as foreign to the real, eternal self was not enough to lead to letting go of the emotional theme. The deeper issue was in how God works in the life of a believer – the acceptance and equipping he provides. Getting down to the bedrock issue of beliefs about God's character and personal love for his children allows a person to give up on the "crutch" of a persistent emotional struggle. And putting greater trust in God's willingness to meet them at their point of felt need – even if that's just a need for alone time or for the ability to say no – leads to the kind of life many people don't believe they can experience – a happy, enjoyable one.

I've never known of a person who said his or her perspective was totally unchanged after praying through an emotional time using "REED" as a guideline. When God is invited into our struggles, he uses that opportunity to reveal his character to us and to redirect our attention from our problems to his goodness and provision. Sometimes, however, our own bitterness and insistence on having our own way are barriers to hearing from God. There have been many times when I so wanted to be involved in a romantic relationship that I just didn't want to see how God was providing for me in other ways. It was going to be what I wanted or nothing. So, you know what that meant: I got nothing – or, worse, a rotten boyfriend. But God would work on me, usually through wise and caring friends or passages of Scripture that I came across even when I refused to open the Bible. There are all sorts of creative ways in which God gets his Word into our line of vision. As he does with all of us, God wanted me to go to him with my disappointments and to hear from him about how he was providing the best for me, which far surpassed what I was willing to settle for. As I turned more and more to him and agreed more and more with his truth, you know what I experienced, don't you? Yes, that freedom I already had in Christ, available all along but not grasped until I'd agreed with God's truth.

When God is invited into our struggles, he uses that opportunity to reveal his character to us and to redirect our attention from our problems to his goodness and provision.

8 FREEING TRUTH ABOUT GUILT, SHAME, AND PUNISHMENT

"Our sins they are many, His mercy is more."[1]
"…there is now no condemnation for those who are in Christ Jesus."[2]
"But you don't know what I've done!"[3]

She looked as though she were about eight months pregnant, but I couldn't tell if that was just how she carried her excess weight. She walked as though she were pregnant, but when she sat down, her stomach went into folds. She was attending a small group I was facilitating for women who struggle with overeating. I had met a number of women who carried weight that seemed unnatural or excessive for their body type, but I'd never seen anyone look so much like she was pregnant. Over the course of our weekly meetings, "Connie" rarely shared during discussion times. She listened intently to what I and the other group participants discussed and seemed to be listening for something to which she could relate. She didn't appear to find much relevance in the topics discussed. I was at the point of deciding to ask Connie for a private meeting when she opened up about what she most struggled with – the fact that she'd had an abortion after she became a believer in Christ.

What baffled Connie was that up until the point of aborting her unborn child, she had not struggled with overeating at all. She'd always been quite slim and had not gotten far enough into her pregnancy to have put on weight. But after the abortion, she steadily started gaining weight and just could not stop eating way past "full" at nearly every meal. She also snacked and grazed all day, every day. As soon as Connie told the group she'd had an abortion, it was apparent that many group members immediately had mental light bulbs go off regarding why Connie carried her weight as she did, why she actually looked pregnant. Connie invited input on why she would start overeating after having the abortion, and many of the small group participants suggested she was trying to fill an emptiness. Connie did feel that was probably a big part of her issue, but then she broke down, crying and confessing how terribly ashamed she felt for doing something she knew was terribly wrong. Through her tears, she blurted out, "I deserve to be ugly. I deserve to be fat." She may have been making herself "pregnant" with food, but she was also punishing herself for her sin by making herself "ugly."

I've met many people over the years who have punished themselves in various ways for their real and/or perceived sins. The punishment tends to accomplish one or both of two purposes: 1) meting out justice for their sin, and 2) providing a consequence that is painful enough to hopefully discourage the person from repeating the sin. Sadly, the punishments never accomplish those purposes. No, Connie did not have another abortion, but she made sure she was reminded every day about how bad she had been and how careful she needed to be to not sin so horribly again. This meant she continued to sin against herself, her husband, and her children every day by living with an all-consuming compulsion to eat and eat and eat.

Many people punish themselves in various ways for their real and/or perceived sins.

My own overeating and weight gain was motivated in large part by my desire to keep myself from ever engaging in anything even close to the sexual activity that had caused me so much guilt and shame during my childhood. Also, I used my eating binges to distract me from the anger I felt toward others, thinking my anger was unforgivable and shameful, deserving punishment and deterrence.

Here are some comments from people who have expressed to me individually or in a small group setting their guilt and shame and attempts to assuage that guilt through self-punishment:

- *I feel so hung over the next day, you'd think I'd remember and not drink that much again.*
- *Every time I feel angry with someone, I know it's wrong to feel that way, so I stuff myself with candy and binge-watch TV shows. I know I'm trying to punish myself to make myself quit, but I still do it again.*
- *If I just hate myself enough, maybe I won't do it again.*
- *I raised my voice again to my mother, and then I pulled out all the hair on the right side of my head.*
- *I've always been such a slut; I deserve it when I pick up men who slap me around.*

Usually, the self-punishment is in the form of activities that only lead to additional guilt and shame and never serve as adequate motivators to prevent repeat bad behavior.

Usually, the self-punishment is in the form of activities that lead only to additional guilt and shame and never serve as adequate motivators to prevent repeat bad behavior. For guilt-ridden, shame-filled people there is a cycle that repeats and repeats and repeats. It leads to hopelessness and periods of just giving up on trying to "be good." They slip into "falling off the wagon" patterns, such as binge-eating, binge-drinking, overspending money, or hours and hours of mindless screen time. "Why bother even trying to be good?" is a familiar refrain.

This shame and self-punishment cycle can be broken, but it is broken through what at first feels quite foreign to someone who has experienced guilt and shame for years.

> Or do you show contempt for the riches of his kindness, forbearance and patience, not realizing that God's kindness is intended to lead you to repentance? (Romans 2:4)

It is actually through putting faith in God's kindness and mercy that we are motivated to turn from sinful behaviors!

There are many Scripture passages about how God has provided totally for our guilt through the shed blood of Jesus on the cross. Here are just a few:

> This is my blood of the covenant, which is poured out for many for the forgiveness of sins. (Matthew 26:28)

> …there is now no condemnation for those who are in Christ Jesus, because through Christ Jesus the law of the Spirit who gives life has set you free from the law of sin and death. For what the law was powerless to do because it was weakened by the flesh, God did by sending his own Son in the likeness of sinful flesh to be a sin offering. And so he condemned sin in the flesh, in order that the righteous requirement of the law might be *fully met* in us, who do not live according to the flesh but according to the Spirit. (Romans 8:1, emphasis added)

> God made him who had no sin to be sin for us, so that in him we might become the righteousness of God. (2 Corinthians 5:21)

> In him we have redemption through his blood, the forgiveness of sins, in accordance with the riches of God's grace that he lavished on us. (Ephesians 1:7-8)

> But now in Christ Jesus you who once were far away have been brought near by the blood of Christ. (Ephesians 2:13)

> …the blood of Jesus, His Son, purifies us from all sin. (1 John 1:7)

Many people find it very difficult to accept that they have been totally forgiven in Christ. They feel as though justice has not been served or they should be penalized for sin, even if they have suffered consequences. They believe there is no motivation to avoid sinning if you know you don't have to suffer punishment for your sins. First, this shows there is an assumption that a person actually can pay for his or her sins. By looking through the sacrifices made by the Israelites, we can see payment for sin was, at best, a very temporary solution – even the Day of Atonement had to be repeated annually (Leviticus 23:26-32). The only adequate payment for sin was made by God himself through the death of the only completely innocent God-man, Jesus.

Many people believe there is no motivation to avoid sinning if you know you don't have to suffer punishment for your sins.

Second, when people try to use self-punishment or just ongoing feelings of guilt and shame as motivators to avoid repeating their sins, they show their misunderstanding about how God actually designed "new creations in Christ" to be motivated. Our motivation to holiness is something God does from within us, not requiring us to "guilt ourselves" into good behavior. God has actually written his law on our hearts (Hebrews 8:10) and created us to be "like God in true righteousness and holiness" (Ephesians 4:24). God has come to dwell within us by his Spirit, who guides us and causes us to desire God's will and glory (John 16:13-14). God is always at work in all believers to give them the desire and power to obey him (Philippians 2:13). These graces from God – his forgiveness, his indwelling Spirit, our spiritual rebirth – are the best motivators in the world, far better than any self-punishment or painful, persistent shame can ever be.

> For the grace of God has appeared that offers salvation to all people. It teaches us to say "No" to ungodliness and worldly passions, and to live self-controlled, upright and godly lives in this present age… (Titus 2:11-12)

When I decided to walk out in the faith that I no longer needed to be "fat" in order to avoid sexual sin, I was still very tempted to commit sexual sin. But God was also very faithful to guide me by his Spirit away from temptation.

> …God is faithful; he will not let you be tempted beyond what you can bear. But when you are tempted, he will also provide a way out so that you can endure it.
> (1 Corinthians 10:13b)

Along a similar line of thinking to the role of self-punishment, many believe that they will and should live with painful, nearly unbearable consequences to their sin or that, worse yet, their sin has permanently scarred the lives of others. I hear this most from mothers who believe they have ruined the lives of their children through their bad behaviors and bad examples. This attitude is evidence of a misunderstanding about God's sovereignty and transforming power. Not only are believers assured by Romans 8:28 that "in all things God works for the good of those who love him, who have been called according to his purpose," but there are many examples in Scripture of how God uses sins and bad judgments to further his good purposes. A dramatic example is the very sin-filled Sampson, who among other failures, married a Philistine woman in direct disobedience to God's law. Although this was truly sinful, Scripture explicitly says that "this was from the LORD, who was seeking an occasion to confront the Philistines…" (Judges 14:2-4). God can and does use even our sins to accomplish good. Another example is when the sinful stoning of Stephen in Acts 7 and the ensuing persecution of the early church was immediately used by God to spread the gospel to Samaria and beyond (Acts 8). The ultimate transformation of sin took place when Jesus was crucified because of trumped-up charges brought by sinful leaders, but God used that death to atone for our sin. My own experiences with an abandoning mother and abusive stepparents resulted in God transforming their sins into my spiritual growth. My extreme ways of coping with the abuse I'd suffered resulted in my emotional collapse, forcing me to address in early adulthood numerous erroneous beliefs, exchanging them for God's freeing truths about who he truly is and who I am in Christ.

The fact of God's transforming power to change one's sin to the good of the sinner and even for the good of those around him or her can lead to the disturbing thought that perhaps there is no need to be concerned about continuing in sinful behaviors. Well, the apostle Paul anticipated this reaction to God's overwhelming grace when he wrote Romans 6:1:

> What shall we say, then? Shall we go on sinning that grace may increase?

Paul goes on to answer that question by explaining how true believers no longer desire to sin because of their changed nature:

> By no means! We are those who have died to sin; how can we live in it any longer? … We were therefore buried with [Christ] through baptism into death in order that, just as Christ was raised from the dead through the glory of the Father, we too may live a new life. (Romans 6:2-4)

Paul continues to expand on this new life by telling believers that "though you used to be slaves to sin, you … have been set free from sin and have become slaves to righteousness" (Romans 6:17-18). We need not fear that God's grace in forgiving and transforming our sins will lead to even more sinning, because we are now enslaved by righteousness. Sinning is foreign to who we truly are in Christ and is not what we actually want to do.

We all want to be free of guilt and shame…except when we think that guilt and shame is doing something vital for us, such as providing justice or motivation to do better.

We all want to be free of guilt and shame…except when we think that guilt and shame is doing something vital for us, such as providing justice or motivation to do better. But as we understand and put faith in the truths that no one gets off scot-free (Jesus paid a very high price), that God has re-created us to actually desire godliness, and that he can even transform our sin into what ends up being good for us and others, we become free from the guilt, shame, and self-punishment that so weighs us down.

A Word about False Guilt

A frequent question that arises when addressing guilt is about how to distinguish between real guilt and false guilt. There are many resources available online about that differentiation and addressing false guilt. (See, for example, see https://tabletalkmagazine.com/article/2023/05/false-guilt/.) Many people told me that, because I was a child molested by an adult, I should not feel guilty for anything I did related to those experiences of molestation. But I did still feel guilty… until I realized I was questioning the efficacy of the blood of Christ to atone for my sin and the intent of God to forgive me in Christ. I also realized I "needed" my guilt, because I thought it was making me try harder to avoid sinning. But it really wasn't helping me as much as God himself wanted to help me through his grace and Spirit! If it's really not authentic guilt, the freedom comes from the same truths that apply to real guilt. Jesus has totally atoned for your sin, so if you *think* you sinned, that atonement applies. And Jesus is the resource for you to move into a godly life. In fact, he's already said that all your shame and guilt and self-punishment won't work when he told you, "…apart from me, you can do nothing" (John 15:5). Reliance upon Jesus – his atoning death and his motivating power – sets you free from guilt and shame.

Reflection

1. Over what do you feel constantly ashamed when you think about it?

2. What are some of the ways in which you have punished yourself for your sin? Has that effectively kept you from repeating your sin?

3. To what degree do you believe you are completely forgiven for all past and future sin?

4. To what degree do you believe that God is interested in enabling you to avoid sinning?

What Others Have Experienced

You can always tell if someone has really "bought into" the truth about total forgiveness and the motivating power of the indwelling Spirit when the self-punishment dials down. For me, I just stopped needing to stuff myself whenever I felt angry or whenever I felt sexual attraction. For many, yes, the self-punishing behaviors cease, but only until there is another instance of either wanting to commit a sin or actually committing one. This is a real challenge to faith in full forgiveness and especially in God's motivating work. This is where the very fundamental understanding of what it means to be a "new creation in Christ" and why new creations still do sin is very important. We will not be sinless until we are in heaven. This life involves being constantly tempted by the world, the flesh, and the Devil. And sometimes we do fall to temptation. But, as new creations, we are not defined by our behavior, but by what God has said is true about us. And the Christian life involves constantly, repeatedly exercising faith and relying on Jesus. In the face of failure, I usually spend some time berating myself and considering hateful things I can do to myself that will really sting. As the years have gone by, this period of self-flagellation has become shorter and shorter. It used to take days to get back to faith in forgiveness and in the guidance and power of the indwelling Spirit, but more recently, there is not even a thought about self-punishment. What good would that do, really?

I've started to see – and encourage others who struggle to see – that every misstep, every painful event, every disappointment in myself is used by God to draw me into greater dependence on him and a deeper understanding of the depth of his unconditional love for me. When I, or someone I know, is swimming in shame, I see the Father beckoning that person with an invitation of "Come here to me. I want you closer to me." Understanding and accepting total forgiveness means we can learn from our mistakes and sins, and more easily move on. It's good to pause and prayerfully ponder what led to the sin – the inappropriate angry outburst, the day wasted on social media, the resentment felt or expressed toward a parent or child – asking God where faith in his goodness was weak. But then we need to allow the Lord to minister to us about how he is providing for and enabling us to walk in the power and love of Jesus.

People who talk with trusted friends and mentors about the degree to which they have trusted in the truth of forgiveness in Christ and the enabling power of Christ seem to be the ones who become more confident in these beliefs. I've seen many within a small group setting benefit from admitting to weak faith and being encouraged by others whose faith has also faltered. Usually someone has an inspiring article or sermon to share or a story of having been uplifted by a particular passage of Scripture. God really does use all the members of his body to build each one up in freeing faith (Ephesians 4:15-16).

Homework

Use the following REED outline to prayerfully explore an instance of guilt, shame, or self-punishment that plagues you:

Recognize: Over what do you feel particularly guilty and how do you try to motivate yourself to avoid repeating the behavior that causes you shame? Through what means do you try to avoid feeling your guilt and shame?

Every misstep, every painful event, every disappointment in myself is used by God to draw me into greater dependence on him and a deeper understanding of the depth of his unconditional love for me.

Express: Tell God all about the guilt and shame you feel. Admit to him what you've been doing to avoid feeling guilty or to punish yourself for your guilt. Admit how effective (or ineffective) your efforts have been.

Evaluate: Ask God to guide you into evaluating your thinking as compared to what he has revealed in his Word. What are the promises God has made to you about your guilt and shame? What has he promised to do for you in the face of temptation? What does God say about how you are motivated to holy living?

Decide: Tell God what decisions you are making about putting trust in his forgiveness and in his desire to lead and empower you.

Homework Follow-up

1. What are some Scripture passages that are particularly good reminders regarding how God sees your sin, guilt, and shame?

2. What are some ways in which you can remind yourself of the truth about forgiveness in and dependence upon Christ? Where in your life is there reinforcement regarding these truths?

Comments on the Homework

Unfortunately, for many believers who struggle with guilt, shame, and self-punishing behaviors, there is much in their lives to reinforce the very opposite of the truth about full forgiveness and the ways God motivates his children to right behavior. Throughout most of my life as a believer, I've heard sermons that used guilt to attempt to motivate congregants to do better, do more, and try harder to live a "good Christian life." Messages abound about confession and repentance that are actually a call to "admit it and quit it," but that never get to the root of what motivates sin and what motivates godly living. There have been numerous altar calls, inviting believers to make new resolutions or vows to obey and not sin again. And then there's been the ensuing deep disappointment and deeper shame that resulted when the resolution or vow was broken.

You may indeed be in the minority among your friends and fellow church members when it comes to the truths that allow you to experience freedom from shame and guilt. But you are not alone.

You may indeed be in the minority among your friends and fellow church members when it comes to the truths that allow you to experience freedom from guilt and shame. But you are not alone. Not only is God reminding you throughout Scripture of his grace and forgiveness, there are also many materials and ministries that promote these truths, such as His Truth Transforms International in Oklahoma City, Oklahoma; Shepherd's Call in Arlington, Texas; and The Grace Church in Lubbock, Texas. In Chapter 12, a list of resources is listed. These reinforce the concepts that have been presented in this book.

What I call "pocket verses" are extremely helpful in reinforcing truths. Some forgiveness-related Scripture passages to consider memorizing or writing down to keep at the ready are the verses already quoted in this chapter, as well as:

> …he does not treat us as our sins deserve
>   or repay us according to our iniquities.
> For as high as the heavens are above the earth,
>   so great is his love for those who fear him;
> as far as the east is from the west,
>   so far has he removed our transgressions from us. (Psalm 103:10-12)

> "Come now, let us settle the matter,"
>   says the LORD.
> "Though your sins are like scarlet,
>   they shall be as white as snow;
> though they are red as crimson,
>   they shall be like wool." (Isaiah 1:18)

> When you were dead in your sins and in the uncircumcision of your flesh, God made you alive with Christ. He forgave us all our sins, having canceled the charge of our legal indebtedness, which stood against us and condemned us; he has taken it away, nailing it to the cross. (Colossians 2:13-14)

> …since we have a great high priest who has ascended into heaven, Jesus the Son of God, let us hold firmly to the faith we profess. For we do not have a high priest who is unable to empathize with our weaknesses, but we have one who has been tempted in every way, just as we are—yet he did not sin. Let us then approach

God's throne of grace with confidence, so that we may receive mercy and find grace to help us in our time of need. (Hebrews 4:14-16)

May these truths from the Word of God penetrate to your very soul and enable you to experience joy-filled freedom from guilt and shame!

9 FREEING TRUTH ABOUT LIVING BY RULES AND STANDARDS

"Do this, don't do that. Can't you read the sign?"[1]
"…sin, seizing the opportunity afforded by the commandment, produced in me every kind of coveting. For apart from the law, sin was dead."[2]
"If I don't have rules, how will I know what to do?"[3]

People love keeping rules, and people love breaking rules. Which rules do people love? The ones they can keep and thereby feel good about themselves, even righteous. For example, as long as I was sticking rigidly to a diet plan, I felt so superior, so in control. And we all know the people who so piously say they'd never watch *that* show or listen to *that* kind of music.

What rules do people love to break? All of them! We are born rule-breakers. God gave Adam and Eve one rule, and they broke it! Since then, give people any rules at all and they'll break them. Just seeing a sign that says "Keep Off the Grass" arouses in us the desire to step on that grass. And apparently this tendency to react to rules by breaking them is known to at least some rule writers. In 1986, in Heathrow Airport, I was amused to see a sign that read, "Please try to avoid smoking." No, it's not a rule you'll feel you have to break; it's just our very polite suggestion, so maybe you'll comply. (I didn't see anyone smoking, so maybe that tactic worked!)

Ever read the Old Testament? Now those Israelites were some hard-core rule-breakers. Even when God spoke directly to them, as soon as Moses went up the mountain to meet with God, the Israelites broke the rules. (See Exodus 20 and 32.) If people are so deeply bent toward rule-breaking, why did God give so many rules?! And we don't have to cope with only God's rules, but also with society's, the culture's, and those of various institutions. Perhaps the rules and standards that are the source of more pain than any others are our family's and our own. Since we are born rule-breakers and there are so many rules everywhere, it's no wonder many Christians become very, very tired and very, very defeated. I've seen Christians respond to the exhaustion they feel in the face of all the rules in two ways: 1) fail and then try harder, or 2) totally give up and leave Christianity.

This chapter falls in this book where it does because of my own painful experience with being confronted about rule following too soon in my discipleship process. When I was in my mid-twenties, during our first meeting, a counselor referred to me as "standards queen." She was alarmed by the many rules I told her I was following "religiously," such as "I must wear size 9 clothes," "I must have 10 perfect nails," "I must never feel angry," and "I must have at least 30 minutes per day for a quiet time with God and memorize at least one new verse per week." When the counselor asked me to list some of my personal rules, there were more than 20 that I was immediately able to jot down.

At the time I saw this counselor, I was hoping for advice about possibly moving back to my hometown to pursue a better relationship with my father. The counselor noticed how controlled I appeared to be and how hard I seemed to want to project being "together," so she asked me about my personal standards. Her implication was that having those standards was not part of a

Since we are born rule-breakers and there are so many rules everywhere, it's no wonder many Christians become very, very tired and very, very defeated.

godly lifestyle. If I had any standard that was supreme, it was that I should live a godly lifestyle. The counselor said I was relying on my own rules in order to live the Christian life instead of relying on the Holy Spirit. She was right, but I really had no idea how to rely on the Holy Spirit. So, I did what I could to change how I was living by trying to give up my rules and standards. And within a few weeks, I emotionally collapsed. Not knowing I could rely on God (since he'd been the one who had subjected me to all the trauma of my childhood); not knowing I was a "new creation in Christ" (because I'd been taught that I was a "dirty, rotten sinner"); and not understanding anything much about the work of the Holy Spirit in the life of a Christian, all I'd had to prop up my sense of self and to motivate "Christian" behaviors were my rules. No rules, no Paula. This is why I always cover the basics of understanding God's character, the role of the Holy Spirit, and new identity in Christ *before* discussing how people were never really supposed to live by rules. In fact, rules always backfire, especially for Christians, because the rules force believers to rely on themselves, not on Christ.

Mine is not a really common story. What is far more common is the "they're all hypocrites so I stopped going" story (i.e., "they broke their own rules so why should I try to keep them"). Or the "I just gave up trying because I'd never be anything but a disappointment to Jesus" story (i.e., "I keep breaking my own rules or what I thought were God's rules"). At the core of these stories – and at the core of why many Christians are completely exhausted – are rules, rules, rules – in other words, God's law, religious legalism, and cultural and personal standards.[4]

By "God's law," I mean all the rules and regulations that are spelled out in the Old Testament. In Romans 7:12, the apostle Paul tells us that the laws of the Old Testament are "holy, righteous, and good." Paul also says of the Law that its purpose was to point us to Christ: "So the law was put in charge to lead us to Christ..." (Galatians 3:24). How did the Law lead us to Christ? By proving to us that we were incapable of keeping it and thus incapable of living up to God's holy standards. Therefore, the Law brought us to the realization that we were in desperate need of a Savior. No one (but Jesus) has ever been able to totally fulfill all the requirements God laid out for a holy life. Therefore, no one has ever been able, through keeping the Law, to achieve the righteousness that would allow him or her to live in union with a holy God. Without special intervention on God's part – without the sacrificial death and miraculous resurrection of Christ – we cannot achieve holiness and righteousness. We could not do this on our own, no matter how hard we tried to follow all the rules. The rules were right, but we chose wrong. The rules actually pointed out to us how far afield we were from holiness. And that is good, because it creates in us an awareness of our need for Jesus.

With the advent of Jesus Christ – in light of his atoning death that, through faith, enables us to enjoy his righteousness and an eternal union with God – how are we then to view God's law, the Old Testament rules and regulations? First, we can see that the Law is an outline of how life was intended to be lived. The Law provides us with wisdom and understanding about the parameters of life as God created it. (See Deuteronomy 4:5-8.) We realize that God never intended for us to worship anyone or anything other than him (Exodus 20:3). We understand that God made us in such a way that it is healthy for us to engage in sex only within the confines of marriage, that lying to one another and stealing from one another is harmful to all involved, that getting rest on a regular basis and stopping to worship God regularly is absolutely necessary to

No one (but Jesus) has ever been able to totally fulfill all the requirements God laid out for a holy life.

our well-being, along with many other guidelines for living. As Bill Gillham said, the Bible is the "manufacturer's handbook"[5] for how people were designed to run smoothly.

In looking at the Old Testament dietary laws from a New Testament perspective, we see that Jesus himself rescinded them. See Mark 7:18-19 and Acts 11:7-9. And, all of the sacrificial laws are completely fulfilled by the "once and for all" sacrifice of Jesus Christ on the cross. See Colossians 2:13-14 and Hebrews 10:1-12. All of the moral and ethical laws are totally fulfilled by Christ living in us and having written his laws on our hearts by means of the Holy Spirit. See Jeremiah 31:33 and Romans 10:4, as well as Hebrews 8:10 and 10:14-16. For the believer, God's law gives us understanding about life and is fulfilled, summed up, and lived out by and through Jesus Christ.

In 1 Timothy 1:8, we see that God's law can be used improperly. This happens when a person or institution believes that acceptance by God is available only through keeping the Old Testament law. This makes performance the basis of obtaining God's acceptance rather than the finished work of Jesus Christ on the cross. This is religious legalism, which puts the emphasis on self-effort and promotes the belief that man actually can fulfill God's righteous standards. The Pharisees of Jesus's day engaged in religious legalism. They even added their own laws to the Law of God in order to make sure they would stay well within the Law's parameters. As Jesus pointed out, though, they failed to actually keep God's law because their hearts were not right. They appeared compliant on the outside, but they were still corrupt on the inside. (See Matthew 23:25-28.) And, sadly, the Pharisees had so much faith in their adherence to the Law making them acceptable to God that many of them totally missed the fact that they needed a Savior – even though he was standing right in front of them!

For the believer, the Law gives us understanding about life and is fulfilled, summed up, and lived out by and through Jesus Christ.

Because no one can possibly live up to God's law, those who practice religious legalism have to contort God's law to fit what they *can* fulfill. Religious legalists emphasize the rules they are able to keep and turn a blind eye to the rules they fail to keep. Look at the Sermon on the Mount in Matthew 5:21-48. When Jesus said, "You have heard that it was said..., but I tell you...," he was telling the religious legalists that they were keeping only part of the Law and not all of it. Haven't you known someone who, for religious reasons, refused to go to movies but thought nothing of watching television or renting DVDs? This is an example of how religious legalism engenders inconsistent behavior and hypocrisy.

When you read the Bible as a set of "oughts" and "shoulds," you get caught up in trying harder and harder to do all those "oughts" and "shoulds." Eventually, you either fail and give up completely by leaving what you perceive to be "the faith" or you have emotional problems from the stress of trying to live the Christian life in your own strength. This is exactly what happened to me when I was in my early twenties. I tried desperately to adhere to all the "laws" I felt I had to keep in order to be a "good Christian." I couldn't do it. I collapsed. But, before I came to the end of myself, I experienced all of the typical symptoms of legalism: panic attacks, bitterness, workaholism, depression, resentment, and being hyper-critical and judgmental.

I tried desperately to adhere to all the "laws" I felt I had to keep in order to be a "good Christian." I could not do it.

Finally, to understand the truth about living by rules and standards, it is important to examine cultural and personal standards. Standards are the rules people develop for themselves and others that may or may not be based on Scripture. These rules are what people feel they *must* do in order to gain acceptance from God, others, family, society, the culture, or just from themselves. Standards are usually "caught" from our families, the culture, peers, authority figures, the media, and religious training. We are often told, either directly or tacitly, that when we do "thus and so," we will be thought of as a "good" person. The basic belief is: *I must be accepted and approved of by others in order to feel good about myself; therefore, I must do "this."* A prime example of standards is how women believe they must be reed thin in order to be acceptable to themselves and others. Many women even feel this is one of God's standards. Another example is how men feel they must provide material wealth (not just a good living) for their families. I know many who can even quote Scripture (out of context) to affirm this worldly standard.

Symptoms of legalism – either the religious kind or the kind that's based on keeping one's own standards – include smugness (*I keep my standards but others don't.*); high expectations of others (*If I have to, why don't they have to keep this standard too?*); being critical of others (*They really don't have very high standards, do they?*); a low tolerance of people making mistakes (*He should have been able to keep that standard!*); fear of failure (*I'll hate myself if I fail at keeping this standard.*); and self-punishing behaviors (*I didn't keep that standard, so I deserve to pull out my hair and look ugly.*). These symptoms are very often evident in people who are on diets or people who keep rules particular to their denomination's traditions.

> *It is difficult to let go of standards when you believe your legalism is what's keeping you in line.*

Even for those who become convinced that living by rules and standards is negative and not productive (even counterproductive), it is difficult for them to let go of their standards because they believe their legalism is what's keeping them in line, keeping them from going off the deep end and getting totally out of control. But just the opposite is true. Not only do laws and rules "lack any value in restraining sensual indulgence," as Colossians 2:23b says, but also, they actually lead us to sin more, not less. According to Romans 7:9, "when the commandment came, sin sprang to life," and according to 1 Corinthians 15:56 "the power of sin is the law." Think about how totally luscious everyday foods, such as butter and mayonnaise, seem when you're on a diet that forbids or limits those foods. Think of how many times you think about looking at Facebook when you're on a "Facebook fast."

> *The alternative to legalism is living life "by faith" and "in the Spirit," living in constant and total dependence upon the indwelling Christ.*

So, if laws, rules, and standards don't enable us to live a godly, moderate life, what does? Read Galatians 3:3, 5, 10-14 and 5:16-26. The alternative to legalism is living life "by faith" and "in the Spirit"; that is, living in constant and total dependence upon the indwelling Christ, humbly asking him to guide and being confident that he will and does. The emphasis at the beginning of this book on understanding the work of the Holy Spirit and one's new identity in Christ as a "new creation" was to serve as the underpinning for grasping why we can trust that the Spirit is at work in us to guide us into right behavior. We do not need to constantly crack the whip and toe the line to make sure we live as we "ought." Instead, we need to humbly rely upon God and his work within our lives. We can accept that he has given us a new heart, that we are motivated from within to be holy and moderate. We can follow the promptings of the Spirit, who directs us, for example, to pause and ask God for help in figuring out why we want to engage in a behavior we feel compelled to do but know is not right. As Galatians 5:16 (AMP) tells us, "...walk *habitually* in the [Holy] Spirit [seek Him and be responsive to His guidance]; then you will certainly not carry out the desire of the [flesh]." This is true because "where the Spirit of the Lord is, *there* is freedom" (2 Corinthians 3:17b, emphasis added).

A very common prayer of frustrated Christians is that God would enable them to control a feeling or behavior they hate and can't seem to stop feeling or doing. But God doesn't usually answer their prayers as they'd like because he wants his children to realize that the only way to live life as he designed it is to live in constant communication with and dependence upon *him*.

He certainly didn't design you to control your emotions and behaviors through rules. When we know the truth about rules and regulations, we find we are not only free from bondage to forever failing to keep them, but also free to enjoy intimacy with our loving, faithful, empowering God.

Comparisons and Judgments

Whenever a person expresses to me the need to maintain a number of standards that are not God's requirements, I know I'm listening to a person who is not secure about his or her acceptance in Christ before God, does not understand the person God has made him or her to be, and/or does not find God's approval satisfying enough and needs additional affirmation by maintaining standards. What goes hand-in-hand with this sort of insecurity is a need to constantly evaluate others according to one's standards. This is the very sort of judgment Jesus commands against in Matthew 7:1. Jesus was not telling people to never make an evaluation – see verses 6 and 15-20. Discerning by making judgments is necessary. The judgments that are unhealthy are the type made by people who want to feel better about themselves by seeing others as "less than" based on standards the insecure person keeps but others do not keep. (See Matthew 7:2-5.) An example that comes to mind is when a friend was disdainful of me for being what he considered to be overweight when he had lost 50 pounds (and was therefore obviously once overweight). Soon after he regained the 50 pounds and more!

Whenever a person expresses the need to maintain a number of standards that are not God's requirements, I know I'm listening to a person who is not secure about his or her acceptance in Christ before God.

The flip side to the smugness that an insecure standard-keeper can feel when judging others is the devastating self-loathing felt when comparing to others who are doing better at certain standards. For example, when my friend did regain his weight but my weight remained stable, he didn't even want to run into me because he compared himself to me, assuming I was in God's good graces and God was punishing him for sin in his life. His feelings of superiority and then of inferiority resulted from a standard about appearances that is not God's. (See 1 Samuel 16:7.)

The two-sided coin of judgments that enable us to feel we're better than others and then negative comparisons that result in withering shame when others do better at our standards than we do are both avoided when one grabs hold of God's true delight in who he had made us to be. He even rejoices over us with singing! (Zephaniah 3:17) When we understand the deep love God has for us as demonstrated through Jesus (Romans 5:8), we do not need to make judgments in order to prop up our egos, and we don't bother to engage in negative comparisons. We can agree with Paul when he said:

> We do not dare to classify or compare ourselves with some who commend themselves. When they measure themselves by themselves and compare themselves with themselves, *they are not wise.* (2 Corinthians 10:12, emphasis added)

Another of Paul's statements to the church in Corinth is a verse I call to mind when I'm tempted to see myself as less acceptable than a more accomplished person or when I think someone is judging me according to his or her standards:

> I care very little if I am judged by you or by any human court; indeed, I do not even judge myself. (1 Corinthians 4:3)

When we understand the truth about the grace God gives that enables us to live godly lives (Titus 2:11-12) and the power and guidance we are provided by the indwelling Spirit, we know the truth that sets us free from the pain of legalism, judgments, and comparisons.

Reflection

1. In what areas of your life do you currently have discipline and why do you think you have it in those areas?

2. What are some of the reasons you are motivated to "do right" (avoid sin, do loving acts, pursue a relationship with God, treat others with kindness, etc.)?

3. What rules are you attempting to follow and how successful have you been in doing so? (If you have trouble identifying your standards, think of the last time you felt superior or inferior to someone else. Based on what standard did you feel superior or inferior?)

What Others Have Experienced

Many discouraged Christians who are asked in what areas they currently have discipline will give a knee-jerk response of "I don't have any discipline!" This indicates they are focusing mostly on their unwanted behaviors and failures at rule-keeping. However, once pressed, they'll all admit they brush their teeth regularly, do laundry as it is needed, pick up the kids after school, go to work consistently, get the shopping done so that there's enough food in the house, bathe regularly, and comb or brush their hair nearly every day. They take these activities for granted and don't realize they are part of the discipline in their lives.

Now, are people disciplined in the areas of their hygiene and taking care of the needs of their families because there is a set of rules that says they must do so? Usually not. Usually, people are motivated to brush their teeth and groom their hair regularly because they enjoy how it feels when they do and they dread the consequences of not doing so. They like feeling clean and don't like feeling grungy. And most people are motivated to engage in activities that meet the needs of family members because of their love and loyalty, wanting to do what's best for people who count on them for nurture and care.

The truth of the matter is that if rules were in place regarding the routine "disciplines" of our lives, we would probably resent them. As long as my husband doesn't tell me he expects me to pack his lunch each day, it's a joy and a gift to get to do so. I can well imagine that I'd frequently

Are people disciplined in the areas of their hygiene and taking care of the needs of their families because there is a set of rules that says they must do so? Usually not.

find excuses to avoid preparing his lunch if I knew he believed it to be my "duty." If there were monitors who checked our teeth every day for cleanliness, don't you know we'd find ways to cheat and bluff?! It's the same with trying to motivate ourselves to "do right" through personal or cultural standards. As long as the rules say we ought to, who wants to?

Now that I no longer try to use rules and regulations to keep myself in line, I'm as motivated to avoid binge-eating, gossip, and smutty movies as I'm motivated to keep my teeth clean. I don't like the way it feels when I'm overstuffed, betraying a friend's trust, or exposing myself to unwholesome images. I like how I feel when I've eaten just the right amount of food to satisfy my hunger, kept my mouth shut when the temptation to gossip arises, or enjoy wholesome activities. Now that there are no rules and I can very personally rely on God to provide for me spiritually, emotionally, and materially, I have the freedom to assess what I really do *want* to do, and I don't *want* to sin (although I do sometimes choose to do so). It just doesn't feel good. And that's evidence of experiencing the "real me," the free-in-Christ new creation who allows the Holy Spirit to direct her.

There are times we are faced with rudeness and we choose not to react in kind. There are times when we are very tired and we choose to help a friend with her garage sale anyway. There are times when we really want to spend time praying or reading the Scripture and don't even think of turning on the TV. What gives us that "umph" to do what is right, especially when doing right is to some degree difficult or inconvenient?

There are two basic categories of motivators for all the "good" that we as Christians do. One motivator is self-centered, doing what is right because it will somehow get us what we want. Many of our "good deeds" are done for very selfish reasons. (In fact, given the fallen condition of our souls without Christ, all good deeds done by those who do not believe in Christ are done, ultimately, for selfish reasons.) This is where doing good because the "rules" say you should is applicable. There is a personal satisfaction we can enjoy when we "do as we ought" or follow a rule. Of course, there can also be other rewards of various types and sizes for "doing good": the appreciation of a recipient, the smugness of knowing we're better than others, the recognition of those who notice our not-so-random acts of kindness. Christians are not exempt from this form of motivation. When we as Christians act out of the flesh, even when we do "good," the motivation is always selfish.

On the other hand, for new creations in Christ, the greatest motivators in the universe are within us; that is, the Holy Spirit and the love Christ puts in our hearts (John 14:16-17; 2 Corinthians 5:14). Because God indwells us and has changed our hearts, it is indeed our nature to act in godly ways. When we turn to God for his power to motivate our behaviors, we act in ways that are Christ-like. Why would we want to set up rules for ourselves that we just end up breaking when we can rely on the Holy Spirit, who is at work in us to make us more and more like Christ in any and every area of our lives (2 Corinthians 3:17-18; Philippians 2:13)?

If you've read this far in this book, it is likely you have struggled with the discouragement of what has been referred to as the "try harder/give up cycle."[6] For a while, you can keep up with all the "have-to's" and then there's a failure that makes you want to give up. Then, maybe after a short time of not even trying, you get back up and try harder at keeping all the rules. Until the next failure…and the cycle continues.

As long as the rules say we ought to, who wants to?

For new creations in Christ, the greatest motivators in the universe are within us: the Holy Spirit and the love Christ puts in our hearts.

Jesus offers a very poignant rescue to those of us who keep trying very hard, especially at keeping rules. To people who had been burdened by not only the impossibility of keeping the law of God from their hearts (as Jesus made clear in Matthew 5:19-48), but also by the many additional rules the Pharisees added to God's Law, Jesus extended this invitation in Matthew 11:28-30:

> "Come to me, all you who are weary and burdened, and I will give you rest. Take my yoke upon you and learn from me, for I am gentle and humble in heart, and you will find rest for your souls. For my yoke is easy and my burden is light."

The yoke that you have been carrying, you've carried on your own – and it's heavy. You're not doing all that well at dragging it along. When you join Jesus in his yoke, he carries the burden. Only he can fulfill all the standards of a holy God, because he *is* God, and he is a *perfect* human being, having obeyed every single aspect of the law. Jesus doesn't crack the whip; he takes the burden and pulls it himself. The rules that you've been trying to keep crowd out Jesus and his work in your life. In fact, according to Romans 6:14, as long as you live by law, sin has the upper hand in your life. When you live by law, you can't bear the fruit of the Spirit (Romans 7:5-6), and you're even empowering sin (1 Corinthians 15:56).

It's not at all easy to know exactly when you're "walking in the Spirit" rather than "walking according to the flesh." We want to be able to measure whether we're doing one or the other. We want a list of "if you do this, then…" But that is not how God created us to operate. Rules and standards are from outside of us. The Holy Spirit – God's very presence – is inside of us and constantly available to turn to for guidance, power, and wisdom. He frees us to live more and more godly lives as we rely more and more on him.

Only Jesus can fulfill all the standards of a holy God, because he is God, and he is a perfect human being.

Homework

Read the transcript of Malcolm Smith's message, "Self-Disciplined Religion," provided with permission in Addendum Two, starting on page 189. The title is a little misleading – it is what Dr. Smith is preaching *against*. Highlight those parts of the transcript with which you particularly identify.

Homework Follow-up

1. What aspects of Malcolm Smith's message pertained to you and the rules you try to keep?

2. What evidence do you see in your life of God's grace and Spirit motivating you to exercise self-control? Does this give you hope regarding areas where you struggle with control?

3. Meditate on Titus 2:11-12. What does this verse tell you about living a godly life?

Comments on the Homework

I especially like the opening of Malcolm Smith's message because Titus 2:11-12 is the passage I use frequently to summarize my understanding of God's solution to "compulsive behaviors." It is the grace of God – the unmerited gift of salvation and our ongoing transformation into the likeness of Christ through the power of the indwelling Holy Spirit – that teaches us, instructs us, to live sensibly with godly moderation! When we look to the Holy Spirit to guide us, he really does do that. When we try to control our lives through our own efforts – through the flesh, no matter how "godly" our actions may appear – we ultimately fail. And we miss the true joy and victory of what it means to be a new creation in Christ and to have an intimate, dependent relationship with God.

Many who have read the transcript of Malcolm Smith's message are struck by his attacks on the "religious." We are so often taught that being "spiritual" actually consists of gritting our teeth and following the rules of whatever sect or denomination in which we're a member. Or we are told that our gratitude to Christ for our salvation should be an adequate motivator to engage in right behavior. Personal willpower and even overwhelming gratitude are not sufficient to enable us to live godly lives. It takes God to be godly. Apart from reliance upon the Holy Spirit, try as we might, we cannot live Christ-like lives.

Many people have tremendous difficulty with a conflict they feel over the religious "oughts" and "shoulds" they have been taught, sometimes since early childhood, and the challenge to take the perspective that these very rules may be the enemy that's defeating their Christian walk. My approach in addressing this is to suggest giving this concept of "walking in the Spirit" a three- or four-month trial. As a result, people discover that they do live up to many of their long-held standards because they are just like the hippies-getting-hair-cuts example in Malcolm Smith's message. God has no objection to certain standards. It's what's going on in the heart that matters. If our motivation is to maintain rules out of our own effort to prove to ourselves or to God that we're "good enough," this will not be permitted to succeed. It's contrary to God's design for Christians. If, however, we ask God to direct our steps and empower our behavior, we may end up looking as though we're being very disciplined and obeying rules when we're actually "walking in the Spirit."

An example of religious rules that can be passed off as "godly" is found in how some church groups dictate, blatantly or tacitly, how women should dress. One church I visited occasionally over the course of several years had an unwritten, but very well-understood rule that all the women wear very modest, loose-fitting, floral print jumpers and ankle-length dresses. The generally accepted understanding was that any article of clothing that clung in any way to one's figure was just forcing the men in the church to lust and, therefore, to sin. One of the women I knew in this church got fed up with the pressure to conform to the church's "dress code" and

When we try to control our lives through our own efforts – through the flesh, no matter how "godly" our actions may appear – we ultimately fail.

started dressing in ways that would assure disapproval from fellow church members. In fact, she seemed to be working very hard at looking downright sex-pot-ish. It was no surprise that in short order she felt criticized and unwanted at this church. She left that congregation about the same time that she started taking classes elsewhere on new identity in Christ and the Spirit-filled life. A few months later, this same woman was wearing all her loose-fitting clothes again, saying that she just didn't feel comfortable in that "tight-fitting stuff" anymore. The rule about clothing had been lifted. The freedom had been granted. And she went back to what was comfortable, as well as less provocative, but not because the rules told her to do so.

Getting out from under the rules is only a part of the solution to living by rules and standards, but it is not at all enough. The more important part of the solution is relying upon the Holy Spirit and believing in who you are at the core of your being as a new creation in Christ. It is necessary to go ahead and step out in faith, and then you will see that God provides you with the grace to live sensibly and righteously (Titus 2:11-12).

An assessment of one's overall Christian experience can help a person recognize that God is already at work in many aspects of his or her life, with their areas of struggle being only a fraction of the areas in which God is transforming them into the image of his Son. Upon reflection, many people realize that they have had victories already thanks to the work of the Holy Spirit within them. They tell of how they sought God's help in controlling their tongues, especially with children or spouses, and saw dramatic success and change. Or they realize that God had enabled them to manage their money and/or time better as they've matured in their relationship with him.

A friend of mine spent years trying to set up rules and self-punishments so that she would arrive at work and appointments on time. For years, she was persistently tardy and even jeopardized her employment because of it. It was when she finally gave up on her own willpower and threw herself on the mercy of God that she started arriving on time at work and appointments more and more often. It is several years later now, and she'd never think of being late for work, church, or appointments. She's practically forgotten what a struggle that once was for her. Another friend could never seem to keep her apartment clean or in any way orderly. This created a problem when she wanted to have people over for a visit. She could invite only those friends she knew would overlook the mess and pick their way through the clutter to sit down or walk across the living room. She looked to God to change this habit and gradually became more and more tidy until she found she was actually uncomfortable when her apartment reached a certain level of disarray.

Look at some of the areas of life that the Bible says are most important – demonstrating love through action, forgiveness, returning good for evil, praying, giving, seeking opportunities to get to know God better, sharing the Gospel with unbelievers. It is very likely that you have gradually made progress in several of these areas. This is because the Holy Spirit indwells you and you have the new heart of a new creation in Christ. If God is at work in you to change you in these areas, why wouldn't he also work in remaining areas of struggle? You don't need rules to keep yourself in line. In fact, those rules are sabotaging not only your ability to have self-control, but also your relationship with God. This is why God doesn't let Christians succeed at rule-keeping. Ironically, a truth that enables you to experience the freedom you already have in Christ is that succeeding at rules and standards is failing at trusting in him.

You don't need rules to keep yourself in line. In fact, those rules are sabotaging not only your ability to have self-control, but also your relationship with God.

10 FREEING TRUTH ABOUT RELATIONSHIPS

> "You light up my life."[1]
> "But seek first his kingdom and his righteousness, and all these things will be given to you as well."[2]
> "And they lived happily ever after."[3]

When it comes to relationships, our culture – including the Western culture and its media, as well as the conservative evangelical Christian culture – sets us up to wear a particular set of blinders or to have tunnel vision. The books and magazines we read, the movies and television programs we watch, and the podcasts we hear continually send a message that love – that is, romantic love – heals all wounds, provides supreme emotional satisfaction, and completes us as individuals. And this love comes from one particular, very special person who is fated (or predestined) to be one's life partner. Once circumstances (or God's providence) bring this person into your life, you will live happily ever after.

NOT!

In fact, the truth is that if you are a born-again new creation in Christ and you believe you're predestined to be Prince Charming or Cinderella, you are definitely destined to be absolutely frustrated or even devastated. Or if you're waiting to meet that certain someone and ride off into the sunset with him or her, before you can *really* live, you're at the wrong bus stop altogether.

Most of the people I have the opportunity to encourage in their faith are women, and one of the most tenacious lies which they rarely surrender to Christ (2 Corinthians 10:5) is the belief that they cannot possibly be "complete" without a loving husband. Of the many men with whom I've enjoyed friendships over the years, several have either abandoned the faith or abandoned a wife because they perceived God as failing to provide a loving, fulfilling partner. One man told me, "God does not want me to spend the rest of my life tied down to someone who can't do all the things I want to do." He was a deacon in his church. He left his wife and his faith and married a younger woman whom he perceived to be more "qualified" to bring him the happiness he "deserved."

Seeing so many of my Christian friends marry with romantic, "happily ever after" motives and then suffer tremendous disappointment and even divorce has caused me to absolutely loathe romantic movies and romance novels (especially the Christian ones and even the "classics").

Perhaps you are single and deeply long to be married. Perhaps you are married and fervently praying your spouse will change and become more attentive, caring, or romantic. Perhaps you believe you're immune to all this romance nonsense because you have bigger fish to fry, such as a persistent struggle with depression or some sort of "addiction." Regardless of your attitude about relationships, you can be sure that you need to know the *truth about* relationships in order to be set free from the *lies about* relationships that can rob you of the joy God designed you to enjoy *within* relationships.

We can look at the words of Jesus to give us a starting point for understanding which relationships are of greatest importance and provide the greatest fulfillment.

If you believe you're predestined to be Prince Charming or Cinderella, you are definitely destined to be absolutely frustrated or even devastated.

> One of them, an expert in the law, tested him with this question: "Teacher, which is the greatest commandment in the Law?" Jesus replied: "'Love the Lord your God will all your heart and with all your soul and with all your mind.' This is the first and greatest commandment. And the second is like it: 'Love your neighbor as yourself.' All the Law and the Prophets hang on these two commandments." (Matthew 22:35-40)

Yes, people are important, but God is of utmost importance.

Jesus prioritizes a love for God over love for people. Yes, people are important, but God is of utmost importance. If you're like me, this can be discouraging. My warm, fuzzy feelings for God are not consistent. However, Scripture gives us great encouragement regarding the truth provided to us so we *can* love God. When we understand God's character and his overwhelming love for us, our natural response is to love him.

> But God demonstrates his own love for us in this: While we were still sinners, Christ died for us. (Romans 5:8)

> Because you are his sons, God sent the Spirit of his Son into our hearts, the Spirit who calls out, "*Abba*, Father." (Galatians 4:6)

> See what great love the Father has lavished upon us, that we should be called children of God! (1 John 3:1a)

> This is how God showed his love among us: He sent his one and only Son into the world that we might live through him. This is love: not that we loved God, but that he loved us and sent his Son as an atoning sacrifice for our sins. … We love because he first loved us. (1 John 4:9-10, 19)

Also, through God's Spirit, we are given the motivation and the power to love God and to prioritize our relationship with God.

> …God's love has been poured out into our hearts through the Holy Spirit, who has been given to us. (Romans 5:5b)

We have Christ within us, motivating us to recognize God as the most loveable person in the universe. Because of God's perfection, because of his steadfast covenant love, because of his sacrificial love, because of his particular, personal, loving care for each of us, we are enabled to enjoy a very personal relationship with him. No matter how much we may feel a pull toward giving love to and receiving love from a tangible human being, there is no human being as splendid, as loyal, as sufficient, and as loving as is the God who revealed himself through Jesus and stirs our hearts through his Spirit.

God baked into human DNA the need to be in relationship with other people.

God is completely and totally sufficient to meet all of our needs, including emotional and relational needs. Nevertheless, when he created mankind, God said, "It is not good for man to be alone" (Genesis 2:18). God baked into human DNA the need to be in relationship with other people. And the first such relationship was marriage – a man and a woman in a unique oneness (v. 24). Then sin entered the picture. We do not know what relationships – the relationships between husband and wife, between parents and children, between siblings, and between friends – would have been like if humankind had remained in perfect union with God. With the Fall, our relationship with God was broken and all human relationships thereafter were marred by sin.

The rest of history is the story of God restoring his people to the relationships they once enjoyed with him, first, and then with others.

A total restoration of relationships will come only when we live in the new heaven and new earth where there will be no more sin (Revelation 21-22) and we will see God clearly (1 Corinthians 13:12; 1 John 3:2). We will fully enjoy our relationship with God as his beloved children. But, as we wait for that day, how should our relationships be conducted? What relationships are most important? In the pages of Scripture, and especially in the New Testament, we see that marriage and family are indeed taken for granted as commonplace. However, marriage points to the far more important relationship between Christ and his church (Ephesians 5:25-32). We see all of human history culminating in the marriage of Jesus to his bride, the church (Revelation 19:6-8). And Jesus makes it clear that marriage has only a temporary place in this present world (Matthew 22:30). Romantic love and the fulfillment found in marriage are acknowledged in Scripture (for example, in Song of Songs), but they are not required for a full and meaningful life. Jesus did not marry. The apostles Paul and John did not marry and led full and meaningful lives. Paul even encouraged people to avoid marriage, if possible, so they could concern themselves with the Lord more (1 Corinthians 7:7-8 and 32-35). Also, over and over again, when believers are encouraged to love one another, it is in the context of relationships with fellow believers. For example, see John 15:12-13 and 1 John 4:7-8.

If we accept that the emphasis in Scripture is not on marriage as the main means by which we express and receive love, this will free us up to receive and give appropriate and wholesome love and affection in the many relationships God gives us. This takes off the blinders that block us from seeing the fulfillment we already have in our relationship with God and in the many types of emotionally satisfying relationships God provides with fellow believers. This widens our tunnel vision of expecting most, if not all, fulfillment in life to come from marriage and immediate family and opens our eyes to see the many means by which God provides for our emotional and relationship needs. And this takes a lot of pressure off of one's spouse!

The big problem with marriage is that it involves people! As we anticipate marriage, we think, *Finally, I'll get all the fulfillment, affirmation, and affection I ever dreamed of!* We don't usually think, *Finally, I'll live up close and personal with another faulty human being who is focusing on what I can do for her just as much as I'm focusing on what she will do for me.* When, in marriage or in any relationship, we look to another person to meet our needs, there will inevitably be disappointment, especially for Christians, because God does not want us to get our needs met through people, but through him. Scripture has quite a bit to say about *God* being the perfect "mate" (Isaiah 54:5; Jeremiah 3:14) and our completeness being found in our union with Christ (Colossians 1:28 and 2:10; Hebrews 11:40). When we try to find our wholeness through marriage and when we try to get a majority of our needs met through a relationship with a spouse, frustration and disappointment are sure to follow – because marriage and spouses were neither designed to make us whole nor to meet most of our needs.

Many have said that marriage is the crucible in which people's true character is tested. Living daily in intimacy with and dependence upon another person and knowing it's "for the long haul" can quickly force to the surface many issues in our lives that might otherwise remain dormant. And various "coping behaviors" can be a response to those issues. Fortunately, we can choose to see our unwanted emotions and behaviors as signals that point out our need to turn to God in

Romantic love and the fulfillment found in marriage are acknowledged in Scripture, but they are not required for a full and meaningful life.

Marriage and spouses were neither designed to make us whole nor to meet most of our needs.

order to ascertain how to do more than merely cope. He then leads us into honestly facing what motivates our coping behaviors and the true healing that not only resolves the negative behaviors and persistent unwanted emotions, but also addresses the more important issues that lie beneath them.

Although the commitment of marriage can spotlight each spouse's weaknesses, any relationship in which people are trying to get needs met though another person is always going to be unhealthy and not very fulfilling. People may be a means God uses to meet some of our needs, but they can never be the ultimate source for any need. Healthy relationships of any sort – family, friendships, marriage, co-workers – require individuals who see their needs as primarily met in Christ (Philippians 4:19). These individuals need not be sinless or without any personal struggles (because they can't be, this side of heaven), but they do need to be growing in the truth about who God really is, how completely dependent they are on him for every aspect of life, and God's desire to meet the needs of his children. Also, as individuals see more clearly who God has made them to be as "new creations in Christ," their sense of self becomes less dependent upon the attention and approval of others, allowing a true flow of Christ's love within a relationship instead of a constant need for affirmation from the relationship.

Any relationship in which people are trying to get needs met though another person is always going to be unhealthy and not very fulfilling.

Because a sense of need for affection and affirmation can be so strong, it is easy to try to get those needs met in ways that "appear to be right" (Proverbs 14:12). This can result in great compromise, such as engaging in premarital or extramarital sexual relationships, hero worship, unhealthy clingy friendships, and all sorts of manipulative behaviors. As these relationships crash and burn, as they almost always do, God brings us back to his great wisdom about how he made us, most importantly to be in relationship to *him*. When we find our needs met in our loving, caring God, who loved us enough to provide fully for our sinfulness that separated us from his holy, perfect presence, we do not need to look for our ultimate fulfillment in relationships with people. We can enjoy how God provides for us through people and enables us to extend love and care to people. The people in our relationships need never be perfect because God is perfect. God uses a vast variety of means to meet our deep longings and desires, but not primarily through relationships, not even through marriage. When we turn to God to provide for us, even in ways we thought only a relationship with a special person could satisfy, we become free to have truly fulfilling relationships in which God is the primary participant and focal point. We experience the freedom to relate to others as we were designed to do, in the freeing love of Christ.

Reflection

1. What are some of your most deeply felt needs that you don't feel God is meeting?

2. How would you like the significant people in your life to change?

What Others Have Experienced

Scores of people have poured out their hearts to me, wondering why God has chosen not to meet their deeply felt needs for affection, sexual intimacy, companionship, and partnership in the tasks and pleasures of life, such as keeping the car maintained and taking vacations. A single friend once admitted with great embarrassment that he engaged in sex he knew was wrong just so he could feel some affection afterward. A young man recently confided to me that he did not believe anything would ever fill the void he feels because he has no girlfriend. A woman I was discipling despaired of ever feeling as through she really was a woman because she could not bear children. Numerous never-married women have asked me, "What is wrong with me that God wouldn't want me to be married?" When I hit 40 and was still single, I told God that if I ever did marry, I'd never, ever say it was worth the wait. (I was terribly mistaken about that!)

What these perceptions of unmet needs all point to is a misunderstanding about the way God has made us and how he wants us to get our needs met. When I told a 30-year-old single woman that the answer to her question of "What is wrong with me that I'm not married?" was "Only your perspective," she was at first put off. As we talked over the truth about how God wanted her to see him as her husband and provider and that she had God's total approval in Christ, she realized that she was insisting on God doing what she wanted him to do and not allowing God to do what he knew was best for her.

Many people believe they cannot possibly live for any length of time without engaging in sexual intimacy. It is very apparent in Scripture that this cannot be true. Too many people never married (Jesus, the apostles Paul and John, and probably Elijah, Elisha, and Daniel). When we see God meeting our needs through various means – through inspiring us from within, through his Word reassuring us of his love, through fellow church members extending care and concern, through our spiritual and genetic family members, through friendly co-workers and loyal friends – the sense of urgency to get needs met through sex is reduced. Yes, Paul tells people it is better to marry than to burn with desire, but in that same letter, he tells people it is better to not marry at all (1 Corinthians 7:8-9).

If God is not providing you with a spouse, then you can be sure God is providing you with all the purpose, love, affection, and helpers you need by other means. Our tunnel vision restricts us in seeing all God has for us in the very creative ways he provides.

For every change a person wants to see in the life of a spouse, parent, sibling, or close friend, there is an expectation for that individual to meet a need God wants to meet another way. I've seen this most pointedly in woman who are heartbroken over how little they feel their husbands love them. Truly miraculous encouragement for these women has resulted from one or both of two avenues: 1) assessing how the husband actually was showing love that wasn't "counted" by the wife, and 2) realizing how God was providing love through other means, primarily through his own deep and perfect love.

An older friend expressed some pretty intense jealousy when she heard that my husband had a large bouquet of flowers, along with a very touching greeting card, sent to me at my office on a day that had no particular significance to us. She hotly told me, "Carl has never sent me flowers or cards, and I wonder if he even loves me at all!" This really struck me because I had long admired their relationship. So, I said to this dear friend, "I thought Carl makes you lunch every day and even packs it when you can't come home on your lunch break." She admitted this was

When we see God meeting our needs through various means, the sense of urgency to get needs met through sex is reduced.

true. Then I said, "I thought Carl makes exactly all your favorites, like chicken salad on special bread, and he goes out of his way to buy you lots of little treats to have in your lunch." Again, she admitted that was true. Seeing where I was going with this, she said, "But he never sends me flowers!" And I said, "And Mike never has made a single meal for me. Which one of us is ahead?" We then talked for a while about all the many ways Carl frequently went to great lengths to make my friend very comfortable and happy – always checking on her car's oil level, doing most of the housework because she worked more hours than he did, sitting on the patio with her while they fed the mockingbird that frequently visited. He hardly ever watched TV because he was so busy doing things for her. She, again, had to admit that the many ways in which her husband served her should be "counted" as demonstrations of love and affection. She wept because she was so happy to realize that her husband did indeed love her.

But sometimes husbands really don't feel love for their wives, and sometimes wives don't feel love for their husbands. This is sad but true. Many people marry to get their needs met and when the spouse does not meet those needs, they "fall out of love." Obviously, they were never truly "in love" in the first place – not the true love of Christ. What was felt was self-love and a desire to get the help of a spouse in loving self. "I'll love you as long as you love me in the ways I want you to." I've known several women who have lived for years with husbands who no longer have loving feelings for their wives. And I'm sure this happens to men just as often. The women who have found joy and contentment in such a situation are those who have relied heavily upon Christ, looking to Jesus to provide the love and acceptance no human being can. One woman even told me that she thanks God her husband cannot truly love her, because she would not have known the deep love of Jesus had she been able to get her affection needs met through her husband.

Many people marry to get their needs met and when the spouse does not meet those needs, they "fall out of love."

Homework

1. Read "Living Well in Marriage," provided with permission in Addendum Three, starting on page 203 of this book. Complete the questions provided in the addendum. If you are not married, apply the information and questions to a significant relationship, such as with a sibling, close friend, or parent.

2. Read "Attitude of Gratitude," a transcript of a recorded message by Bill Ewing. This transcript is provided with permission in Addendum Four, starting on page 211 of this book.

Homework Follow-up

1. What stood out to you about ways you are trying to get needs met by another person and how God is meeting those needs in other ways?

2. In what ways has God equipped you to love the people he's put in your life even when they are not showing love to you?

3. What do you perceive as flaws in the significant people in your life, and how might God be using those flaws for your good?

Comments on the Homework

We've all said it: "God works in mysterious ways!" That's not an exact quote from the Bible, but it's sure biblical! (See Isaiah 55:8-9, Habakkuk 1:5, and Romans 11:33 for just a few examples.) Our transformation into the image of Christ is a mysterious and sometimes painful process. One of the means by which God makes us more and more like Jesus ("sanctification") is through relationships. When we have the perspective that God works all things for our good (Jeremiah 29:11; Romans 8:28), we are more able to "go with the flow" even in the face of the inevitable disappointments that occur in relationships. This never means unemotional stoicism or passive fatalism. We are allowed to express our grief and disappointments to God (as mentioned in Chapters 6 and 7 of this book and as evidenced by many of the writers of the psalms). But we cannot simply moan and complain, because God wants us to experience him as completely sufficient for all of our circumstances. This brings me to a truism I call the "Miserableness Quotient": The degree to which you believe God has good plans for you, despite your circumstances, is the degree to which you minimize your misery.

Corrie ten Boom is quoted as saying, "Every experience God gives us, every person He puts into our lives, is the perfect preparation for a future only He can see."[4] My guess is that, given all she suffered and the fact that she never married, she was putting that thought together with 2 Corinthians 4:17: "For our light and momentary troubles are achieving for us an eternal glory that far outweighs them all." An attitude that "fixes our eyes not on what is seen, but on what is unseen" (2 Corinthians 4:18) enables us to focus on all that God is doing for us, in us, and for others, rather than focusing on what we want but don't have.* We will be much likelier to accept that we do not really know what we need, but God does know. And the truth is that we *do* have all we need (Philippians 4:19). May God grant you the eyes to see what you already have and thereby enable you to experience the freedom you already have to find fulfillment by sharing the love of Christ in any and all of your relationships.

The degree to which you believe God has good plans for you, despite your circumstances, is the degree to which you minimize your misery.

---

* This chapter is not intended to address the issues of abuse within relationships and should not be read as recommending that anyone silently or stoically withstand abuse. If you are experiencing abuse, please seek help immediately.

11 FREEING TRUTH ABOUT BAD THINGS PEOPLE HAVE DONE TO YOU

"Something deep inside of me shattered."[1]
"Record my misery; list my tears on your scroll—are they not in your record?"[2]
"Something like that will scar you for life."[3]

A man was on the other end of the phone line, and it was immediately obvious that he was feeling overwhelming panic. I had answered the phone on one of the Tuesday nights when I filled in as receptionist at the biblical counseling ministry where I worked. "My son was just raped!" What a horrific greeting. I was stunned and could only say, "I'm so terribly sorry to hear that." Then the man said, "I guess he'll become a homosexual now." I could hardly believe that was what was uppermost on this man's mind. His son was no doubt suffering, confused, and wounded in body, mind, and soul, but his father's greatest terror was that, having been sodomized, his son would be doomed to become a sodomite. The self-centered fears of this father truly angered me. As the receptionist, I had no place to say anything, but I reacted with, "He'll only become a homosexual if you expect him to be. How you look at what has happened will make all the difference in how your son processes this event. This has happened because someone has sinned against your son, not because anything is wrong with your boy. This will only be as damaging to him as you make it." He was not fully reassured and asked, "You mean this isn't going to turn him into a homosexual?"

Wow, that was a deeply entrenched belief and, although I've never encountered this exact belief since, I have encountered many people who have very similar beliefs as a result of horrible things someone has done to them. "I will never be whole again." "I will never be clean." "I guess I deserved this." "I brought this on myself." "God knew I could handle this and wants me to help others." These and many more beliefs about rape, incest, sexual molestation, being beaten, being robbed, or having a loved one killed by a drunk driver have been heart-wrenching to hear. Such statements reveal a very unfortunate aspect of having been sinned against that gets heaped on top of the trauma itself; that is, what we think about ourselves as a result of having been sinned against.

One of the cruelest aspects of sin is how *self*-centered it is. Sin is all about getting what *I* want, doing what *I* want to do, and putting *my* perceived needs ahead of all other considerations. This was true of the very first sin. Adam and Eve wanted godhood for themselves and heedlessly disregarded the dire consequence of death in order to get what they wanted by doing what they wanted, putting their perceived "need" to be like God ahead of all other considerations. Sin is very often not well thought out. It is a response to the erroneous belief – not always a fully conscious belief – that "I need this to be happier."

To live life as a human being is to commit sin, because we are born enslaved to sin and separated from the power and love of God that is needed before we are able to choose love and wisdom over sin. (See Romans 3:23, 5:12, and 6:17-18.) And many of the sins people commit are against others, causing deep wounds in those who are sinned against. The pain of being sinned

A very unfortunate aspect of having been sinned against that gets heaped on top of the trauma itself is what we think about ourselves as a result of having been sinned against.

against – through such sins as rape, molestation, incest, overly harsh punishments, verbal abuse, relentless criticisms, neglect, abandonment, physical assault, and threats of violence, to name a few – is not the only result of being used, misused, or mistreated. The person who has been sinned against mentally processes what has happened to him or her and forms beliefs about God, self, and life that are not usually based in the truth, the real truth that can come only from God. Those sinned against form erroneous beliefs because they too are influenced by sin and process what has happened "in the flesh"; in other words, they process traumatic events through their own personal lens and not from God's vantage point. Perpetrators and their victims are sinful. The sinful beliefs of the perpetrator allowed him or her to do an act that hurt another person. Then, because of the victim's own self-centered thinking, the victim is devastated by his or her own beliefs about what has happened. The victim thinks, *What does this offense that happened to me say about me? What does it say about God?* Assumptions are formed, internalized, and rarely questioned as to their accuracy.

This is not the same as "blaming the victim." This is just the bald fact about how people self-centeredly interpret events and circumstances because of indwelling sin. The tragedy is not just in having a heinous sin perpetrated against you. An added tragedy is in the victim viewing that sin as reflecting on him or her in ways that are not true. For example, here are statements I've heard from people who have been violently and/or sexually sinned against:

> *This has ruined my entire life.*
> *I am gross, dirty, and disgusting.*
> *I will never get over this.*
> *I have been completely and forever dirtied.*
> *I guess I'm just a worthless piece of s*#t.*
> *I am trash and should just be thrown away.*
> *There's no one to protect me. I have to protect myself better.*
> *Everyone knows there's something wrong with me.*
> *God doesn't love me as much as he loves other people.*
> *God has forgotten me.*
> *I asked for this.*
> *No one who knows this has happened to me will ever be able to love me.*
> *I will never be a normal person.*

If you didn't see what you've thought about yourself thanks to the traumas you've suffered, write down your beliefs about yourself and God. These thoughts and beliefs are absolutely reasonable to have, given the experience of a traumatic sin against you. Anyone who experienced what you experienced would quite naturally have such beliefs.

Hopefully, you saw a common theme in the statements I listed. Even though nearly anyone could sympathize with the people making these statements, the beliefs expressed are very me-centered. You've probably heard it said that "sin" has an "I" in the middle. Well, that's true not only in the English language, but sadly that is true for every single person, even when a person is horrendously sinned against. After the initial trauma, the one sinned against becomes a victim again, but this time a victim of his or her own thoughts and beliefs about what the trauma means about God, self, and life.

Does this mean the person who was sinned against should beat himself or herself up for the sin of seeing the trauma in a self-centered way? Absolutely not! The death of Jesus Christ on the cross has fully atoned for sin. "There is now no condemnation for those who are in Christ Jesus" (Romans 8:1). In fact, as a believer in Jesus and therefore a new creation in Christ, there is a choice available that is not available to non-believers. A believer in Christ can review his or her erroneous beliefs and start to believe differently. This does not require guilt, shame, or self-punishment. This can end the sin being perpetrated against oneself as a result of believing what is untrue.

The truth is that when someone sins against you, it is *not* because of *you*. It is because of the perpetrator's sin. No sin against you has to be taken personally. No one has been so innocent and so sinned against as was Jesus. However, nothing that people said or did to him – and not even being completely loaded with every sin that was ever committed – affected Jesus's sense of self or his understanding of his worth. With your own identity and worth fully secured in Christ, it is no longer necessary to evaluate yourself based on what someone else did to you.

In my own life, and in the lives of others who have felt emotionally crippled by traumatic events they experienced at the hands of others, I've seen a pattern emerge as victims experience freedom from the ongoing pain they feel. These observed typical steps to freedom are listed below as suggestions for the reader to consider:

1) Admit to yourself and to at least one other person what happened to you and how you felt then and feel now about it.
2) Write down what you've always believed about yourself and about God as a result of what happened to you.
3) Ask God to give you faith and trust in him even though you aren't certain about him since he allowed such painful sins to be perpetrated against you.
4) Make a conscious decision to forgive those who sinned against you. In other words, turn the people who sinned against you over to God, investing trust in God's ultimate justice.
5) Acknowledge your own sins – real or imagined – surrounding the actual traumatic events or in your mental processing of the events. For example, you may have been available to a perpetrator because you disobeyed a parent. Of course, nothing excuses the perpetrator's sinful act against you, but your own sin need not forever plague you if you acknowledge it and accept God's total forgiveness of it through the atoning death of Jesus. Another example is realizing that you believed you were forever sullied by being sinned against when, in fact, Jesus has made you forever redeemed and cleansed. In light of the truth about you in Scripture, you can make a choice to believe differently about yourself.
6) Recognize that being sinned against was not about you but reflected the perpetrator's choices to sin. You can identify with Jesus, who knew it was not because of what he did or even because of who he was that people hated him and sinned against him. It was because of people's sinful, self-centered desires and erroneous beliefs that they sinned against him. The same is true of you. Even if the perpetrator did single you out, that was because of his or her sinfulness, not yours.
7) Decide to agree with Scripture that no one and nothing can ruin who God has made you to forever be – his perfect, acceptable, Spirit-filled, and beloved child.

With your own identity and worth fully secured in Christ, it is no longer necessary to evaluate yourself on the basis of what someone else did to you.

8) Meditate on eternal truths and the promise of heaven, seeing this life as a dot on your eternal timeline of bliss, which is made more powerfully wonderful because of what you have suffered. (See Romans 8:18 and 2 Corinthians 4:17-18.)

I, and many I know who have suffered trauma, have found it helpful to meditate on what Jesus suffered when he took on every sin ever committed and then endured the righteous wrath of God for those sins. Although this is beyond our comprehension, it is possible, especially for deeply wounded people, to understand Jesus's torment to some extent. Taking upon himself every human sin was what I think of as the ultimate rape. Early in my Christian walk, Hebrews 4:15 seemed like a joke to me. How could Jesus have been tempted in every way I've been tempted? He was never a small girl who had been repeatedly molested, assaulted, and told she didn't even deserve to breathe the air. He had been loved, not just by his parents, but also by his Father in heaven. However, because I knew full well that the Bible was 100 percent true, I started "prayerfully pondering" how the writer of Hebrews could accurately say Jesus was "tempted in every way, just as we are…" (Hebrews 4:15). As many have realized before, I realized that you don't have to suffer the exact same traumas to be tempted in a way that is common to everyone. Jesus was repeatedly tempted to believe Satan's lies and take shortcuts to bypass the excruciating pain he knew was on his horizon. Unlike the rest of us, though, he never bought into a lie and never suppressed or repressed the full reality of his suffering. Even though he did not sin in response to his trauma, he does understand how it feels to be horrendously sinned against and deeply betrayed, even by the very people who should have welcomed and adored him.

Can you see Jesus identifying with you in what you suffered? We do not fully understand why God allows suffering to be an often deeply painful part of life, but we know he himself has been there and shows us the way to reflect on our suffering so that it no longer warps our thinking and no longer motivates sinful coping behaviors on which we rely for comfort or for distraction from our pain. And it's important to realize that the pain doesn't just show up; it's actually generated by our thoughts. When we change how we think about what has happened to us, this changes the amount of pain we feel.

The following Scripture passages are my well-worn "pocket verses" (verses I figuratively keep in my "back pocket" to have at the ready when needed) that reassure me in the face of temptation to think negatively about myself and about God because of the ways I have been sinned against: 2 Corinthians 4:6-18; Hebrews 4:14-16; and 1 Peter 2:23.

Any sin against you or committed by you is definitely worthy of your sadness. There need never be a day when you "just don't feel anything" about a trauma you've suffered. If it had happened to another person, you certainly would believe it to be wrong and you would hurt for that person. However, you can move away from experiencing crippling emotions over and over again in regard to the sins people have committed against you. You can know the truth about who you are in Christ and be free!

Reflection

1. Over what past events do you feel repeated pain? About what past events do you avoid even thinking or fear hearing that others have gone through similar circumstances?

Many who have suffered trauma have found it helpful to meditate on what Jesus suffered when he took on every sin ever committed and then endured the righteous wrath of God for those sins.

2. For each event you listed in response to the above question, what did someone do to you or fail to do for you?

3. What emotions do you fear might overwhelm you if you were to think through a past traumatic event and the beliefs you formed as a result of it?

What Others Have Experienced

When individuals repeatedly feel pain about a past event or feel they cannot even "go there" because their own emotions will devastate them, it reminds me of what I used to call the "Max box." This was the imaginary box in which I stored away all the feelings and thoughts I had about having been repeatedly sexually molested by my first stepfather. I once drew a picture in a journal of what I feared would come out if the "Max box" were opened: a giant, fire-breathing dragon. I'm reminded how the most difficult aspect of entering into healing the torment from traumas is being willing to "go there," to think through what happened and especially to think through what beliefs were formed as a result of what happened.

With help from biblical counselors, I gradually came to understand that the pain and fear of being overwhelmed by my own emotions were symptoms of having not yet fully accessed the healing available to me in Christ. I asked Jesus to give me his courage and his resources – his Spirit to comfort, his people to guide and extend caring, his Word to be personally and specifically applied – so that I could receive his balm being poured into my wounds. He enabled me to boldly, in his power, face the lies I'd believed about myself and about God as a result of having been molested by my stepfather and having been told by him that I'd asked for it.

My experience, and what I've observed in others, is that the most difficult aspect of any traumatic sin one has experienced at the hands of another person is the guilt the victim feels about his or her role in bringing on the event. For example, what tormented me more than what my stepfather did to me was the fact that I had purposely put myself in his way several times after the first instance of molestation. I knew he would molest me in the car on the way home on the Sunday nights when he dropped off his children at their mother's home. I now realize I was so starved for attention and affection that I would take any sort of attention offered, even though I had a sense that what was being done to me was wrong and frightening. Then when my

He enabled me to boldly, in his power, face the lies I'd believed about myself and about God as a result of having been molested by my stepfather.

stepfather told me I'd asked for it, this affirmed my thinking that I was at fault. Of course, there is absolutely no excuse for any adult to molest any child, even if that child were to very specifically ask to be molested! The adult knows that is not good for the child and that no such thing should ever be done to a child under any circumstances. But you can see how I'd feel I had some culpability, no matter how much people told me that it's never the victim's fault. It was necessary for me to admit this guilt and, whether anyone saw it as sin or not, to recognize that the blood of Jesus on the cross totally and completely covered my sin and cleansed me from it.

Many women have told me similar stories of having worn clothing that was seductive, having hung out with friends their parents had warned them against, having been somewhere they knew they should not have been, or of having gotten drunk and, therefore, rendered themselves more vulnerable to assault or rape. There is *nothing* we do that gives any person an excuse to sin against us, but we do indeed sin sometimes in proximity to or seeming connection with that perpetrator's sin. There is no amount of "the victim is never at fault" that can assuage guilt as effectively as the total forgiveness available to each of us in Jesus Christ.

There is no amount of "the victim is never at fault" that can assuage guilt as effectively as the total forgiveness available to each of us in Jesus Christ.

Homework

Remembering at least one traumatic sin that someone perpetrated against you, complete the following:

1) Tell a trusted person what happened to you and how much this has hurt you – what you felt then and what you continue to feel now.

2) Write what you believed about God, yourself, and how life works as a result of having been sinned against in this way.

3) Ask God to give you faith and trust in him even though he allowed this trauma to happen to you.

4) Write down your forgiveness of the person who hurt you, putting the ultimate meting out of justice into God's hands.

5) Write what you've felt guilty about in regard to having been sinned against in this way.

6) Write a few sentences expressing that the traumatic event reflects on the perpetrator and his or her sin. Acknowledge that nothing anyone does to you can change who God made you to be.

7) Write at least one Scripture verse that assures you that you are totally forgiven for any sin you may have committed in connection with the trauma you experienced. Write a Scripture that reassures you about who God has made you to be.

8) What eternal truths do you need to keep in mind when you're tempted to see your life as ruined by being sinned against?

Homework Follow-up

1. As a result of doing the homework, have you changed your mind about the way you see yourself? If so, in what way?

2. Has God provided you with a trusted friend or friends with whom you can be open about needing help in getting a better perspective about what has happened to you?

Comments on the Homework

In changing our minds about what the sins that have been perpetrated against us say about us, the model of Jesus informs us of what could be our response if we were not corrupted by our "flesh," the sin that remains within us even though we are "new creations in Christ." Although it is totally understandable that we would take personally sins perpetrated against us, it is not necessary to do so. Every person who has been sinned against (all of us) can choose to see that sin as reflecting the offender's sinful choices, even if it was directed very specifically toward the victim. It is always wrong to sin against another person, regardless of circumstances. The one sinned against may have sinned in some way, but there is never a justifiable reason for anyone to sin against another person. Understanding this fact can and should make a huge difference in how victims think about themselves. For example, I did talk back to my mother, but that did not mean she was right in throwing a knife at me and pinning my hair to the wall. It was possible for her to react to my sin in a sinless manner through appropriate discipline. Her sin against me highlighted *her* sinfulness, not mine. My sin did not generate hers.

Outrage and shame can sometimes paper over the more painful issue of how a person sees himself or herself as a result of having been sinned against. Some people have told me there is nothing wrong with them except that justice was never done. However, it's apparent that there is quite a bit "wrong" because of ungodly behaviors, such as compulsive eating and never-ending weight gain or fits of rage at family members who have done or said things others would find only slightly irritating. With such individuals, I have emphasized God's character and justice – how he can be trusted to make all things right in eternity, even though not everything is just in this life. Putting justice into God's hands frees people to start examining erroneous beliefs about themselves that are motivating their unwanted behaviors.

If you do not *feel* bad about yourself but you can see you are engaging in behaviors you wish you didn't do, this is a "red warning light" that tells you prayerful pondering is needed. Ask God to reveal to you what you have shoved down so far that you no longer feel it. It's apparent by your behavior that you are coping with deeply-held beliefs and their resultant emotional pain. Because the Holy Spirit is the Counselor, he can be trusted to minister to you in the areas where your pain needs to be acknowledged and your mind needs to be renewed.

This chapter was not intended to cover every single possible sin a person may have had perpetrated against him or her. Although each situation can be vastly different from another, there are nearly always very similar responses in terms of the victim considering himself or herself greatly devalued or permanently marred as a result of being sinned against. No matter what you have endured or how damaged you believe yourself to be, ask Jesus to provide you with caring fellow believers with whom you can discuss your painful thoughts. You may need

Although it is totally understandable that we would take personally sins perpetrated against us, it is not necessary to do so.

to ask a pastor to refer you to a counselor or a mature, caring member of the congregation. Many of the women who have sought out my input were referred to me by a ministry leader, church elder, or women within a church who knew me. Letting someone know you need caring and advice allows the body of Christ to operate as it is intended – building "itself up in love, as each part does its work" (Ephesians 4:16). Going it alone and continuing to shove down your feelings about having been sinned against is not in line with the freeing truth God has revealed about his love for you, his work in you, and his work through his people.

12 WHERE DO YOU GO FROM HERE?

> "Seems we just get started and before you know it, comes the time we have to say so long."[1]
> "It is for freedom that Christ has set us free."[2]
> "I never knew half this stuff."[3]

There are many topics this book does not cover, such as a thorough treatment of prayer, spiritual warfare, sex and sexuality, and communication skills. These have been purposely omitted. There are many excellent treatments of these topics that can be found elsewhere. What has been included in this book are the ever-needed foundational truths that undergird every aspect of living a life of faith in Christ and his Word, the truths that led me to freedom from compulsive behaviors and persistently painful emotions and that I've seen lead many others to similar freedom.

The chapters of this book were in a very particular order, starting with truths about God. When you understand the true character of God, especially as opposed to your previously unexamined inaccurate assumptions about him, you are able to trust God. Trusting God is the basis for every aspect of personal growth into the image of Christ. If you don't trust God, you read a verse, such as 2 Corinthians 9:8, and think, *Yeah, yeah, but...* You don't really believe God's rich promises because you don't really believe in the real God, who is always engaged in actively loving and guiding each of his people (Philippians 2:13).

When you understand who you really are in Christ, who you have been born again to be for all eternity, you need no longer see your "flesh" as your identity. You contend with the flesh and the flesh is tempted to follow its own lead, but that's not who you are at the core of your being. When you see who God has made you to be – "created to be like God in true righteousness and holiness" (Ephesians 4:24) – you can know that God is indeed sanctifying you – making you more and more like Jesus every day – and you can consider your sins as foreign to the "real you." Knowing the true character of God and your true, eternal nature makes it much easier to "come boldly unto the throne of grace, that we may obtain mercy, and find grace to help in time of need" (Hebrews 4:16, KJV). Our constant turning to Jesus and his truth (Scripture) is what leads us to the freedom we so deeply desire and that has already been given to each born-again believer in Christ.

Once there is a basic belief in God's character, especially as seen through the life, death, resurrection, and ascension of Jesus, and a basic belief in the extremely radical change that occurs in the believer's life at the point of trusting in Christ, then it is much easier to address the most common issues with which Western evangelical Christians (at least the ones I've encountered over the last 35-plus years) struggle: legalism; alarming and unwanted emotions; maintaining loving relationships; and overcoming persistent sinful behaviors. Numerous types of struggles have not been specifically addressed in this book. Instead, core principles have been covered that enable every Christian to address any struggle he or she might encounter, because when any struggle is faced with true faith in our loving God, we *can* believe in 2 Corinthians 9:8.

Once there is a basic belief in God's character and a basic belief in the extremely radical change that occurs in the believer's life at the point of trusting in Christ, then it is much easier to address the most common issues with which Christians struggle.

And God is able to bless you abundantly, so that in all things at all times, having all that you need, you will abound in every good work.

Most people have not had much exposure to the topics covered in this book. Therefore, it may be advantageous to work through the book more than once. The best way to do that is to invite others to join you in a small group experience. Facilitation of a small group utilizing this book is very simple, and a short Facilitator's Guide is provided on pages 225-228. Group members can even take turns acting as facilitator. Absolutely no experience with small group facilitation or with the topics covered is needed.

Materials and ministries that explain the same concepts as those presented in this book can be very helpful in reinforcing the reader's trajectory toward greater freedom in Christ. Here are some suggested resources by topic:

Understanding the True Character of God and Building Trust in God
- *FatherCare* by Jim Craddock and Christi Taylor (available as a booklet online and reprinted by permission as Addendum One of this book)
- His Truth Transforms International, a ministry in Oklahoma City that provides books, booklets, handouts, and seminars. Contact them at 405-603-2020 or histruthtransforms.org.
- *Our Heavenly Father* by Robert Frost (not the poet)
- *The Father Heart of God* by Floyd McClung
- *Knowing God* by J. I. Packer

Understanding Who You Are as a New Creation in Christ/How to Address Emotions and Beliefs
- *Classic Christianity* by Bob George
- *Lifetime Guarantee* by Bill Gillham
- *Handbook to Happiness* by Charles R. Solomon
- *Seeing Yourself Through God's Eyes* by June Hunt
- His Truth Transforms International has several booklets and handouts on these topics.
- *The Marvelous Exchange* by Dick Flaten
- Shepherd's Call, a ministry in Arlington, Texas, providing in-person and online personal counsel and classes in how the Scripture applies to struggles Christians frequently face. 817-459-8488/scall220.org

Getting Out from under Legalism, both Subtle and Overt
- *The Torah Syndrome*, a booklet available at histruthtransforms.org/store
- *The Weight of Grace* by Paula Neall Coleman, especially addressing compulsive eating/dieting
- *Grace Works* by Dudley Hall

Engaging in God-Centered Relationships
- Living Well, a ministry in Oklahoma City, providing numerous handouts (available for download from their website) regarding Christ-centered relationships/marriage and communication at livingwellokc.org/enrich
- *Caring Enough to Confront* by David Augsburger

Overcoming the Pain of Being Sinned Against
- *Rid of My Disgrace* by Justin S. Holcomb and Lindsey A. Holcomb

When God brought the Israelites into the Promised Land, Moses explained to the people that the Lord would drive out the wicked nations from the land little-by-little, not all at once (Deuteronomy 7:22). Sanctification – that is, growing in holiness and becoming more like Jesus – is a lot like that. It's a process that can often test our patience and even our faith. We want total freedom, but God tells us:

> The path of the righteous is like the morning sun,
>   shining ever brighter till the full light of day. (Proverbs 4:18)

Until we reach heaven, our path to total freedom is a gradual journey with several bumps and unexpected roadblocks. God tells us why this is:

> For God, who said, "Let light shine out of darkness," made his light shine in our hearts to give us the light of the knowledge of God's glory displayed in the face of Christ. But we have this treasure in jars of clay to show that this all-surpassing power is from God and not from us. (2 Corinthians 4:6-7)

The light gets brighter and brighter as we realize we cannot rely on ourselves, but only on God. Sometimes instant "success" is not success at all if it builds *self*-confidence rather than *God*-confidence. Our struggles and failures constantly remind us that we really do have to live the John 15:5 life. Apart from Jesus we can do nothing. We cannot pull ourselves up by our bootstraps. We have no bootstraps and we have no pull! The greatest truths with the greatest power to lead to the freedom that we yearn for are that Jesus transforms us, Jesus supplies us, Jesus empowers us, Jesus works within us, and as we encounter him, we gradually become like him.

When it comes to your struggles, God does not want you to gut it out and *make* yourself feel or act better. He knows full well that you cannot transform yourself. Only he has the ability to transform you. Much of that work has already been done: He has transferred you from darkness into his wonderful light (1 Peter 2:9). He has radically changed your very nature, giving you new motivations and the desire to love and obey him. Believing in him and in what he has already accomplished is a huge step in the direction of experiencing freedom. To continue to grow in that freedom – to experience it more and more in more and more areas of your life – requires your continued reliance upon and faith in Christ.

Turning to Jesus is where transformation takes place. In fact, as we engage directly with him and meditate on him, we become more and more like him.

> And we all, who with unveiled faces contemplate the Lord's glory, are being transformed into his image with ever-increasing glory, which comes from the Lord, who is Spirit. (2 Corinthians 3:18)

Unlike Moses, whose face shone with the glory of God after personally interacting with him but then veiled his face as the radiance faded, we behold God and have no need of a veil because, instead of fading, the glory of God increases in our lives. Each struggle we experience is an invitation from Jesus, saying, "Come to me. See, you need me, and I am here for you. Behold me

Our struggles and failures constantly remind us that we really do have to live the John 15:5 life. Apart from Jesus we can do nothing.

and be transformed and freed." (See 2 Corinthians 3:17!) Jesus wants each of us to know him and experience the love, joy, and peace he has for us. (See Matthew 11:28-30; John 10:10, 14:27, and 15:9; and Galatians 5:22-23.)

There can be a great hindrance to moving more and more into freedom. I've met several people whose anger over injustices suffered kept them stuck in perpetual behavior initially chosen to self-soothe but ultimately keeping them in a hideous prison of dependence on a substance or on self-defeating activities, such as gambling, compulsive tattooing and piercing, skin picking, or binge-eating. Many expressed that their anger was with an individual, but ultimately, they had to confess their anger was with God.

Repeatedly feeling angry with God is a pattern with which I'm sadly too familiar. It makes sense, doesn't it? If you have been wronged or if you've gotten caught up in a self-destructive behavior from which all your heart-felt prayers have not yet freed you, isn't a sovereign God ultimately to blame for your suffering? As hard a pill as it has been for me to swallow repeatedly over the years, the answer to that question is "Yes and no." As mentioned in Chapter 10, Corrie ten Boom, a woman who suffered horribly in a concentration camp, once said, "Every experience God gives us, every person He puts in our lives is the perfect preparation for a future that only He can see."[4] Joni Eareckson Tada, who has spent most of her life as a quadriplegic, often suffering unrelenting pain, has written, "God permits what He hates, even the awful cross at Calvary, to accomplish what He loves; and that is, salvation for a world of sinners. And that is gloriously good news for anyone today who has experienced any tragedy."[5] I am humbled and inspired by these women, who have suffered so terribly yet still see God's plan and purposes in what they've suffered.

Our reaction to suffering really does come down to our own humility, which is the flip side of the "fear of the Lord." When we insist that we know what is just or how our lives *should* have been, we declare ourselves to be god and do not recognize God as having more wisdom than we have. Instead of railing at God about not protecting us from wrongs suffered or not releasing us sooner from besetting sins for which we expected a dramatic, instant deliverance, we can choose to put faith in how God is using every hardship, trauma, or struggle we've ever faced – whether brought about by another's sin or by our own or even when no sin was involved (such as a birth defect or tragic accident) – as God's call to head straight to him for all we need (2 Corinthians 9:8; Hebrews 4:16-18).

Our struggles are also a call to take an eternal perspective. This life is not all there is. We are being prepared for an eternity of bliss and glory (Romans 8:18, 2 Corinthians 4:16-17). Our anger at God is actually our insistence on having our way *now*. But our way is deeply flawed, and God's way, though sometimes painful and surprising, is perfect – and has eternal, positive consequences.

> As for God, his way is perfect: The LORD's word is flawless; he shields all who take refuge in him. (Psalm 18:30)

> Trust in the LORD with all your heart and lean not on your own understanding; in all your ways submit to him, and he will make your paths straight. (Proverbs 3:5-6)

I've met several people whose anger over injustices suffered kept them stuck in perpetual behavior initially chosen to self-soothe but ultimately keeping them in a hideous prison of dependence on a substance or on self-defeating activities.

Humble yourselves, therefore, under God's might hand, that he may lift you up in due time. Cast all your anxiety on him because he cares for you. (1 Peter 5:6-7)

The truth of God's wisdom, perfection, love, and mercy – not always easy to perceive in the haze of suffering and sin – is what ultimately sets us free, free to enjoy all God has for us, free to leave our sinful ways of coping because there's nothing with which to cope – or because we have learned to "cope" by turning to the Lord. When the "God of all comfort" (2 Corinthians 1:3) is in charge, instead of you, your life can be experienced in the way you were designed to live. You are free to be the real you, in more and more dependence on the real Jesus, who told you that you desperately need him more than anyone or anything else (John 15:5).

The Ever-elusive "Quiet Time"

As you have seen throughout this book, in order to experience freedom in Christ, there are many patterns of thought and deep-seated beliefs that need to be exposed and exchanged for God's truths, which are revealed in Scripture. Although God, through his Spirit enables and effects these changes, it is clear in Scripture that God calls us to intentionally participate in that process by the renewing of the mind (Romans 12:2), taking thoughts "captive to the obedience of Christ" (2 Corinthians 10:5), "putting off" and "putting on" (Ephesians 4:22-24), and exercising faith in God and his Word (John 6:28-29; 8:31-32). Our need to change our thinking to align with God's truth points to our need to engage with God in Bible study and prayerful reflection on a regular basis. And on that point I cannot tell you how many times I've heard something along these lines, "I've tried to have a quiet time every morning, but I can't ever stick with it." Yes, I know; me too.

This continued discouragement about having a regular "quiet time" (QT) is almost always due to approaching daily Bible study and prayer as a "duty" or work that must be done in obedience to God. And that's a subtle form of legalism that's bound to fail. (See Romans 7:9-11.) Legalism is something we do "in the flesh"; i.e., in our own strength – and we really do not have enough strength to do it!

The alternative to a legalistic approach to QTs that has led me, and many to whom I've suggested it, to truly enjoy and deeply long for regular special times of engaging with God in Bible study and prayer is this: Ask God to show you the times he has carved out for you to meet with him. Every time this prayer is prayed, over the course of a few days or weeks – and sometimes immediately – that prayer is answered. But, it's not always answered in the way you'd expect. Your QT may not be every single day or at the same time of day each time. And, certainly, when circumstances change, asking God for new guidance about when to meet with him is necessary. Changes that necessitate asking God, "When is our meeting time *now*?" might be a new work schedule, a relative or neighbor needing regular assistance, or the ever-evolving routines of rearing growing children.

To experience success in regularly meeting with God, the emphasis needs to be on how *God* is providing and guiding, instead of how you are "fulfilling your duty." Our reliance upon God's presence, power, and desire to lead us is crucial to every aspect of our lives, even when and how we spend intentional times with him.

Reflection

1. Over what aspect of your life do you feel angry with God (or you think God has treated your unfairly)?

2. What would happen to you if you no longer relied on your most persistent means of coping with life (e.g., bouts of depression; self-isolating; anesthetizing yourself with food, alcohol, or marijuana; pulling out your eyelashes or hair; cutting; or binge-watching television or social media)?

What Others Have Experienced

There are certain injustices that happen to people, even to people I don't know, that tempt me to rage against God: sex slavery, child abuse, rape, and similar suffering that I think God should never allow to happen to anyone. Sometimes when I hear of such sins being perpetrated, I go through a period of what I call "the antenna has fallen off my TV." I just can't seem to get anything "tuned in" correctly in my mind regarding God and his kindness or love. Because this has happened several times over the years, I no longer become alarmed over my own rage, doubt, and hopelessness. Sometimes I just can't even get out of bed for a day or two and wallow for hours (it used to be days) in depression and anger because I so lack faith in God's goodness, and a myriad of fears arise. Is there really a God? Am I really born again? Will God cause something awful to happen to me to make me believe again?

And I know I'm not alone in being overwhelmed by painful emotions regarding suffering and injustice, even when that injustice doesn't directly affect me. Most people I've known who are hit hard in this way are people who have felt tremendous emotional pain as a result of trauma, and when they hear of something horrendous having happened, they fear the pain they'd feel if it happened to them. Or they deeply empathize with how they envision the people affected are likely feeling. It's easy to imagine the worst but leave out the comforting and empowering grace God gives in the midst of trials.

Also, most people I know who are hit hard by atrocious injustices perpetrated against others are also hit hard by what others might view as rather small injustices they experience, such as being kept waiting at a doctor's office for hours past an appointment time or being given a smaller portion than another restaurant diner received at the next table. And most people who are hit hard by exposure to injustices turn to their usual ways of coping (secret behaviors or emotional patterns of anger or depression) to distract themselves from their emotional pain, because they see no hope in turning to God, whom they see as the ultimate perpetrator since he allows the

It's easy to imagine the worst but leave out the comforting and empowering grace God gives in the midst of trials.

injustices to occur. It's easy to remain pain-centered and not invest faith in God using even our pain for our ultimate good (Romans 8:28; 2 Corinthians 4:16-17).

I used to eat my way into oblivion when the "antenna fell off my TV," when I just could not perceive the presence or goodness of God, as a result of hearing a news item or being told about what a friend or acquaintance had endured. Other people I've known pull out their eyelashes, drink to drunkenness, or start using a legal or illegal drug they haven't used in years. To the person suffering from "trauma-informed empathy," it feels as though there is no option but to engage in self-numbing in order to cope with their feelings of pain, fear, and rage against God.

This is exactly where the mercy and steadfast love of God come in. Time and again, I have seen him call me back from my emotional abyss. In fact, although I may spend a day or two with the "emotional flu," I no longer even think about turning to food in order to distract myself from the confusion and pain I feel when in the midst of times of doubt about God's goodness. I may not always turn to God in faith, but because I am a new creation in Christ, I cannot help but pray, even if the prayer is as desperate as some of the psalmists', who were railing against the injustices they were experiencing (e.g., Psalm 73:21-22). God has repeatedly, faithfully turned my mind back to the truth about how justice wins when life is seen as eternal. (See how the writer of Psalm 73 came back to the truth in verses 23-26.) If you are still quite angry with God about aspects of your life, tell him plainly about it and then ask him to show you a perspective that will set you free from that anger, because it's crippling you and keeping you in bondage to your unhealthy ways of coping with it.

Even though people are horribly ashamed of turning again and again to a pattern of behavior, such as gambling, drug abuse, overeating, or viewing pornography, and no matter how unwanted their behavior may be, many do acknowledge their fear of how naked and vulnerable they think they'll feel if the behavior were no longer a part of their lives. This can also be true for emotional patterns of depression or anger. Even though everyone longs for freedom from emotional pain and embarrassing behaviors, there are very real fears about living "in victory." Who would I be if this aspect of my life were resolved? Would stress be totally overwhelming because there would be no distraction from it? Would being more "together" mean having more responsibilities or having to serve as a role model to others? Would pride and self-satisfaction be a temptation if the besetting sin were no longer there as a reminder of my lowliness and inadequacy? Would humility vanish along with the distasteful behaviors or debilitating emotions? If the obnoxious behavior or emotions weren't there to keep people away, would relationships abound and invade personal space and time? Might the rejection I always thought was certainly because of my overweight, sulking, smoking, drinking, or etc., turn out to actually be rejection of the "real me"?

Fears of letting go of the behaviors and emotions we've trusted for so long can and should be acknowledged and faced while holding the hand of Jesus. Throughout the Bible, God's people are told, "Fear not." In many of these instances, we are also told *why* we need not fear.

> Be strong and courageous. Do not be afraid; do not be discouraged, for the LORD your God will be with you wherever you go. (Joshua 1:9)
>
> …I will fear no evil, for you are with me… (Psalm 23:4)
>
> The LORD is with me; I will not be afraid. (Psalm 118:6)

If you are still quite angry with God about aspects of your life, tell him plainly about it and then ask him to show you a perspective that will set you free from that anger, because it's crippling you and keeping you in bondage to your unhealthy ways of coping with it.

> Fear not, for I am with you... (Isaiah 41:10, ESV)
>
> The Lord is near. Do not be anxious about anything... (Philippians 4:5b-6a)
>
> "Never will I leave you; never will I forsake you." So we say with confidence,
> "The Lord is my helper; I will not be afraid." (Hebrews 13:5b-6a)

Our release from our fears about "what if" – what if I don't cope with stress by going on a shopping spree or by binge-eating donuts and ice cream or by sneaking off to watch outrageous sexual acts on the computer – is found in acknowledging and putting trust in the loving presence of Jesus. This is why I have thoroughly studied the Gospel of John and refer frequently to many passages in it. John referred to himself as "the disciple whom Jesus loved" (e.g., John 13:23). He knew and felt the love of Jesus. And he ended up living a long and fearless life, including exile for his faith (Revelation 1:9) and probably arrest and torture.[6]

Meditating on and directly engaging with Jesus, who loves you and gave himself for you (Galatians 2:20), enables you to prayerfully think through worst-case scenarios for each "what if" and see Jesus guiding you through them. You can be completely honest with Jesus about what you fear and even how limited your faith is regarding his trustworthiness in being there for you when you need him. He will speak to you to reassure you and build your faith in his adequacy and nearness in every circumstance. But how will he do that? As mentioned in a previous chapter, Jesus has come to dwell within you through his Spirit, who illumines God's Word so that you will understand how God's truth applies to you personally.

> ...as it is written:
>
> "What no eye has seen,
>   what no ear has heard,
> and what no human mind has conceived" –
>   the things God has prepared for those who love him –
>
> these are the things God has revealed to us by his Spirit. ... What we have received is not the spirit of the world, but the Spirit who is from God, so that we may understand what God has freely given us. (1 Corinthians 2:9-12)

As you read God's truth, hear solid Bible-centered preaching, discuss God's truth with wise counselors and mature believers, listen to God's truth as it is sung in biblical songs and hymns, and as God reminds you of his truth by bringing Scripture passages and principles to your mind, you will be able to exchange your long-trusted coping mechanisms for the freedom God has already given you in Christ.

Homework

1. Complete the following study regarding the freedom God has already granted to you as his born-again child and new creation in Christ. (Answer key provided on in Addendum Five on page 224.)

FREEDOM IN CHRIST
John 8:32, 36 / 2 Corinthians 3:17

Freedom from...

Acts 13:39; Romans 6:6-7, 14, 17, 22 _____

Romans 8:1; Colossians 1:22 _____

Romans 6:23; Colossians 1:14; 1 Thessalonians 1:10 _____

John 8:12; Ephesians 5:8; Colossians 1:13 _____

Galatians 5:13-16, 24 _____

John 14:1-3; Romans 8:2; Hebrews 2:14-15 _____

Romans 7:6, Galatians 3:13, 23-25 _____

2 Peter 1:4 _____

2 Corinthians 2:11; 10:4-5 _____

1 Thessalonians 5:9 _____

Freedom to...

Jeremiah 31:34 _____

John 1:12; Romans 8:15-16; Galatians 4:6-7 _____

John 14:15; 1 John 5:3 _____

Galatians 2:20; Ephesians 2:8 _____

Romans 6:22; Titus 2:11-12 _____

2 Corinthians 5:21; Ephesians 4:24 _____

2 Corinthians 3:18 _____

John 14:16-20, 1 Corinthians 6:19 _____

Ephesians 3:12; Hebrews 4:14-16 _____

Ephesians 1:11-12, 2:10 _____

John 3:16; 1 John 2:25 _____

2. Read through the following review of the information presented in this book. Prayerfully think through whether you believe these concepts are true for you. Make notes regarding those points you find difficult to believe and why it's difficult to believe them.

EXPERIENCE THE FREEDEOM YOU ALREADY HAVE IN CHRIST REVIEW

Experiencing the freedom you already have in Christ takes place as you progress in the following:

1. Understand and believe wholeheartedly that Jesus reveals the true character of God the Father and that you probably have misunderstood God and responded to him in ways that are more in line with what your parents/authority figures were like than what God is actually like. Change your mind about God's love, acceptance, and approachability.
2. Understand and believe deeply that the Holy Spirit is present within you and interested in guiding your desires, thoughts, will, and understanding of the truth. Turn more and more to the Spirit for power in everyday situations and especially when discerning the underlying motivations for ungodly emotional and behavioral patterns.
3. Understand and invest faith in the difference between who God has made you to be in Christ and what your flesh is. Recognize that your flesh is not who you are now or who you will be for all eternity. The flesh is what remains from having been born separated from God and having found ways of coping with life through your own devices. It's so familiar it feels like it's the real you, but that's not at all true. Meditate on who God has made you to be as a "new creation in Christ." Amazingly, who you are for all eternity is "created to be like God in true righteousness and holiness"! (Ephesians 4:24)
4. Start seeing all your behaviors and emotions – good or bad – as motivated by your beliefs. Your beliefs lead to your thoughts, and your thoughts lead to your emotions. Your erroneous thoughts and negative emotions lead to reliance on the coping strategies of the flesh. When your beliefs are firmly planted on the truth about God's character, your total forgiveness, God's work to turn all things to the good, and your new identity in Christ, then your thoughts and emotions will lead to wholesome behaviors instead of reliance on the flesh.
5. With the Spirit's help, recognize what you believe that is not in line with truth. Then reject the lies and replace them with truth. This is a lifestyle and a crucial aspect of your personal relationship with God.
6. Express your emotions to God. He can handle it and welcomes this sort of expression. Ask for God's help in understanding what beliefs are resulting in painful emotions. Check those beliefs against what God says is true in his Word, and choose God's truth over your erroneous beliefs.
7. Forgive those who offend you or sin against you. Remember that you cannot forgive ahead of time. Just because you've forgiven someone before, doesn't mean you don't need to forgive again when sinned against again or when a past sin affects you in a new way. Realize that justice is in eternity and not always in this life.
8. Accept the total forgiveness provided to you through the death and resurrection of Jesus Christ. Start recognizing your self-punishing thoughts and behaviors and change your mind about how effective those are in curbing "besetting sins."
9. Understand that legalism leads to greater and greater feelings of compulsion and desire to sin, but accepting the love and grace of God leads to more and more freedom to be yourself, which is a person who actually wants to live as God intends, since that's how God designed you as a new creation in Christ.
10. Let go of comparisons. Accept your total adequacy in God that equips you for the life he has given you. Realize that no one has it great. What you usually see is another's best moments and then compare that with your worst.
11. Realize that absolutely every human being in the world does disappoint. Jesus does not. Expect less of people and look more to Jesus for what you feel you need.

12. Understand that there is absolutely nothing that anyone can do to you that can ruin you or ruin your life. God completely transforms all our suffering into our good in this life or in the next. Anything a person does to you is a reflection of that person's sin and does not reflect on your worth, which is totally determined by God, who has proclaimed you to be his beloved child. Accept the adequacy of Christ's blood for any guilt you may feel in connection to having been sinned against.

Homework Follow-up

1. What Scripture passages do you see as your "friends" or "pocket verses" (verses you put into your "back pocket" to have at the ready when needed for reassurance or guidance)?

2. Which concepts presented in this book do you find hard to believe? What are the reasons for not believing them, and what do you believe instead?

Comments on the Homework

There are certain passages of Scripture that have been extremely helpful for me to have "on hand;" in other words, those I have memorized. Because I often doubt that any progress is being made in my becoming more like Christ, the verse I repeat most often to myself is Philippians 2:13 (GNT): "God is always at work in you to make you willing and able to obey his own purpose." Because the Scripture is God's Word, Bible passages are not only encouraging words, but also tools for the Holy Spirit to use in renewing our minds. Keeping some key passages stored on your hard drive, so to speak, gives the Spirit an opportunity to pull them up onto your "desktop" and work all that more effectively in lining up your thinking with God's truth.

Bible passages are not only encouraging words, but also tools for the Holy Spirit to use in renewing our minds.

Occasionally someone mentions theological reasons why they do not agree with the concepts I frequently present. But that hasn't happened all that often. Most of the people who have objections, when they truly explore why they do not agree with the principles presented, cannot find Scripture to contradict them. Instead, what does contradict the concepts are their own deeply felt, long-held inaccurate beliefs about themselves and God. For them, the hardest hurdle is believing in something that doesn't *feel* right. This is where I suggest just trying out new beliefs for a while, going ahead and behaving as if one is a new creation in Christ with a pure heart and as if God really cares about personal struggles, but doing so for just a few weeks or months and then evaluating the outcome. (Yes, I did mention this previously, but see 2 Peter 1:12-13.)

Scripture tells us that our love for God is demonstrated in our obedience to his commandments, and that his commandments are not burdensome because God has equipped us to overcome the world through our faith in Christ (1 John 5:1-5). Our love for God is not just a mushy feeling, but provides the power to act in faith. And this is almost always apart from our feelings, at first. There are several behaviors and concepts that feel foreign to us, but that is only because they are untried. The ways we have been used to behaving and what we have been used to believing have resulted in emotional pain – frustration, hopelessness, guilt. Though familiar, those behaviors and beliefs are what's actually foreign – to the person God created you to be.

Ask God to help you assimilate the concepts presented in this book that he knows will be most transforming for you.

Ask God to help you assimilate the concepts presented in this book that he knows will be most transforming for you. Prayerfully explore some of the suggested additional materials and helpful ministries that present concepts along the same lines. The Spirit is the one who guides us into all truth (John 16:13), as long as we are willing to hear it from him and are not blocking the truth with our own preconceived notions.

God is extremely interested in leading you into the freedom that you already have in Christ.

So if the Son sets you free, you will be free indeed. (John 8:36)

As you pursue your relationship with Jesus, based on the truth of his Word, you will *experience* his grace and truth and know what it is to "live self-controlled, upright and godly lives in this present age" (Titus 2:12). Now that's freedom!

Addendum One

FatherCare, a booklet reproduced by permission of
His Truth Transforms International
Oklahoma City, Oklahoma
histruthtransforms.org

FatherCare

A Fresh Perspective on the Character of God

Copyright 1993 Jim Craddock
All rights reserved

INTRODUCTION

Jesus came to reveal the Father! (John 1:18; 10:30; 14:7,9) All that He did, all that He said, all the miracles He performed demonstrated this amazing truth. It was in the humanity of our Lord Jesus that the Father found full and free expression as our Father. The life that Jesus lived and the death that He died was a deliberate act of revealing to humanity God the Father.

In essence, Jesus was the Father here on earth! Time and time again Jesus reiterated this truth – John 5:19-26; 8:18,29,42,54; 10:30; 14:1-13. It is an inescapable fact that Jesus was on earth what the Father is in heaven. **God stepped out of heaven and became a man in the Person of our Lord Jesus Christ so that a Father's love and care could and would be demonstrated in person to heal and comfort those who were so desperately hurting.**

My own personal experience in counseling and ministering to literally thousands of Christians demonstrates that most believers hold an erroneous view of God as Father. What has happened is that they have based their own concept of the Father, not on the inspired Word of God, but on their own past relationship with their earthly fathers, good or bad. It is no small wonder then that the Church is weak and frail – **it knows not the Father!**

You don't trust a stranger, much less love him. To a great host of believers, the Father is some vague, spiritual being or some "cosmic policeman," who is ten million light years away. For all practical purposes He is a stranger to them. **How can we put any confidence in One we hardly know?** (See Psalm 9:10.) The answer is that we don't! Yet, James warns us of the emotional consequences when we lack confidence in God (James 1:6).

How can we break this belief system that has substituted an earthly father for the Heavenly Father? **The answer to this dilemma lies in the Person of our Lord Jesus Christ.** We must learn to see the Father in Him. As we do, the Holy Spirit will begin to change our own erroneous concepts of the Father into the correct one with all of the accompanying benefits.

Within the confines of our evangelical faith we have so sought to identify with Jesus that we have failed to see Him in His primary role, that of revealing the Father. Also, in an emphasis on seeking the Spirit and His gifts, we have also lost sight of the Father. **Jesus is not a substitute for the Father; He is the essence of the Father on earth.**

Paul wrote to the believers at Colosse:

> **For in His physical body every attribute of the Godhead continuously and permanently dwells.** Colossians 2:9, paraphrase

Simply stated, this means that every attribute, every characteristic of the Father exists in the Person of our Lord Jesus Christ. All that the Father is, is in Jesus. **So, we must view Jesus as revealing the Father.** Otherwise, we will miss what he came to do – **UNVEIL THE FATHER.**

FATHERCARE

Life is made up of relationships – some good, some bad – but all necessary. The Bible is God's inspired textbook on relationships. It is important to recognize the basic common denominator inherent in all relationships; that is, the foundational relationship from which all relationships originate, man's relationship to God, the Father/child relationship. It is this Father/child relationship that made Adam's interaction with God so unique, and it was the Father/child relationship that was lost at the Fall, thereby making man's life so desperate.

History shows us that men have always sought after God. Even from the earliest and most primitive of cultures, there has been a pattern of worship – of man's attempt to restore the lost Father/child relationship. However, it does not lie within the capabilities of man to restore this lost relationship. It has to be done by God. From God's perspective, the restoration of the Father/child relationship was so important that He stepped out of heaven in the Person of Jesus Christ to initiate and accomplish the process of restoring the Father/child relationship.

At the same time, the restoration of the Father/child relationship is so frighteningly threatening to Satan that he has made every attempt to hinder and confuse the process of that restoration (2 Corinthians 4:4). For a child of God to know God as Father brings that child into such intimacy with God, producing such worship of God and service for God, that the whole hierarchy of the evil one is threatened.

As we being this study, I want you to do an exercise. Write out a paragraph on who your father was to you as a person. Stop reading here and do that now:

_____

_____

_____

_____

Believe it or not, years of having counselees do this exercise show that you have just described your concept of God as Father! That's right, most people transfer their experiential knowledge of their earthly fathers to the Heavenly Father. This is Satan's masterstroke of confusing the issue, and it is the reason why the vast majority of Christians have either an erroneous or, at the least, a very nebulous concept of God as their Father.

I once asked a missionary, who had come for counseling, to write out who her father was to her as a person. Later, I had her write out who the Father was to her as a Person. It stunned her to realize that she had written out basically the same thing for both. That was not an isolated case. I have found that most Christians have done this. Read a few of the comments that were received from hundreds of surveys taken with teens. The surveys asked them who their fathers were to them and who the Heavenly Father was to them as a Person. The surveys were taken at Christian conferences across the country and those surveyed indicated that they were Christians, active both in their churches and in the organization that sponsored the conferences.

Jennifer, age 15: *My father is a two-faced, irresponsible, mean S.O.B. Always perfect, nobody can ever do anything right. He is selfish and cruel. ... There is no way I can picture God as my Father.*

Lee Ann, age 14: *My dad always seemed sort of far away. It's like he wants to love me, but he doesn't know how to. ... God is sort of distant and hard to reach.*

Kristy, age 17: *Don't have and never knew my real father. ... God is someone who sits on a white throne.*

Tammi, age 15: *My daddy loves me a lot, I think, but I am not sure 'cause my parents are divorced and I haven't seen my father in five years. ... The Father to me is my protector and guide. Sometimes I feel like He doesn't love me as much as other people.*

Chris, age 19: *I hardly know my father. He has always been too busy working to spend time with me and the rest of the family. ... My heavenly Father I think of similarly as my earthly father in that at times I think He's far off and too busy.*

I could multiply what was said by these young people hundreds of times by the adults who have come in for counseling. What I have found is a profound ignorance on the part of Christians about who God is as their Father. The result of this ignorance is far-reaching, affecting the Christian both spiritually and emotionally.

This phenomenon is particularly disturbing when we realize the importance that the Bible puts on knowing God. In fact, for us to know God as our Father is so critically important that God, in the Person of Jesus Christ, stepped out of heaven to reveal Him. The Bible demonstrates that all Jesus did, all that He said, was for this one single purpose of revealing God as our Father. What man had lost at the Fall – the Father/child relationship that existed between Adam and God – God was determined to restore through Jesus Christ!

Studying how Christ revealed the Father is a study that can revolutionize your life, because it brings you into an intimacy with God as your Father that you have not experienced before. The importance of this knowledge is attested to, not only in Scriptures, but by the great authors of Christendom. For example, J. I. Packer, in his book, *Knowing God*, says, "It is the most practical project anyone can engage in. ... Knowing about God is crucially important for the living of our lives."[1]

Kittle's *Theological Dictionary of the New Testament* says this:

> The glorifying of God's name is effected by Christ's work, and to this again it belongs that Jesus should reveal God's name to men as that of the Father. God's name is obscure to men; it is strange and general. But to those whom the Father has given Him, Jesus makes this name manifest, certain, and plain, so that it again acquires specific content: Father.[2]

I have stated over and over again, not only to counselees, but to Christian groups everywhere, that it is imperative for the Christian to know God as Father. A great deal of the Christian's emotional and spiritual problems can be laid at the feet of ignorance, ignorance of God and who He is as Father.

Why Is It Important to Know God as Father?

First, it is important to know God as Father because the Bible commands that we know God.

... that the God of our Lord Jesus Christ, the Father of glory, may give to you a spirit of wisdom and of revelation in the knowledge of Him. Ephesians 1:17, NASB

> But from there you will seek the LORD your God, and you will find Him if you search for Him with all your heart and all your soul. **Deuteronomy 4:29, NASB**

> And He said to them, "You shall love the Lord your God with all your heart, and with all your soul, and with all your mind." **Matthew 22:37 NASB**

> And those that know Thy name will put their trust in Thee. **Psalm 9:10a, NASB**

> I have manifested Your name—I have revealed Your very Self, Your real Self—to the people You have given Me out of the world. They were Yours, and You gave them to Me, and they have obeyed and kept your Word. **John 17:6, AMP**

To know God intimately, as God desires us to know Him, we need to know Him as Father. It is one thing to know God through His attributes, but it is quite another to know Him as Father. To know God only through His attributes tends toward a sterile, non-intimate relationship, while knowing Him as Father creates an awesome intimacy.

It is an astounding thing to read the Scripture and realize that God, the absolute Sovereign of the universe, desires that we should know Him, and that He should make it possible for us to do so. I repeat, **Christ's primary purpose of coming to this sin-ridden planet was to reveal God as Father, so that we, as his children, might enjoy that Father/child relationship that once existed between God and Adam.**

The very fact that God in the Person of Jesus did come to this earth to reveal the Father shows the importance God attaches to knowing Him. All that Jesus did and all that He said was to make God known as Father. By His life He gave content to the word "Father." It is interesting to note that the word "father" is used 418 times in the New Testament, and over half of the references, some 264, are of God as Father.

Jesus said:

> I and the Father are one. **John 10:30, NASB**

> If you had known Me, you would have known My Father also; from now on you know Him, and have seen Him. ... He who has seen Me has seen the Father. ... Do you not believe that I am in the Father, and the Father is in Me? The words that I say to you I do not speak on My own initiative, but the Father abiding in Me does His works. **John 14:7, 9b, 10, NASB**

> But He answered them, "My Father is working until now, and I Myself am working. ... Truly, truly, I say to you, the Son can do nothing of Himself, unless it is something He sees the Father doing; for whatever the Father does, these things the Son also does in like manner. For the Father loves the Son, and shows Him all things that He Himself is doing; and greater works than these will He show Him that you may marvel." **John 5:17, 19-20, NASB**

Not only are we commanded to know God, but second, knowing God as Father is important for giving meaning to our lives. Packer puts it well:

> Knowing about God is crucially important for the living of our lives. As it would be cruel to an Amazonian tribesman to fly him to London, put him down without an explanation in Trafalgar Square and leave him, as one who knows nothing of English

or England, to fend for himself, so we are cruel to ourselves if we try to live in this world without knowing about the God whose world it is and who runs it. The world becomes a strange, mad, painful place, and life in it a disappointing and unpleasant business, for those who do not know about God. Disregard the study of God, and you sentence yourself to stumble and blunder through life blindfolded, as it were, with no sense of direction and no understanding of what surrounds you. This way you can waste your life and lose your soul.[3]

Third, it is important for the Christian to know God as Father for his emotional and spiritual well-being. A person cannot and will not trust a stranger. If God as Father is a stranger to us, for whatever the reason, we cannot and will not trust Him (Psalm 9:10). If we can't trust Him, we will doubt Him. And our doubts about God, while we try to live for God, produce a contradiction in our lives that creates tremendous emotional and spiritual stress (James 1:6). I have yet to have someone come in for counseling who was suffering from emotional stress and turmoil and had a good, Biblical concept of God as Father.

As you progress in this study, you will see how crucial it is to your spiritual development to know God as Father. In fact, as you begin to grasp this great truth of God as your Father, you will realize the tremendous spiritual and emotional benefits that accrue to the Christian who gains this knowledge.

What Are the Benefits that Come from Knowing God as Father?

No relationship is more crucial to children than that of the parent/child relationship. In our culture, we sometimes forget how important the father/child relationship is. I have often stated that every daddy needs a little boy or little girl, and every little boy and little girl needs a daddy. What a loss when we realize that the average father spends approximately six minutes a day with his children. We live in a society that not only condones, but encourages, absentee fatherhood. What a refreshing and astounding difference it makes when we realize that God is our Father and is never absent, but always available to us every moment of every day.

Two passages of Scripture, among many others, confirm this fact of God's fatherhood to us:

> **A father of the fatherless, and a judge and protector of the widows, is God in His holy habitation.**
> Psalm 68:5, AMP

> **"And I will be a Father to you, and you shall be sons and daughters to Me," says the Lord Almighty.**
> 2 Corinthians 6:18, AMP

Allow me to digress here for a moment to demonstrate how easily we have been deceived into erroneous thinking about God. In this passage from the Psalms, you will note that God selects two segments of society to specifically mention, widows and orphans. It is interesting to note that at the time of this writing, both widows and orphans were considered a detriment to society, a non-productive drain upon the culture.

In this passage, God is called a "judge." Now what image comes to your mind when you think of a judge? Normally, we see in our mind's eye an image of a judge behind his bench, dispensing justice from his perspective – and we feel guilty. Place this mental image of a judge over onto God and we come up with the concept of a "cosmic policeman" just waiting for us to step out of line.

However, God is not a judge in that sense. First, all judgment has been placed in Christ (John 5:22). Second, there is no condemnation to those who are in Christ (Romans 8:1). Third, all of our punishment was placed on Christ (Isaiah 53:5). Fourth, God doesn't remember our sins and transgression (Hebrews 10:17). Fifth, our transgression is forgiven and our sins covered (Psalm 32:1). So, if God is not a judge in the way we conceive of a judge, then how are we to define the way "judge" is used in Psalm 68:5?

The way that the word "judge" is used here is "one who evaluates worth"!!! Get this, for it is important – God as Judge is not one who condemns, but one who evaluates what is of worth. In this passage, He is evaluating as worthy the two segments of society which were considered worthless. **Therefore, God doesn't judge you in the sense of passing judgment unto condemnation, but He evaluates your absolute WORTHINESS!!!**

Now, what is a father? William Barclay says this:

> There are two English words which are closely connected, but whose meanings are widely different. There is the word "paternity" and the word "fatherhood." "Paternity" describes a relationship in which a father is responsible for the physical existence of a son; but, as far as paternity goes, it can be, and it not infrequently happens, that the father has never even set eyes on the son, and would not even recognize him if in later years he met him. "Fatherhood" describes an intimate, loving, continuous relationship in which father and son grow closer to each other every day.[4]

It is this "fatherhood" that describes God's relationship to us. Thus, this is the greatest benefit of all in knowing God as Father – a continuing, growing intimacy with the Father.

However, this tends not to be our experience because on what basis do we build our concept of the Father? Humanly speaking, we establish father concepts through experiential relationships with our earthly fathers. Unfortunately, this produces erroneous concepts of a true father, because there is no absolutely perfect human father who can provide a role model for us.

Therefore, it is only through the Bible, our absolute standard of truth, that we can know what a father truly should be. It is the Bible that shows us, in the humanity of Jesus as He lived His life here on earth, the perfect role model as to what a true father is. It is there in the pages of Scripture that we see Jesus as the Father, a real Father in action.

What I am saying is that our normal father concepts tend to be erroneous, and it is only through the love and care of God, as we know Him as Father, that we can establish the proper concept of "father." It is in this Biblical dimension that we discover what a father truly is, that is, by seeing, in the Person of Jesus Christ, the Father at work here in our lives on earth!

A true father, a perfect father, a caring father is one who has the ability and desire to meet his children's deepest needs. And, what are our deepest needs? Let us discuss six of them:

- the need to worship
- the need to be loved and to belong
- the need for well-being
- the need to feel secure
- the need for approval
- the need for acceptance

The Need to Worship

Most people would probably not list worship as one of their deeply felt needs, but it is man's most vital need because man was created for worship and to worship. Worship denied or wrongly expressed can and will cause wrong and/or harmful spiritual and emotional problems, as well as wrong behavior.

The word "worship" comes from the Anglo-Saxon word *weorthscipe*, which evolved into the word *worthship* and then into "worship." Worship is ascribing worth to someone or something. Man was not designed to live independent from God, but to commune intimately with, and totally depend upon, God. In order to live life as it was meant to be lived, to its fullest, man must ascribe to God His ascendant, infinite, absolute worth, His "first-place-ness." Man must worship. Without worship, we do not have God in His rightful place and, therefore, everything else in life is totally out of place. Right worship is ascribing to God His worth and worthiness.

It is through worship, right worship, that we come to know God and experience His love and care. Worship and intimacy are related. The greater the worship, the greater the intensity of intimacy. This is what our Father desires, an intimate relationship with us, His children. When His Spirit indwells us at our rebirth in Christ, He gives us the ability to rightly worship Him, to place Him in His rightful position, to honor Him and, therefore, to return to our deep dependence upon Him in every aspect of our lives – in other words, to be in an intimate, right relationship with our Father.

In a day and age where "self worth" is said to be man's basic need, we need to realize that worth, true worth – a true understanding of who we really are – can only come through worship, right worship – a true understanding of who God really is as the One of ultimate worth. In a sense, that is what this study is all about – to introduce you to who He really is: our loving heavenly Father, the One who meets all our needs out of His love, the One who is worthy of our worship, the only One who can fulfill our need to worship, because of His perfection and greatness and selflessness.

The Need to Be Loved and to Belong

Probably no other word so characterizes Christianity as does the word "love." The profound mystic of the Christian faith is the overwhelming, overpowering, compelling unconditional love that flows from the pages of God's Word. It is a very basic, deeply felt need in all of our lives. We crave love – not a conditional love based on what we have or on what we are able to achieve, but an unconditional love, based upon who we are.

We need to love and be loved. It is the indispensable dynamic of our existence. And, our ability to love and be loved is directly related to our knowledge of God as our Father. The Bible says it best:

We love, because He first loved us. 1 John 4:19, NASB

Two words characterize our Father's love for us and to us. The first word is found in Ephesians 2:4, where the word "great" is associated with God's love for us. The second is found in 1 John 3:1, where the word "manner" (KJV) is associated with God's love.

The word "great" in the Greek is *polus* and signifies "much, many, or abundance." Here I think the word "magnificence" would best describe this love – a superabundance and overflowing of love from our Father to us. The word "manner" in the Greek is *potapos*, and Kenneth S. Wuest says, "The word speaks of something foreign. The translation could read, 'Behold what foreign kind of love the Father has bestowed upon us.'"[5] Actually, our words "exotic" or "incredible" would be suitable translations.

What we are being told about our Father's love to us and for us is that it is **INCREDIBLY MAGNIFICENT!!!**

It is said that the love of God must have arms, and we are the arms through which the love of God is demonstrated. Let me share an incident that illustrates God's love for us. My wife, Doris, and I have five children – four boys and a girl. Our daughter is the youngest and the first girl in three generations of Craddocks. You can imagine the fuss made over this little piece of femininity when she pushed her way into this world. But the impact upon Danny, the youngest of the four boys, was something else. What do you do when you have three older brothers and, suddenly out of nowhere, comes a sister who steals the limelight? What you do is break the mold, and that is just what Danny did.

I could write a book about Danny. I will someday when I can safely change the names to protect the guilty. This boy could do more, get into more trouble, find the dirtiest mud hole, create more commotion than all the rest of our kids put together.

When Danny was a preschooler he was always going to marry one of the cute girls on our staff. He invariably had a crush on one or more of them, depending on who was the cutest and most responsive. One Sunday afternoon we had a rather formal tea to introduce new staff members. One young woman, Arlys, was a lovely brunette who came dressed in the prettiest, filmiest, whitest dress you ever saw. She was absolutely breathtaking.

As we adults were chatting, in came Danny, moving along with his dust cloud and looking like he just invented twelve new ways to incorporate dirt and mud into his four-year-old body. Just as he was about to head out the front door, out of the corner of his eye he caught a glimpse of this lovely girl in white and, in a second, he was up in her lap, hugging the life out of her.

I almost fainted. All I could see was a dirty, grimy little guy who was messing up the whitest dress in the room. But all Arlys could see was a little guy who needed loving, and she just loved on and hugged on him as though he were the only little guy in all the world.

God taught me something in that moment. We tend to look at ourselves as though we are the dirty, grimy guys, but God as our Father sees us only as little guys and gals who need lots of loving, and that is why His love is **INCREDIBLY MAGNIFICENT!**

Belonging to God allows us to fulfill the flip side of this need, that of belonging to others. God created us as social beings. He meant for us to relate to one another. In Genesis 2, God said that it wasn't good for man to be alone. The word "alone" in the Hebrew means "to be isolated." No one is an island unto himself. We need to belong.

If we are rightly related to God, enjoying the intimacy of right worship, then He becomes the prime mover in bringing other people into our lives to fulfill the need for belonging. How? He does this through the Church! – a family of like-minded people, born of His Spirit, enjoying oneness in His Spirit, learning to care for one another. Here is where the need to belong can be and should be met.

The Need for Well-Being

Solomon wrote, "All a man's labor is for his mouth and yet the appetite is not satisfied" (Ecclesiastes 6:7, NASB). Man is driven to secure the basics of life – food, clothing and shelter. And once these are secured, man looks for emotional well-being.

However, our Lord made it quite clear in Matthew 6 that a sense of well-being comes, not through what we have or what we can get, but from who our Father is!

> ...do not be anxious for your life, as to what you shall eat, or what you shall drink; nor for your body, as to what you shall put on. Is not life more than food, and the body than clothing? Look at the birds of the air, that they do not sow, neither do they reap, nor gather into barns, and yet your heavenly Father feeds them. Are you not worth much more than they? ... Observe how the lilies of the field grow; they do not toil nor do they spin, yet I say to you that even Solomon in all his glory did not clothe himself like one of these. But if God so arrays the grass of the field, which is alive today and tomorrow is thrown into the furnace, will He not much more do so for you...? Do not be anxious, then, saying, "What shall we eat?" or "What shall we drink?" or "With what shall we clothe ourselves?" For all these things the Gentiles eagerly seek; for your heavenly Father knows that you need all these things. But seek first His kingdom and His righteousness; and all these things shall be added to you.
>
> Matthew 6:25-26, 28-33, NASB

We are to seek, first, His kingdom and His righteousness, and then all these things *will* be ours. Our Father promises to meet all of our needs, but only *He* can meet them. Our pursuit of them only leads to failure and frustration. As we relate to our Father, He opens our eyes to see His abundant provision, to see that our well-being is a need He eagerly desires to fulfill.

The Need to Feel Secure

A father is one who provides security. **God our Father guarantees personal security**. This personal sense of security is affirmed and reinforced by the use of the term "Abba Father" in the Bible (Mark 14:36; Romans 8:15; Galatians 4:6). The word *abba* is a transliteration from an Aramaic word that signifies the first words a little baby says of its father. Our modern-day counterpart would be "da da." In other words, the best translation of the word *abba* would be "daddy"!! That is right. God is our "Daddy"! And I am not being disrespectful in the least.

The two words used in unison, "Abba Father," have great significance. The first demonstrates the childlike faith the believer is to have in his heavenly Father, followed by an adult appreciation of that childlike faith.

Let me share a personal chapter out of my own life that will illustrate the security that a daddy brings. When I was quite small, one of the "fun-est" things of all was to get a penny or two and go to Pinelli's corner grocery store and buy some candy. In those days a penny could go a long way toward corrupting a five-year-old addicted to candy. I can remember going to that store and yearningly looking over every piece of candy displayed in the case. I would pick and choose, drooling over what I couldn't afford, changing my mind constantly, asking dozens of questions, taking forever. (Of course, I was driving "old Man Pinelli" crazy in the process.)

However, there was a problem with getting my candy. To get to Pinelli's grocery store, I had to go up a block and over two blocks. This wasn't so bad, but situated at the strategic point midway between my house and Pinelli's was the biggest, ugliest four-foot bully you ever saw. He made the Incredible Hulk look like a ballet dancer. This bully and his buddy had a nasty habit of shaking me down for my pennies. (By the way, when you are three and a half feet tall, a four-foot bully looks immense.) Whenever this happened, I would return home blubbering about the threat to my life and the assault on my funds. I remember my dad telling me to stand up for my rights, but being of sound mind, and not necessarily suicidally depressed, I rejected that advice forthwith.

About the third time this degrading, depriving experience occurred, my dad told me that he would sneak up the alley, and if these two nemeses of my candy run interfered, he would handle them. Well, I can't begin to tell you the difference in my attitude. I was cock-o'-the-walk. I made faces at those two bullies. I flipped my pennies to let them know I was going to get some candy. In short, I was acutely obnoxious. However, I kept looking over my shoulder to make sure that my daddy was there. As long as I knew he was there, I had all the security in the world.

Of course, the moral to the story is that when we know God as our Father, as our *Abba*, our "Daddy," then we have that profound sense of personal security and safety. No matter what we face, the obstacles that lie in our paths, the struggles in our lives, our Father is there!!! He will never leave us nor forsake us! (Hebrews 13:5)

The Need for Approval

Approval comes in many forms, and we all desire it. Everyone desperately seeks parental approval, and when it is not forthcoming, it creates real problems. As Christians we constantly seek God's approval. Jesus said, "Well done thou good and faithful servant" (Matthew 25:22). Proverbs says to give a pat on the back to whom it is due (Proverbs 3:27). Approval is a basic need of life. Through my counseling I have found that men who are younger than forty drive for success, while men over forty seek significance. Both are indicative of a need for approval. Since significance is so closely related to approval, let us look at it for a moment.

Have you ever thought what it is that gives significance? The early Greeks felt that it was determined by parentage. They felt a noble mind and virtue were inherited and could not be acquired.[6] In the rabbinical culture of Paul, his significance was based upon his being Jewish and a Pharisee, on belonging to the tribe of Benjamin and on his learning within the rabbinical schools (Philippians 3:5-6). In our day and age, significance is based upon performance, on what we are able to achieve, on credentials and on what we have. Notice in all these that significance is based on external factors, not internal ones.

Why is significance so important to us? Because it makes us "someone." It allows us to stand apart and above the crowd. It gives us the sense of approval we so deeply desire. But more importantly, in this mixed up, crazy world of ours, it is our way to try to gain a sense of worth. In the world system in which we operate, our approval and, hence, our significance, does not come from our inward sense of worth, but from our accomplishments achieved outwardly. The Biblical pattern is just the reverse.

The drive for approval is so strong that men will neglect their families, their health, all that they have, to gain it. Women will risk their happiness, their children, their futures, everything, to gain it. Why? Because we want so deeply to be somebody, to stand apart from the crowd, to leave an indelible mark on history, to stand approved before men. This drive explains why one survey I saw in a newspaper showed 82 percent of all American men were unhappy with their present employment and were considering changing jobs. A great number of men make a change as they enter their forties because they feel it is their last chance to make an impact upon their world and, thus, their last chance for gaining approval.

The Bible tells us that God gives His approval unconditionally in Christ! (Colossians 1:22) But how do we then, as Christians, gain a sense of this approval/significance? Is it through performance or achievement? Is it doing, is it having, or is it through some other means? Obviously, it is through God's means and not through man's efforts. Our Father is far more concerned with who we are than in what we do. In other words, as far as the Bible is concerned, approval and significance is related to **BEING**, not doing. Real, lasting approval comes from a relationship with the Father that insures us that we are His children.

I have mentioned some aspects of what a father is, but there is another factor which would normally go without saying, and that is that a father is one who has children. Really profound, you say! Yes, it is when you consider who the Father is and what that makes us as His children. Under the inspiration of the Holy Spirit, Paul quoted to the Corinthians an astounding truth from 2 Samuel:

> **And I will be a Father to you, and you shall be My sons and daughters, says the Lord Almighty.** 2 Corinthians 6:18, AMP

God, the almighty, majestic God of the universe is our Father!!! This means that we really do have a Father who is **consistent**, who is **kind** and **caring**, **loving** and **thoughtful**. We have a Father who **cherishes** us, who is happy when we are happy, sad when we are sad. He is a Father who brings immeasurable fullness into our lives.

On what basis can I as a Christian really know that I am truly a child of God? How can I have that personal security and knowledge that God accepts me and saves me once for all, for all eternity – that I have the ultimate approval? The assurance that we need can be summed up in one Biblical word, "**ADOPTION**"! However, it is important that you realize that the Biblical concept of adoption is totally different from our idea of adoption today. Our use of the word "adoption" involves children, while the Biblical use of the word involves adults. In other words, we are adopted by God as adult sons and daughters, not just as small children.

The word "adoption" in the Greek is *huiothesias* and is used only five times in the New Testament. This kind of adoption was peculiar to the Romans and was unknown to either the Greek or Jew.[7] It spells out in detail what God has in mind when he uses it in regard to us. William Barclay gives us a most graphic description of Roman adoption in his commentary on Romans 8:12-17.

> It is only when we understand how serious and complicated a step Roman adoption was that we really understand the depth of meaning of this passage. Roman adoption was always rendered more serious and more difficult by the Roman *patria potestas*. The *patria potestas* was the father's absolute power over his family; that power was absolute; it was actually the power of absolute disposal and control, and in the early days it was actually the power of life and death. In regard to his father, a Roman son never came of age. No matter how old he was, he was still under the *patria potestas*, in the absolute possession, and under the absolute control, of his father. Obviously this made adoption into another family a very difficult and a very serious step. In adoption a person had to pass from one *patria potestas* to another. He had to pass out of the possession and control of one father into the equally absolute possession and control of another. There were two steps. The first was known as *mancipatio*, and it was carried out by a symbolic sale, in which copper and scales were symbolically used. Three times the symbolism of sale was carried out. Twice the father symbolically sold his son, and twice he bought him back; and the third time he did not buy him back, and thus the *patria potestas* was held to be broken. After the sale there followed a ceremony called *vindicatio*. The adopting father went to the *praetor*, one of the Roman magistrates, and presented a legal case for the transference of the person to be adopted in his *patria*

potestas. When all this was completed then the adoption was complete. Clearly this was a serious and impressive step.

But it is the consequences of adoption which are most significant for the picture that is in Paul's mind. There were four main consequences. (i) The adopted person lost all rights in his old family, and gained all the rights of a fully legitimate son in his new family. In the most literal sense, and the most binding legal way, he got a new father. (ii) It followed that he became heir to his new father's estate. Even if other sons were afterwards born, who were real blood relations, it did not affect his rights. He was inalienably co-heir with them. (iii) In law, the old life of the adopted person was completely wiped out. For instance, legally all debts were canceled; they were wiped out as if they had never been. The adopted person was regarded as a new person entering into a new life with which the past had nothing to do. (iv) In the eyes of the law the adopted person was literally and absolutely the son of his new father.

That is what Paul is thinking of. He uses still another picture from Roman adoption. He says that God's Spirit witnesses with our spirit that we really are the children of God. The adoption ceremony was carried out in the presence of seven witnesses. Now, suppose the adopting father died, and then suppose that there was some dispute about the right of the adopted son to inherit, one or more of the seven original witnesses stepped forward and swore that the adoption was genuine and true. Thus the right of the adopted person was guaranteed and he entered into his inheritance. So, Paul is saying, it is the Holy Spirit Himself who is the witness to our adoption into the family of God.

We see then that every step of Roman adoption was meaningful in the mind of Paul when he transferred the picture of adoption into the family of God. Once we were in absolute possession of sin, in absolute control of our own sinful nature; but God, in His mercy, has brought us into absolute possession of Himself. The old life has no more rights over us; God has an absolute right. The past is canceled; the debts of the past are wiped out; we begin again a new life, a life with God. We become heirs of all the riches of God. If that is so, we become joint-heirs with Jesus Christ, God's own Son. That which Christ inherited, and inherits, we also inherit.

It was Paul's picture that when a man became a Christian he entered into the very family of God. He did nothing to earn it; he did nothing to deserve it; God, the great Father in His amazing love and mercy, has taken the lost, helpless, poverty-stricken, debt-laden sinner and adopted him into His own family, so that the debts are canceled and the unearned love and glory inherited.[8]

What Biblical adoption means is that, as a Christian, you are a chosen child of God and God is your Father. He has adopted you as a son or daughter into His family. It means that nothing can ever change that fact – nothing you can do or ever will do changes the fact that you are an adopted child of God. You are indelibly written in the Lamb's book of life forever and ever. And because you are adopted, you are destined to an eternity with the greatest Father in all the universe.

What does this have to do with approval? Medical science tells us that we are the sum total of our parents' genes, a blending of the two. To a large degree, I am what they are. So it is with the new birth. I become one with my Father in heaven. I become in reality an image-bearer, having been created in the image of God. What greater approval and significance can there be than to realize that, as Christians, we are children of the Most High and Holy God? What is so amazing is that God gives so unconditionally – His love, His care and, of course, His approval.

One time, after I led a Bible study, a young mother approached me and requested to see me for counseling. Later, in the privacy of my office, she shared with me about a childhood with a demanding, demeaning father. No matter what she did, it was never good enough. She could never quite measure up to her father's expectations. Even though her father had been dead for a number of years, she was still in a desperate search for his approval.

I wish this were an isolated case, but it isn't. One of the strongest drives of a person's life is for parental approval. And, the higher the expectations of the parent, the harder it is to gain a sense of his or her approval.

What makes it all so hard is that God created man to be loved, accepted, approved, and understood unconditionally. I mean by this that there is innately in us the expectation and need to be received unconditionally. However, we are born into a world system that receives no one unconditionally, but only conditionally based on what a person is able to do, achieve or have. Every person born into this world discovers that there is a direct contradiction between the desire to be received unconditionally and the world's refusal to honor that need. This contradiction produces enormous stress, especially in light of the tremendous drive that we all have for approval.

At the Fall, man's concept of God was shattered and replaced with an erroneous mindset. Man then had no absolute basis of worth, so his own identity was shattered. Because man had no basis of unconditional worth, he had to compensate. He did this by adopting a compensating system of self-imposed standards, which would allow him to gain conditionally what was denied him unconditionally. He tried to gain worth and significance through his performance rather than in his being as was God's original plan before sin entered into the picture.

What happens is that a person is born into a world system with no basis of unconditional worth. This guarantees a poor identity or poor self-image. Therefore, a person doesn't consider himself worthy enough to receive anything unconditionally. Still, those inward drives and needs for approval must be satisfied, so we all opt for a compensating system of self-imposed rules and regulations, standards by which we can measure ourselves and gain the "strokes" we feel we need.

I call this compensating system the "Torah Syndrome." In Hebrew, *torah* means "the embodiment of the law." What we do is impose upon ourselves a standard or "law" to gain "strokes." In other words, if I don't get what I need unconditionally, I impose upon myself a standard which, if I keep it, can give me conditionally what I desire emotionally. For example, I might decide, "If I make straight A's, then I'll know I'm worthy." Usually we have an elaborate set of such rules for ourselves. They enable us to measure our worth through performance.

Reflect back for a moment to your own childhood. Think of the system you adopted to gain approval from your parents. What did you do to be thought of as a good little boy or girl? Every family has their limits and standards. Approval comes, not from who we are, but from our ability to meet these limits and standards. If you do "this and this and this," then you receive the approval you are looking for. This forces you into a performance bias, which sets the stage for the "Torah Syndrome" you create for yourself as an adult.

The moment we impose upon ourselves standards to gain approval, we deny the innate desire for unconditional approval and acceptance. Therefore, we are doomed to failure. We can never do enough, achieve enough, have enough to satisfy that longing. We keep thinking that more standards will provide that sense of approval, but what we really want is *unconditional* approval. Getting caught up in this "Torah Syndrome" causes many Christians to suffer nervous breakdowns.

However, our Father, who created us to be received unconditionally, does receive us unconditionally. His approval is given on the basis of who He has made us to be in Christ, not on the basis of what we do. He loves us, he accepts us, he approves of us as His children.

A story, again involving Danny, my youngest son, demonstrates this unconditional receiving. Danny was accident-prone. Twice, firemen in large ladder trucks had to rescue him from the heights of enormous trees. His body is riddled with the scars from hundreds of stitches. When he was two and a half, it took seven stitches to repair his head when he got too curious about the neighbor digging out a cistern. At three, he cut his finger off in a car door. (Thankfully, a surgeon restored it.) When he was four, it took over a hundred stitches to repair a leg cut open when he fell. What all this did was to build into Danny a healthy fear of anyone in a white smock!

So, when Danny began to complain of a toothache, I took him to a dentist friend of mine; but when Danny saw the white smock, he figured that here was more pain. He fought for his life. In about fifteen minutes, my friend came out and asked me to take Danny somewhere else (like to a home for incorrigible children).

I had another friend named Charley Brown (really), who was a dentist. Charley told me that he could handle Danny. He said he had had twenty hours of child psychology and this was a good opportunity to put into practice what he had learned.

When we arrived at Charley's office, I offered to help out, but it was felt that I would be more of a hindrance than a help. So, I sat in the foyer listening to the shouts, cries, thudding, etc., until finally Charley came out and asked me to come in. It seemed that when he held Danny's arms with one hand and the drill with the other, with the nurse holding Danny's feet, there was no way to get Danny to open his mouth. Here I am afraid that I destroyed in twenty minutes twenty hours of child psychology. I took off my belt (I refer to this as B-therapy) and told Danny if he didn't open his mouth, I would apply B-therapy.

For four sessions, Charley labored with Danny, along with "the belt and I," through all the strugglings, cryings and fightings that only a pain-enlightened four year old can produce. Finally, when it was all through, we were seated in Charley's office when Charley came in, sat down and, without a word, caught Danny up and hugged and loved on him and said, "Danny, I love you!"

Now Danny knew that he had done nothing to deserve this kind of unconditional approval. In fact, if he had gotten what he deserved, he wouldn't nor couldn't sit down for a week. But all the way home, Danny kept saying over and over again to me, "Daddy, that man really loved me!"

The moral of this story is that we have done nothing to deserve God's unconditional love or approval, but He gives it anyway, not on the basis of what we have or haven't done, but on the basis of His Beloved Son. You can't earn God's approval. All of your little systems to gain God's "strokes" won't work with Him. He gives you His approval unconditionally. You simply are to receive it in faith! We could say then with Packer:

> There is tremendous relief in knowing that His love for me is utterly realistic, based at every point on prior knowledge of the worst about me, so that nothing I can do will disillusion Him about me.[9]

The Father knows it all, and He gives you His approval still.

The Need for Acceptance

Approval and acceptance are very closely related. If we feel approved, we will feel accepted. Unfortunately, many Christians do not feel approved or accepted by God. This happened in my case. As a new Christian, I was taught that God didn't love me, but rather he loved the Christ in me. In fact, I was told by many a preacher that there was no good thing in me and that, because of sin, God could only stand to look at me through "rose-colored glasses." The rose-colored glasses represented the blood of the Lord Jesus. All of this really tended to reinforce my own poor self-image.

What a tragedy that a lie of the pit is preached as though it were the truth of heaven. How ridiculous! God doesn't love the Christ in me. **He loves me!** Of course, He loves His Son. That isn't even the issue. The issue is that He loves me, He accepts me unconditionally. It isn't the Christ in me that makes me acceptable to God. It is what Christ did on the cross that makes me acceptable to Him. And God, my Father, accepts me, Jim Craddock, with all my hang-ups, with all my sins, with all my idiosyncrasies, as a person, unconditionally.

For years, as a Christian involved in Christian work, I never believed that God could or would accept me unconditionally. How could He? There was no good thing in me. Well meaning men did me and many, many others a great disservice by telling me this. But, it was through the greatest crisis of my life up to that time that I discovered the truth that was to change my life.

In the ministry I was in, tremendous animosity had arisen between the president and the top directors, of which I was one. On our part, there was an unreasonable reaction to the productivity demands and a frustration over what seemed to us a dictatorial style of leadership. On the president's part, there was a lack of understanding and communication. During those tense, almost unbearable hours, as charge and countercharge were made and many unfortunate statements were said, I was struggling with my own deepened sense of inadequacy and failure. I felt that I couldn't bear what was happening to the ministry I loved and the people I respected.

During one of the breaks in the meetings, when everything seemed so hopeless, one of the directors turned to the president of the organization and said, "You know, I haven't loved you unconditionally as I should, and I just now realized it. Will you forgive me?" This was the breaking point, for from that moment on, God had the victory.

But for me, in that moment, it suddenly dawned on me that God loved me unconditionally – not the Christ in me. It was not what I was able to do for Him, but that He loved me as me. He loved me as a person, not the Christ in me, but Jim Craddock with all of his weaknesses.

It took time, but I came to experience personally His unconditional acceptance. What a relief it was not to have to struggle for his acceptance or His love and approval, but just to receive them by faith. How great it was and is to be unconditionally loved and accepted by the Father in heaven.

Relationship

I mentioned that a father is one who has children and meets the needs of those children, but there is another facet of fatherhood which I want to develop, and it is crucially important to both father and child. It is that of relationship – a relationship involving three factors: a **continuing** relationship, a **growing** relationship and an **intimate** relationship.

A true father/child relationship is always a **continuing** relationship. We see this in the parable of the prodigal son (Luke 15:11-32). Nothing that the son did affected the relationship of the father to the erring son. The father maintained a continuous relationship with the son. What this parable means to us is that our Father maintains a continuous relationship with us. Nothing can affect it. This is important because every child needs a parent that remains unchangeable even in the face of a changeable child. As a father, I am not to respond in kind to my children's outbursts or inconsistent behavior. I am to be unmovable and unchangeable in my love. Unfortunately, I fall short of this, but my Father in heaven does not! (However, it is important to remember that although nothing affects God's relation to us, sin in our lives can and will affect *our* relation with Him.)

If I am faithless, He is faithful (2 Timothy 2:13). If I am impossible, he is kind. If I am angry with Him, He is patient. In other words, what I need desperately is the security of a Father whose attitude of love, kindness, acceptance and approval is not subject to the whims of vacillating emotions. And we do have a Father who is consistent in His relationship with us.

Having had my own teenaged daughter, I have struggled with thoughts and feelings about what I would do if she were immoral and ended up pregnant out of wedlock. Consequently, when the daughter of a friend of mine bore a child out of wedlock, I asked him how he had handled the obviously difficult and painful situation. His reply was, "I loved her as my daughter before this happened, and I love her as my daughter now that it has happened." He had a continuing relationship with his daughter that transcended her behavior.

Don't get me wrong. He didn't condone what she had done. He hated the sin, but he allowed nothing to affect his relationship with his daughter. He deeply loved her and the child she bore. This is illustrative of God's continuing relationship with us. We are his children by His choice, not ours, and having made that choice, He allows nothing to destroy it!

Not only is our relationship with our heavenly Father a continuing one, it must be a **growing** one – one that grows deeper every day. There is one relationship that we have with our children as babies and quite another as they enter into puberty. When my children were small, we packed them everywhere. We couldn't afford babysitters, so we had to. But then, that wasn't really a problem. We loved showing them off. As they grew older, we would take them with us whether they wanted to or not. We would carefully instruct them on what to do, how to act, to be polite, etc. But when the time came for them to be perfect little men and women, they would allow their mother's genetic side to come through and blow the whole thing!

As my children became young adults, it was a different story. By then my relationship with them had taken on new dimensions. When the kids were in junior high and high school, I would have luncheon dates with them. Once a week we would have a date, and off we would go to scarf down a hamburger and a coke. (They referred to this as a "gut-bomb and a belly-wash.") This gave us time to talk, more like adults.

Now that they are adults, my children and I relate as adults. Our relationship has been one that has continued to grow. Unfortunately, this is not true of all father/child relationships. I'll never forget one young lady who approached me after a meeting in a sorority house where I'd spoken. My topic had been on the father/child relationship. She came up afterwards and said, "My father deserted our family when I was two, and I made up my mind that I didn't need a daddy!" Then she dissolved into tears and cried on my shoulder over and over again, "Oh, but I do need a daddy, I do need a daddy!"

Our Father guarantees us a **continuing** relationship with Him, but the growth of that relationship is a great deal dependent upon us. In his book, *Enjoying Intimacy With God*, J. Oswald Sanders graphically describes the various positions of the disciples with Christ:

> Each of the disciples was as close to Jesus as he chose to be, for the Son of God had no favorites. ... It is a sobering thought that we too are as close to Christ as we really choose to be.[10]

Out of this continuing and growing relationship with our Father, there develops **intimacy**. This intimacy with the Father is not a luxury, but a necessity for our well-being. The whole purpose of this study is to enable you to develop an ever deepening intimacy with the Father as you come to know Him through the Person of His Son, Jesus Christ.

The question is, just how badly do you want this intimacy? Again, quoting from Mr. Sanders, "It would seem that admission to the inner circle of deepening intimacy with God is the outcome of **deep desire**. Only those who count such intimacy a prize worth sacrificing anything else for are likely to attain it."[11] (emphasis mine)

Isn't it astounding that our Father would make such provision for this type of relationship with us, His children? As I said previously concerning His love for us, and I say it again, His love-relationship with us is **INCREDIBLY MAGNIFICENT**!!!

What then is a father? One who begets children, who raises and nourishes them, who meets their needs, and who encourages an ever growing, continuing relationship with them. But, more than all of this, a father is one who loves his children dearly and who tenderly watches over them, cares for them, understands them, talks with them, listens to them, and is vitally concerned for them. This is *our* heavenly Father.

Beginnings

Before we enter into the practical phase of our study, let me share with you how this particular study came about. It all began with a phone call from a tearful young wife and mother (I'll call her Pat), who was requesting an appointment. Because she was so emotionally upset, I set an appointment for the next morning. Pat arrived early, and as we began our discussion, she poured out her feelings. Having grown up in the church, she understood what it meant to be a committed Christian. In the course of our conversation, she related that, although her grandfather had been a pastor and the church an integral part of her family life, her father had divorced her mother when Pat was quite young. This had caused a lot of disillusionment and bitterness on her part.

In the course of our counseling, I had Pat write out who God was to her as a person. She wrote that God was an all powerful, all loving, all knowing being. Later, for some reason, I had her write out who the heavenly Father was to her as a person. I was astounded to see that she had written out that, to her, the Father was a liar, a thief and a sneak.

I pointed out the contradiction to Pat, and we worked through his misconception. But my curiosity was aroused, so I began to ask a number of people the same two questions. Far too often, they did just what this young woman had done, in that they described two different persons! They had one concept of God as God and another of God as Father.

Then I began having counselees write out who their fathers were to them as a person and who the Father was to them as a person. Again, I was astonished to find that almost everyone was saying the same thing about two different persons. It was obvious that they were patterning their concept of God as Father after their experience with their earthly fathers. Two conclusions seemed to emerge: (1) many Christians are "double minded" as it concerns God as God and God as Father, and (2) most Christians pattern their concept of God after their earthly fathers.

The next stage of my own discovery of this great truth of knowing God as Father came as I was speaking to a class of young ladies at Louisiana State University. During some interaction before my evangelistic presentation, I discovered that most of the class was made up of fairly conservative Jewish girls. However, although my message was about Christ, they proved a very attentive and appreciative audience.

Following the class, I was approached by one of the Jewish girls who told me that, if I was willing to listen, she could tell me how I could become world famous. Of course, anytime a cute young lady wants to tell me how to become world famous, I will listen. So, I told her that I would buy her a Coke and off we went to a quiet part of the student union. We had no sooner seated ourselves than she stated, "What you have to say is not only interesting, but imperative for people to hear. However, by mentioning the name of Jesus you cause people to turn off." She then very earnestly begged me to no longer speak of Jesus, but only of God.

This led to a lively discussion – she talking of God and I of Christ. But she had a peculiar habit that was very disturbing to me. Whenever she spoke of God, great tears would come to her eyes. Her sense of the awesomeness of God was amazing. She seemed to have an awareness of God that was missing from my life. Of course, I had Christ, but I came away from that encounter knowing that I did not know God in the way that I ought.

New Dimensions

The more I thought about God as my Father, the more I realized that I really did not know Him as a Father. My intimacy was with the Son. I knew Jesus. I had served Him for years, but I remained ignorant of the Father.

It was during this time of new awareness about God as Father that I received word that my father was dying. I rushed to his bedside, but he had only hours to live. During the confusion of the next few days, I was too busy to think much about this death, but when I caught my plane to go to my next conference speaking engagement, I contemplated my relationship with my father. The thought kept going over and over again in my mind, "I never really knew him!" My father was a good man, a provider. He had his problems, including a bout with alcoholism, but he had "taken the cure" and hadn't had a drink in 25 years. As I thought of the good times and the bad times, I thought over and over, "I never knew the man."

Suddenly, it occurred to me that I had the same feelings about God the Father. I really didn't know Him as Father. It all seemed to come together, for I too had projected the image of my earthly father onto my heavenly Father. When I returned home, I began to search through the Psalms, for the first time seeking out God as my Father. I reveled in the great and graphic descriptions of the majesty of God found in Scripture. I read every book that I could get my hands on concerning God. I studied His attributes, then His names. It was a thrilling experience.

But the greatest thrill of all was when I discovered that Jesus had come to reveal the Father. This was His primary purpose in coming to this sin-ridden planet. By studying the life of Christ, I could see in detail the Father at work here on earth. In Jesus I could see all the characteristics of the perfect Father.

It was in Jesus loving that I saw a loving Father. It was in Jesus caring that I saw a caring Father. It was in Jesus approving that I experienced a Father's approval. It was in Jesus's kindness that I saw a kind Father. It was in Jesus's gentleness that I saw a gentle Father. It was in Jesus's acceptance that I knew a Father's understanding. It was in Jesus's security that I knew the security of a Father. It was in a patient Jesus that I saw a patient Father. It was in Jesus that my knowledge of the Father began to become complete.

Let me illustrate this from Scripture. Take the marriage feast at Cana (John 2:1-10). You are familiar with the story. Jesus's mother was in charge of the wedding. She had planned it, executed it, and was obviously anxious over it. Then the unexpected occurred and they were running out of wine. This could have been disastrous. It would have embarrassed the bride and groom and humiliated Mary. But was Jesus going to let this happen? Would he allow the wedding feast to be spoiled and His mother to suffer the indignity of failing in her preparations for the feast? Of course not. He cared! He cared even for the insignificant things in the lives of people. This was the Father at work. The Father cares. Jesus made this very plain in John 5:19-23.

Take the young man born blind (John 9). People were calloused in that culture. To be born blind could only mean that either you or your parents were under God's judgment. This meant a life of total rejection and ridicule, a life of begging, of groveling in the dirt for every measly morsel. Even the disciples were caught up in this mindset.

Why did Jesus heal the young man? To show His own greatness, to give vent to his deity? Of course not! When Jesus looked at that young man, he didn't see a dirty, filthy beggar. He didn't see a man destined to live out his life under the supposed judgment of God. What He saw was a young man who wanted desperately to be able to see. It was the caring Father in the Person of Jesus who cared enough for that young man that He healed him of his affliction. It was the Father at work, a caring, loving Father.

Take the leper in Matthew 8. If you know anything about leprosy, you will know that it is one of the most horrible of diseases known to mankind. Even today, if a person contracts leprosy, he becomes an instant outcast. In the time and culture of Jesus, leprosy was considered a most dreaded disease, one to be greatly feared lest it spread. Being a leper meant a life of living death, outcast from any normal type of life, doomed to eke out an existence with other lepers, fighting desperately for life while scavenging for food among garbage dumps. A leper knew nothing of what it meant just to talk with someone, to be held and touched, to have someone look at him without flinching. A leper could not enter the city nor attend the synagogue. Lepers were ostracized from their own families. For a leper to approach a normal, healthy person meant instant death through stoning.

Yet, here in Scripture we are witness to an incredible event. Driven by desperation, fearing life more than death, a leper walks right up to Jesus. The leper could have been stoned for this. He falls at Jesus's feet and pleads for healing. And what did our Lord do? An incredible thing! He actually reached out and touched that loathsome leper. He put His great arms around the filthy leper and held him and told him, "I will cleanse you! I will heal you!" I wonder, in that pregnant moment, with all the bystanders gaping aghast, what it meant for that man to feel those strong arms of Jesus around him and to hear that soothing, gentle, loving voice say, "I will heal you!"

Why did Jesus do such a thing? Because the Father cared! It was the Father at work in Jesus. When He looked at that leper, He didn't see the loathsome, despicable, dross of human society. He saw a man intensely desperate to be healed, to be normal. Jesus cared – the Father cares!

And what about the little street prostitute who invaded the private garden party of Simon the Pharisee (Luke 7:36-50)? What a potentially embarrassing moment. Here was Jesus, known for His purity and holiness, reclining in the open courtyard of Simon's house. Not only were there guests, but the townspeople were crowded around the courtyard walls waiting to listen to this young teacher who was stirring up all the people. What would they think? I wonder what the reaction would be today if a well-known prostitute ran up to a famous preacher during Sunday services and threw herself at his feet. He would probably be run out of town.

Notice Jesus's amazing reaction. He allows this young woman to wash His feet with her tears and to dry them with her hair. He actually allows her to anoint Him with perfume. Does He leap up in indignation? No. Does He scream at her for her actions? No. Does He cast her out? No. What does He do? He receives her. He doesn't humiliate her or reject her. He is protecting her, a common street prostitute! Why? Because the Father is at work. Now, you can see why I call the love of God the Father **INCREDIBLY MAGNIFICENT**!!!

We know the Father as our own Father through our Lord Jesus! **It is as we see Jesus as a Father that we come to know the Father!**

> **O taste and see that the LORD is good; how blessed is the man who takes refuge in Him!**
> Psalm 34:8, NASB

This relationship with God as Father is two-sided. It was initiated by Him, carried on by Him, but it demands a response on our part. As to God's part, Packer puts it well:

> What matters supremely, therefore, is not, in the last analysis, the fact that I know God, but the larger fact which underlies it – the fact that *He knows me*. I am graven on the palms of His hands; I am never out of His mind. All my knowledge of Him depends on His sustained initiative in knowing me. I know Him because He first knew me and continues to know me.[12]

And to man's part, Sanders says:

> Both Scripture and experience teach that it is we, not God, who determine the degree of intimacy with Him that we enjoy. We are at this moment as close to God as we really choose to be.[13]

The Bible calls God's part of the relationship "grace," and the part which is ours is faith." Grace has been called the "divine adequacy." Faith is the human response to our Father's adequacy. As we grow in awareness of His adequacy, we grow in our experience of the love and care and peace of the Father.

Why is it important for us to see the Father in Jesus? Mainly because we are told by Jesus that the Father is spirit (John 4:24), but we can't identify with spirit. Being flesh and blood, we only relate with flesh and blood. How then was the Father to reveal Himself? Obviously, through the Son. Therefore, to know God as Father, you must know Him as such through our Lord Jesus!

Reparenting

There are nine Bible studies in the application section of this booklet. These are to help in a "reprogramming" or a "reparenting" process to replace wrong ideas about God with right ideas about

God. These wrong ideas about God have been programmed into us over the years through experiential relationships with our earthly fathers and form a basic part of what we call our "belief system."

Our "belief system" is everything we believe about God, about ourselves, about others and about the world around us. Unfortunately, much of our "belief system" is erroneous; thus, it needs to be changed. God's means of changing our "belief systems" is through the **renewing of the mind** (Romans 12:2). In regard to how we view God as Father, our term "reparenting" is used interchangeable with "renewing of the mind." This process of renewing or reparenting consists of two basic elements: (1) the **putting off** of the wrong ideas about God and (2) the **putting on** of the right ideas about God.

This "putting off" and "putting on" process takes time. This is why the Bible studies at the end of this booklet are designed to be done over a number of weeks. You should schedule your time to spend a minimum of two weeks on each of the studies.

You will note that there are two sections in the back of this booklet: the workbook section and the application section. The workbook section involves a Bible study consisting of questions and answers. Look up the verse related to the question and then write out the answer in the space provided. It would be helpful to also read the passages of scripture both before and after the verse being cited.

The application section is a combination of Scripture memory and prayer. This section has two parts. First, there is a "Relationship Test," which covers ninety characteristics of the Father. Each group of ten characteristics is correlated with a Bible study page in the second part of the application section, which applies the results of the "Relationship Test" to a practical exercise of Scripture memory and prayer.

WORKBOOK SECTION

Jesus came to reveal the heavenly Father, and the purpose of this study is to reinforce this truth in your own mind so that you might enjoy the benefits which are yours as a child of God.

1. In John 10:30, what did Jesus tell the Jews? _____

2. Read John 14:8. What was it that Phillip wanted to see? _____

3. Read John 14:9-10. What was Jesus's reply to Phillip? _____

4. Read John 14:6. How can we come to know the Father? _____

5. Read John 5:18. Why were the Jews trying to kill Jesus? _____

6. Read John 5:19. What was Jesus's statement concerning what He said and did? _____

7. Read John 5:43. In whose name did Jesus come? _____

8. In John 8:58, Jesus refers to Himself as the "I AM." Read Exodus 3:14 and comment on the connection. What was Jesus claiming to be? _____

9. Read John 17:26. What did Jesus say that He came to do? _____

10. According to 2 Corinthians 6:18, what are we as Christians and who are we told that God is to us?

11. Explain Psalms 68:5 in your own words. Before you do, reread "The Need to Feel Secure" section of this booklet (pp. 219-220). _____

_____

_____

_____

12. If God is a Father – a Father to us – we need to know some of the characteristics of God as Father. For example, Paul says in 2 Corinthians 1:3 that God our Father is the God of mercies and comfort. Therefore, two characteristics of our Father are that He is merciful toward us and that He comforts us. From Psalm 3:3-5, list at least four characteristics of what God is to you as a Father.

_____

_____

13. According to Zephaniah 3:17, what is your Father's attitude toward you?

_____

14. In 1 John 4:10, what are you told is God's attitude toward you?

_____

In Romans 15:7? _____

15. Do you feel it is important to you to know God as your Father? Why or why not?

_____

_____

16. In the following passages, God is described by certain characteristics of a Father. For example, in 2 Corinthians 1:3, God is called the Father of mercies. Look up each passage and fill in the descriptive word or phrase that describes a characteristic of the Father.

Matthew 5:48: "… as your Heavenly Father is _____."

Matthew 6:18: "… your Father who sees in secret will _____

_____."

Luke 11:13: "… how much more shall your heavenly Father _____

_____?"

John 14:2-3: "In my Father's house _____."

John 16:23: "… if you shall ask the Father for anything, He _____

_____."

Romans 1:7b: "_____ from God our Father."

Romans 8:16: "The Spirit himself bears witness with our spirit that _____

_____."

2 Cor. 1:3b: "… the Father of _____ and God of

_____."

Eph. 1:3: "Blessed be the God and Father of our Lord Jesus Christ, who has blessed us

with _____

_____."

Eph. 1:17 "that the God of our Lord Jesus Christ, the _____

_____ may give to you ___ _____

_____."

Eph. 3:14-19: "For this reason, I bow my knees before the _____

from whom every family in heaven and on earth derives its name, that He would

grant you, according to _____

to be _____

so that _____

_____

_____

_____

_____

_____."

James 1:17:   "Every _____

is from above, coming down from _____

_____."

1 Peter 1:3:   "Blessed is the _____

who according to His great mercy has _____

_____

_____."

APPLICATION SECTION

RELATIONSHIP TEST INSTRUCTIONS

This test is designed to allow you to rate your relationship with the heavenly Father. Because it is subjective, there are no wrong answers. To ensure the test reveals your actual feelings, follow the instructions carefully.

1. To arrive at an accurate relationship rating, it is imperative that you answer openly and honestly. Do not answer the questions from a theological knowledge of God, but from a personal, experiential knowledge. Do not answer from what your relationship ought to be or what you hope it will be, but from what your relationship is with the Father right now. *In other words, if this test is to achieve its purpose, you must be absolutely candid in your answers.*
2. Some people feel that God might be displeased with them if they indicate a negative factor in answering the questions. Nothing could be further from the truth. Ask the Holy Spirit to guide you as you rate your relationship with the Father. He already knows how you feel and accepts you.
3. To guide you as you begin this test, you may find it helpful to phrase questions around each characteristic. For example, "To what degree do I really feel God loves me?" or "To what degree do I really know and experience God's majesty?" Your answers will form the subjective values that you assign each question.
4. It might be helpful to recall times of stress and difficulties as well as normal situations. *Who was God to you during these times?*
5. Moving from left to right, rate your relationship with the Father in terms of the degree to which each characteristic describes your experiential relationship with Him. *Rate yourself according to the following scale, circling the appropriate number that indicates your choice.*

    1 - ALWAYS   2 - VERY OFTEN   3 - OFTEN   4 - SOMETIMES
    5 - SELDOM   6 - HARDLY EVER   7 - NEVER

AFTER THE TEST:

1. Wherever you have circled a "3" or higher, put an "X" in the column just to the left of the characteristic.
2. Once you have marked all the X's, transfer them to the corresponding columns in the FatherCare Bible study exercises that follow. There are ten characteristics under each FatherCare heading. For each are listed verses and phrases which will help you in the "reparenting" process.
1. Choose a verse from among the key verses listed for each characteristic and begin to memorize the verse you choose. Establish a consistent prayer time when you can begin to pray out loud and choose to "put off" the wrong ideas about God and "put on" the right ideas about God. An example prayer is given at the end of this booklet. It is a good practice to write out your verses several times in longhand as well as to meditate on them.

RELATIONSHIP TEST

FatherCare:

___ Caring   1 2 3 4 5 6 7
___ Loving   1 2 3 4 5 6 7
___ Kind   1 2 3 4 5 6 7
___ Understanding   1 2 3 4 5 6 7
___ Strong   1 2 3 4 5 6 7
___ Calming   1 2 3 4 5 6 7
___ Pleasant   1 2 3 4 5 6 7
___ Approving   1 2 3 4 5 6 7
___ Sensitive to you   1 2 3 4 5 6 7
___ Listens   1 2 3 4 5 6 7

FatherFriend:

___ Friend   1 2 3 4 5 6 7
___ Faithful   1 2 3 4 5 6 7
___ Patient   1 2 3 4 5 6 7
___ Delights   1 2 3 4 5 6 7
___ Truthful   1 2 3 4 5 6 7
___ Counselor   1 2 3 4 5 6 7
___ Supportive   1 2 3 4 5 6 7
___ Humble   1 2 3 4 5 6 7
___ Joyful   1 2 3 4 5 6 7
___ Discerning   1 2 3 4 5 6 7

FatherKing:

___ King   1 2 3 4 5 6 7
___ Majestic   1 2 3 4 5 6 7
___ Awesome   1 2 3 4 5 6 7
___ Great   1 2 3 4 5 6 7
___ Victorious   1 2 3 4 5 6 7
___ Gracious   1 2 3 4 5 6 7
___ Worthy of honor   1 2 3 4 5 6 7
___ Just   1 2 3 4 5 6 7
___ Good   1 2 3 4 5 6 7
___ Righteous   1 2 3 4 5 6 7

FatherProvider:

___ Provider   1 2 3 4 5 6 7
___ Trustworthy   1 2 3 4 5 6 7
___ Adequate   1 2 3 4 5 6 7
___ Generous   1 2 3 4 5 6 7
___ Fair   1 2 3 4 5 6 7
___ Steadfast   1 2 3 4 5 6 7
___ Wealthy   1 2 3 4 5 6 7
___ Concerned   1 2 3 4 5 6 7
___ Satisfies   1 2 3 4 5 6 7
___ Giver   1 2 3 4 5 6 7

FatherSavior:

___ Redeemer   1 2 3 4 5 6 7
___ Merciful   1 2 3 4 5 6 7
___ Forgiving   1 2 3 4 5 6 7
___ Compassionate   1 2 3 4 5 6 7
___ Gentle   1 2 3 4 5 6 7
___ Beautiful   1 2 3 4 5 6 7
___ Cleanses   1 2 3 4 5 6 7
___ Holy   1 2 3 4 5 6 7
___ Pardons   1 2 3 4 5 6 7
___ Reasonable   1 2 3 4 5 6 7

FatherProtector:

___ Protective   1 2 3 4 5 6 7
___ Secure   1 2 3 4 5 6 7
___ Preserver   1 2 3 4 5 6 7
___ Alert   1 2 3 4 5 6 7
___ Deliverer   1 2 3 4 5 6 7
___ Defender   1 2 3 4 5 6 7
___ Cherishes   1 2 3 4 5 6 7
___ Advocate   1 2 3 4 5 6 7
___ Mighty   1 2 3 4 5 6 7
___ Sheltering   1 2 3 4 5 6 7

FatherLove:

___	Loving	1 2 3 4 5 6 7
___	Considerate	1 2 3 4 5 6 7
___	Comforting	1 2 3 4 5 6 7
___	Encouraging	1 2 3 4 5 6 7
___	Lover	1 2 3 4 5 6 7
___	Accepting	1 2 3 4 5 6 7
___	Intimate	1 2 3 4 5 6 7
___	Pleasant	1 2 3 4 5 6 7
___	Rewarder	1 2 3 4 5 6 7
___	Appreciative	1 2 3 4 5 6 7

FatherTeacher:

___	Instructor	1 2 3 4 5 6 7
___	Wise	1 2 3 4 5 6 7
___	Creative	1 2 3 4 5 6 7
___	Helpful	1 2 3 4 5 6 7
___	Lovingly kind	1 2 3 4 5 6 7
___	Disciplines	1 2 3 4 5 6 7
___	Imparts hope	1 2 3 4 5 6 7
___	Bestows favor	1 2 3 4 5 6 7
___	Light	1 2 3 4 5 6 7
___	Respectful	1 2 3 4 5 6 7

FatherLeader:

___	Guide	1 2 3 4 5 6 7
___	Bold	1 2 3 4 5 6 7
___	Confident	1 2 3 4 5 6 7
___	Perfect	1 2 3 4 5 6 7
___	Devoted	1 2 3 4 5 6 7
___	Commander	1 2 3 4 5 6 7
___	Authoritative	1 2 3 4 5 6 7
___	Loyal	1 2 3 4 5 6 7
___	Sufficient	1 2 3 4 5 6 7
___	Decisive	1 2 3 4 5 6 7

FATHERCARE – THE CHARACTERISTICS OF THE FATHER

As you do each of the following studies, ask yourself these questions:

1. Does this passage clearly support the point made in the characteristic?
2. Are there any cross references which might better highlight or emphasize that characteristic?
3. Have I personally had an experience with God in which this trait was made clear to me? If not, do I have trouble believing God is this way?
4. As I meditate upon this trait in God's character, what emotions come to the surface and what do they tell me about the condition of my belief system?
5. How does this characteristic motivate me to greater love for God Himself rather than just to "serve in His name" or to see His gifts?

When you conclude each Bible study, write out a prayer to God, thanking Him for who He is and for how He has shown Himself to you and asking Him to continue to reveal Himself to you as the perfect Father He is. There is a sample prayer on the last page of this section.

NOTE: Unless indicated otherwise, the Scripture references in this study are based on the wording in the New American Standard Version of the Bible. Wording may vary slightly in other translations.

FatherCare:

1. **Caring:** Matthew 6:26; 1 Peter 5:7
   - ___ He cares for me as only a loving father can care for his child.
   - ___ He not only cares for me, but He cares about me.

2. **Loving:** John 3:16; Romans 5:8; Ephesians 3:14-19
   - ___ He loves me for who He made me to be, not for what I do
   - ___ His love for me is unconditional and unceasing.

3. **Kind:** Psalm 103:13; Romans 2:4; Ephesians 1:4-5
   - ___ Our Father is a kind and considerate Person to us, His children.
   - ___ He always has a kind and encouraging word for me.

4. **Understanding:** Psalm 103:14; 139:1; Hebrews 4:15
   - ___ My Father understands me as a person.
   - ___ He understands me in my moods, my feelings, my thoughts, my actions.

5. **Strong:** Psalm 93:1; 105:4; 106:8; Ephesians 6:10-13
   - ___ My Father is strong and powerful on my behalf.
   - ___ His strength becomes my strength. He is the strongest of the strong.

6. **Calming:** Psalm 37:7; Matthew 11:28; John 14:1
   - ___ I find my tranquility in my Father's calmness. He is never hurried or harassed.
   - ___ He calms the anxious heart and takes senseless activity and turns it into creative productivity.

7. **Pleasant:** Psalm 16:11; 21:6; 147:1
   - ___ My Father is absolutely pleasant. What a pleasure it is to be in His presence.
   - ___ He is altogether lovely.

8. **Approving:** John 6:27 with Colossians 3:3
   - ___ My Father gives me unconditional approval.
   - ___ His approval is based on who I am in Him and not on what I do or have.

9. **Sensitive to you:** Psalm 94:9; 139:1-6, 17-18; Hebrews 4:15
   - ___ My Father is sensitive to my every mood and thought.
   - ___ He is sensitive to my needs and desires.

10. **Listens:** Psalm 55:17; 102:17; 116:1-2
    - ___ My Father listens to me. He takes time to be involved in who I am and what I do.
    - ___ He knows what I have to say is important. It is important to me; therefore, it is important to Him.

FatherKing:

1. **King**: Psalm 47:7; 95:3
   - ___ My Father is the sovereign king of the whole universe. He is the Kind Most High!
   - ___ I am a child of the King (John 1:12). I am a prince/princess. He enables me to think as a child of the King, act as a child of the King, be the child of a King.

2. **Majestic**: 1 Chronicles 29:11-13; Psalm 93:1
   - ___ My Father is majestic. He rules and reigns on high. How great He is!
   - ___ He desires my participation in His majesty. He freely shares it all with me.

3. **Awesome**: Exodus 15:11; Psalm 99:3
   - ___ My Father is awesome in His ability to love and protect me.
   - ___ He is awesome in His strength, power and holiness.

4. **Great**: Psalm 86:10; 99:2
   - ___ Greatness Becomes my Father. He is before all things, above all things; He presides over all things.
   - ___ He makes me an integral part of His greatness. I find my greatness in Him.

5. **Victorious**: Psalm 98:1; Zephaniah 3:17
   - ___ My Father is victorious over all things – the world, the flesh and the devil.
   - ___ His victory allows me to be victorious.

6. **Gracious**: Psalm 86:15; 111:4; 119:132; Ephesians 1:7-8
   - ___ He is gracious to me no matter how I act toward Him.
   - ___ He lavishes His grace on me as His precious child.

7. **Worthy of honor**: Philippians 2:9; 1 Timothy 6:15-16
   - ___ My Father is distinguished and upright. His name is above every other name.
   - ___ I am so very proud of Him. I am proud to call Him Father.

8. **Just**: Deuteronomy 32:4; Psalm 89:14; 99:4
   - ___ My Father is absolutely just. I know that He is impartial.
   - ___ I know that He will be just with me no matter what.

9. **Good**: Psalm 34:8; 100:5; 106:1
   - ___ My Father is good, a good Person in every sense.
   - ___ He is so good to me. He insists on giving me everything out of the goodness of His heart.

10. **Righteous**: Deuteronomy 32:4; Psalm 11:7; 111:3; 119:137
    - ___ My Father is absolutely righteous, even though He had been tempted in every manner just like me.
    - ___ Because He is righteous, He has made me to be righteous, not because of what I do, but because of who I am in Him.

FatherSavior:

1. **Redeemer**: Psalm 19:14; Isaiah 63:16; Jeremiah 50:34
    ___ My Father cared enough to redeem me out of the authority of darkness.
    ___ He redeemed me from the power of sin and from the hold of Satan, and He put me into His kingdom.

2. **Merciful**: 2 Samuel 24:14; Psalm 86:15; Ephesians 2:4
    ___ My Father is always merciful to me, regardless of my circumstances.
    ___ In the dark storms of self-reproach and condemnation, He is always merciful.

3. **Forgiving**: Psalm 86:5; 103:10-12; Hebrews 10:17
    ___ He has forgiven me completely and totally for all my sins and transgressions, past, present and future.
    ___ He forgives, He forgets – He wipes the slate of my heart clean.

4. **Compassionate**: Psalm 103:13-14; Matthew 9:36; Mark 6:34
    ___ My Father's heart is full of compassion for me for He has shared intimately all my pain and hurt and sorrows.
    ___ Through His compassion, He affirms and supports me.

5. **Gentle**: Psalm 18:35; Matthew 11:29; 2 Corinthians 10:1
    ___ He is a gentle Person. He deals with me so gently.
    ___ My Father's gentleness permeates my being, making me a gentle person.

6. **Beautiful**: Psalm 27:4; 96:6
    ___ He is the lily of the valley, the bright and morning star, the fairest of ten thousand.
    ___ My Father is a beautiful Person, and He believe me to be a beautiful person.

7. **Cleanses**: Isaiah 1:18; Acts 15:9; 1 John 1:9
    ___ The blood of Christ cleanses me from all unrighteousness.
    ___ No matter the defilement, my Father cleanses, moment by moment.

8. **Holy**: Psalm 99:3,5,9
    ___ The beauty of holiness shrouds my Father.
    ___ He is absolutely holy; thus, He makes me holy.

9. **Pardons**: Psalm 103:3; Romans 8:1; Hebrews 10:17
    ___ He freely pardons me – all my sins, all my transgressions; even the defilement is pardoned. I am free.
    ___ The Father took me as His precious child and sacrificed His Son to pardon me.

10. **Reasonable**: Isaiah 1:18; 1 Corinthians 10:13
    ___ To think that my Father would reason with me. How important that makes me feel.
    ___ He never demands more than I am able to really give. In every way, He is so very reasonable.

FatherFriend:

1. **Friend**: Exodus 33:11a; John 15:13-15; James 2:23
   ___ My Father is my friend. He is closer than a brother.
   ___ Since He is my friend, I can call on Him at any time; He is never too busy for me.

2. **Faithful**: Numbers 23:19; Psalm 89:1,2,5,8; 100:5; Lamentations 3:22-23
   ___ My Father is absolutely faithful to me as a person.
   ___ His faithfulness to me never lags and will never end.

3. **Patient**: Psalm 86:15: 103:8; 1 Corinthians 13:4
   ___ My Father is so patient with me. Nothing affects His patience where it concerns me.
   ___ I cannot provoke Him, nor does He ever hold anything against me.

4. **Delights**: Psalm 18:19; 27:4; Zephaniah 3:17
   ___ My Father delights in me because I am me; that is enough for Him.
   ___ He is a delightful and pleasing Person.

5. **Truthful**: Psalm 119:160; Isaiah 45:19; John 14:6; 16:13
   ___ My Father is always truthful to me, to everyone. He cannot be untruthful.
   ___ He builds into me truthfulness. I can be truthful because He is truthful.

6. **Counselor**: Job 12:13; Psalm 73:24; Isaiah 9:6; John 14:26
   ___ There is nothing that I cannot bring before my Father and seek His counsel on.
   ___ He never condemns or belittles what I ask Him. His advice never fails.

7. **Supportive**: Psalm 37:23-24; Isaiah 41:10
   ___ My Father supports and cares for me.
   ___ I know that whatever I attempt, He is there. What He requires of me, He give me the strength and power to do.

8. **Humble**: Matthew 11:29; Philippians 2:6-8
   ___ To think that the King of kings humbled Himself for me.
   ___ Out of my Father's humbleness, I find my humility.

9. **Joyful**: Isaiah 62:5; Zephaniah 3:17; John 15:11
   ___ My Father is always joyful and full of joy. He is a Father of joy.
   ___ His joy for me and in me produces my joy. I can rejoice in Him.

10. **Discerning**: 1 Samuel 16:7; Jeremiah 17:10; Mark 2:8
    ___ My Father is so very discerning. He knows my heart and nothing is hidden from Him.
    ___ I can be myself. I don't have to be a phony since He knows my heart.

FatherProvider:

1. **Provider:** Psalm 23; Matthew 6:25-34; Philippians 4:19
   ___ My Father provides for my every need – emotional, spiritual and physical.
   ___ I can rest secure knowing that He will provide for me as He has promised.

2. **Trustworthy:** Psalm 9:10; 18:2-3; 2 Corinthians 1:20
   ___ In every way, in every circumstance of life, my Father is trustworthy.
   ___ He is worthy of the trust I place in Him.

3. **Adequate:** 1 Chronicles 29:12; Psalm 73:25-26,28; 2 Corinthians 3:5
   ___ My Father is totally adequate for all my needs. He is, in and of Himself, totally adequate.
   ___ His adequacy is the basis for my own personal adequacy. My adequacy is in and of Him.

4. **Generous:** Matthew 7:9-11; John 3:34; Romans 8:32
   ___ My Father withholds nothing good from me. He lavishes the riches of His grace upon me.
   ___ He freely and bountifully gives me all good things.

5. **Fair:** Deuteronomy 32:4; Psalm 98:9; 99:4
   ___ How fair in all of His dealings with me is my Father.
   ___ I know that He will never, ever be unfair with me.

6. **Steadfast:** Psalm 31:3; Isaiah 40:8; Hebrews 13:8
   ___ What security I can have because my Father is steadfast and unmovable.
   ___ He is like a rock; I can truly trust Him.

7. **Wealthy:** Psalm 50:10-11; 2 Corinthians 8:9
   ___ My Father owns the cattle on a thousand hills. He is rich beyond comprehension. His wealth is my wealth right now as my present possession.
   ___ My Father's real wealth is me. I am His inheritance.

8. **Concerned:** Matthew 6:28-32; 10:29-31; 1 Peter 5:7
   ___ My Father is deeply concerned with the intimate details of my life.
   ___ I can trust Him because He cares about me.

9. **Satisfies:** Psalm 103:5; 107:9; 128:1-4
   ___ In my Father I am fulfilled.
   ___ He satisfies beyond my wildest dreams.

10. **Giver:** Psalm 37:4; John 3:34; Romans 8:32; James 1:17
    ___ No good thing does my Father withhold from me, His child.
    ___ He brings gifts and gives them to me – the gift of the Sprit, spiritual gifts and material blessings.

FatherProtector:

1. **Protective**: Psalm 91; 118:6-9; 2 Thessalonians 3:3
   ___ My Father protects me because He loves me.
   ___ As His precious child, He protects me.

2. **Secure**: Psalm 18:2; Proverbs 3:25-26; 29:25
   ___ In an insecure world, my Father gives me security.
   ___ The world offers no sanctuary of security; that only comes in Him.

3. **Preserver**: Psalm 97:10; Isaiah 54:17: John 10:29
   ___ My Father preserves me and keeps me from all harm.
   ___ He maintains (preserves) His righteousness in me.

4. **Alert**: 2 Chronicles 16:9a; Psalm 121:3-4: 139:1-12
   ___ If His eye is on the sparrow, then I know He watches me.
   ___ My Father watches over me even in the night watches. I am never alone.

5. **Deliverer**: Psalm 97:10; 107:6; 1 Corinthians 10:13
   ___ My Father delivers me from the hand of the enemy.
   ___ He delivers me from all temptation.

6. **Defender**: Psalm 7:10; 10:17-18; 27:1; 28:7-8
   ___ My Father protects and defends me from myself and my enemies.
   ___ He stands up for me and is a shield to me.

7. **Cherishes**: Psalm 18:19; Zephaniah 3:17; Ephesians 5:29
   ___ My Father delights in me.
   ___ He cherishes me as a person dear to His heart.

8. **Advocate**: Hebrews 7:25; 1 John 2:1
   ___ My Father speaks up for me and defends me.
   ___ He proclaims to Satan that I am "not guilty."

9. **Mighty**: Isaiah 40:10-26; Mark 10:27; Luke 1:37
   ___ My Father accomplishes with ease that which man finds impossible.
   ___ He is mighty to conquer His enemies and mine.

10. **Sheltering**: Psalm 61:3-4; 91:1-2; 121:5-8
    ___ My Father shelters me with his protective care.
    ___ He protects me from both seen and unseen enemies.

FatherLove:

1. **Loving**: 1 Corinthians 13:4-8a; 1 John 4:8-10
   ___ My Father is altogether loving. He is full of love and embodies love.
   ___ He inspires love and affection in me.

2. **Considerate**: Isaiah 54:4-6; Jeremiah 29:11; Mark 5:22-42
   ___ My Father is so considerate of me. Even when I am wrong, His consideration does not change.
   ___ He never neglects nor ignores me. To Him I am so very important and he is considerate of my needs.

3. **Comforting**: Psalm 68:5; 94:19; 2 Corinthians 1:3-4
   ___ He comforts me in all the trials and tragedies I face.
   ___ My Father's comfort extends even to the most intimate areas of my life. There is nothing I can't share with Him.

4. **Encouraging**: Isaiah 40:28-31; Romans 15:4-5
   ___ My Father encourages me constantly.
   ___ No matter what I face, the pain I feel, the hurt I experience, He is always encouraging me.

5. **Lover**: Romans 5:8; Ephesians 2:4-5; 3:17-19
   ___ He is the lover of my soul. He tenderly watches over and cares for me.
   ___ I am secure and confident in my Father's aggressive, yet tender, love for me.

6. **Accepting**: Romans 14:18; 15:7
   ___ My Father accepts me as a person, with all my hang-ups, all my sins, all my guilt. He accepts me just as I am in Christ.
   ___ He accepts me on the basis of who I am, not on the basis of what I do.

7. **Intimate**: Psalm 139; Proverbs 3:32; John 17:26
   ___ My Father is not someone who is ten million light years away; He is with me at all times.
   ___ He is not vague, but real. He is someone who does care and love.

8. **Pleasant**: Jeremiah 15:16; Matthew 11:28-30; John 1:14
   ___ What a pleasing Person my Father is. His presence is like the radiance of the sun.
   ___ Not only does He try in every way to please me, but He makes me desire to please Him.

9. **Rewarder**: 2 Timothy 4:7-8; 2 Corinthians 9:6-11; James 1:12
   ___ My Father has promised crowns to me.
   ___ Knowing Him intimately is reward enough in eternity.

10. **Appreciative**: Matthew 24:45-47; Luke 6:38
    ___ My Father always shows His appreciation for my efforts on His behalf.
    ___ He appreciates me as a person.

FatherLeader:

1. **Guide**: Psalm 73:24; Isaiah 58:11; John 16:13
   ___ I know, no matter what the call, my Father guides my way step by step.
   ___ His will is not elusive and will-o'-the-wisp, but a definite statement of His desires for me.

2. **Bold**: Psalm 76:4-9; Hebrews 4:15-16; Revelation 19:11-16
   ___ My Father is bold, bold for me.
   ___ He imparts boldness to me. He makes me to be bold.

3. **Confident**: Isaiah 41:13; 42:8; 45:5; 2 Corinthians 3:4-5
   ___ My Father is supremely confident. He knows what He is about.
   ___ Out of His confidence, He builds confidence in me.

4. **Perfect**: Deuteronomy 32:4; 2 Samuel 22:31; Psalm 18:30; Hebrews 7:28
   ___ Can anyone be as perfect as my Father? He is perfect in and of Himself. He is perfect to me.
   ___ He is the perfect Person for me, to make me everything that I could never be in and of myself.

5. **Devoted**: Hebrews 13:5-6; 1 John 3:1-2
   ___ My Father is devoted to me. He pours out His affection and love on me.
   ___ His devotion for me drove Him to the Cross. I am that worthy in His sight.

6. **Commander**: 2 Chronicles 13:12; Psalm 33:9; 91:11
   ___ My Father is the Commander of the host of the Lord.
   ___ He is in charge. Need I fear anything?

7. **Authoritative**: Matthew 7:28-29; 9:6; 28:18
   ___ My Father speaks with authority.
   ___ He commands the attention and obedience of all.

8. **Loyal**: John 10:27-30; Romans 8:31-39; Hebrews 13:5
   ___ My Father's loyalty to me as His child never ceases.
   ___ He protects loyally. He never embarrasses nor humiliates me. He cares that I remain loyal and obedient to Him.

9. **Sufficient**: 2 Corinthians 9:8; 12:9
   ___ My Father is sufficient for every need, for every situation and circumstances of life.
   ___ His sufficiency guarantees that in my weakness His strength will be made perfect.

10. **Decisive**: Psalm 33:9; 2 Corinthians 1:19-20
    ___ My Father is decisive. He speaks and it is done.
    ___ He knows where He is going and how to get there. My indecision is to be swallowed up in His decisiveness.

FatherTeacher:

1. **Instructor**: Psalm 25:8-9; 32:8; John 14:26; 2 Timothy 3:16-17
    ___ My Father carefully, patiently instructs me in everything.
    ___ He prepares me fully to live a life for Him.

2. **Wise**: Job 9:4; 12:13; Psalm 104:24; Romans 16:27; James 1:5
    ___ My Father is wise beyond imagination. I cannot fathom His wisdom, but it is always the best for me.
    ___ He imparts His wisdom to me, so that I might be truly wise.

3. **Creative**: Psalm 104:5-24; John 1:3; Ephesians 2:10; 2 Corinthians 5:17
    ___ In His creative genius, He carefully fashions all that is.
    ___ My Father created me twice – once in His image, and again in spirit.

4. **Helpful**: Psalm 54:4; 121:1-2; John 14:16-17; Hebrews 13:6
    ___ My Father is my Helper.
    ___ What I find impossible in my own strength, I find possible in His.

5. **Lovingly kind** (steadfast love): Psalm 25:6; 89:1; 103:10-13; Titus 3:4-5
    ___ My Father's loving kindness is constantly extended toward me.
    ___ His loving kindness forms a shield over me, a guard in front of me, a hedge behind me.

6. **Disciplines**: Psalm 94:12; Isaiah 30:20-21; Hebrews 12:5-11; Revelation 3:19
    ___ My Father will not allow me to stray into danger.
    ___ He tenderly corrects me so that I may live life at its best.

7. **Imparts hope**: Jeremiah 29:11; Romans 15:4; 1 Peter 1:3
    ___ My Father never gives up on me; He's always optimistic for me.
    ___ He gives me hope out of the great hope within Him.

8. **Bestows favor**: Psalm 30:5; 89:15-17
    ___ I find my Father's favor in my intimacy with Him.
    ___ His favor suffices. It strengthens and keeps me.

9. **Light**: Psalm 27:1; John 1:4-5,9; 8:12
    ___ My Father is the light of life, the light of the world.
    ___ In the darkness of my path of life, His light carefully guides my way.

10. **Respectful**: John 15:15; Hebrews 2:11-13
    ___ My Father respects me because He loves me as a person.
    ___ I don't have to earn His respect; He gives it to me freely.

SAMPLE "REPARENTING" PRAYER

A prayer like the one that follows would be appropriate after each of the preceding Bible studies. In your prayer, acknowledge the characteristic of God that you now believe to be true according to His Word. This prayer is an example for the characteristic of "loving."

> **My Father, I always considered You an unloving God, but now I know that You are a *loving* Father to me. I choose now in faith to put off my false belief and I choose to believe that You are loving to me. I choose to believe what Your Word has to say about You rather than my feelings or reason or past experiences, and I know that Your Word says that You love me as a person and that your love is not based on my performance or on what I have or achieve. Thank You, my Father, for loving me unconditionally.**

Addendum Two

"Self-Disciplined Religion," a transcript reproduced by permission of
Unconditional Love Fellowship
PO Box 1599
Bandera, TX 78003
830-460-4000
unconditionallovefellowship.com

SELF-DISCIPLINED RELIGION

By Malcolm Smith
Transcribed from an audio recording with permission from
Unconditional Love Fellowship
PO Box 1599
Bandera, TX 78003

Copies of this and other messages by Malcolm Smith may be ordered from
Unconditional Love Fellowship: (830) 460-4000
unconditionallovefellowship.com

Let's turn to Titus – Paul's letter to Titus – [chapter 2,] verse eleven:

> *For the grace of God has appeared, bringing salvation to all men, instructing us to deny ungodliness and worldly desires and to live sensibly, righteously and godly in the present age.* Titus 2:11-12, NASB

The grace of God has appeared. And if you notice, it tells us that this grace, when it comes, does two things to us. It tells us to renounce – or your word in the Bible I'm reading from is "deny." It's a very strong word, very strong. The word "deny" doesn't really say it unless you get inside the word "deny" and stamp your feet a bit. The word "deny" – it means to renounce, repudiate, reject, absolutely have nothing to do with. The grace of God has appeared, teaching us or instructing us to reject, deny all ungodliness and worldly desires. So that is the first thing, when a person has received the grace of God, they will turn upon sin and have nothing to do with it.

But, secondly, it says, "...and to live sensibly, righteously and godly in this present age." So it isn't only that they have renounced their lifestyle of ungodliness. That's only one side of it. They have embarked upon a new kind of a lifestyle, which is characterized by three words: to live sensibly, righteously, and godly.

Now, I don't have enough time for three words. But I do have time for one word, which I think, actually, could be the most important word in that sentence. I'm not sure about that, but it could be. And the word is "sensibly." If you are born again, you have renounced – done with – ungodliness, and you have taken up a new lifestyle that is called here "being sensible." Now, I know that didn't sound too exciting, and actually I would like to have translated that word by another word. I'm not sure what your version might say. Maybe it says what I would like to have translated it as. That word, in my opinion, should be translated "self-control."

Now, in actual fact it is translated "self-control" elsewhere in the New Testament by this [translation of the] Bible, New American Standard. But here they've chosen "sensibly," and for the life of me, I don't know why. "Self-control" is the word. It's a very important word in the New Testament describing the new-birth kind of life. In fact, right here, in Titus, it keeps on coming up. When he talks about elders, leaders of the church, one of the great characteristics of them, according to verse eight, is that they are self-controlled. You jump down to chapter two, and it says the older men in the church – they should be characterized by being – it says "sensible" in my Bible – self-controlled. It says the older women should be characterized by being self-controlled – in verse five. Then in verse six it says, "…and likewise, the young men should be self-controlled."[1] Then he says here that, in fact, it is the characteristic of everybody. Once the grace of God has come to you – one of the characteristics that stands out – you become self-controlled.

You might remember that when Paul was addressing Felix. (Now this I find fascinating.) When Paul was addressing Felix, a heathen, he's preaching the Gospel to him, and what does he address this man about? Self-control. It would suggest to me that all these people, according to Titus, are to realize that self-control is the center of this Christian life. And when he addressed Felix, self-control was part of the Gospel that he presented.

And then, of course, another one that leaps out is Galatians 5. The fruit of the Spirit is… And down that list is "self-control." This has got to be a very important word – self-control. So, I must ask, "What is this self-control?"

Now, I don't want you to get confused here. It's very easy. In fact, there are some Bible commentators that got terribly confused here. You see, in the days of Paul, there were certain philosophies. There were certain Greek moralists. You know what I mean? You do realize that being moral is not being Christian. You do understand that, don't you? There is no such thing, actually, as Christian morality. We won't get into that. But, morality is not being a Christian. So, the "Moral Majority" can include a lot of human beings. They don't have to be Christians. Because being moral is the cry of what's left after the Fall has blitzed man. Man is not totally lost in terms of not knowing right from wrong, though man is lost unless he comes to Christ. Even in his lost-ness, he does know God is there somewhere, and he does know there's right and he does know there's wrong. In that sense, he's not totally lost. The devil doesn't know right from wrong. Do you understand what I mean by that? The devil thinks right is wrong and wrong is right. He's totally immersed forever into wrong-ness. Man was deceived, so he can tell the difference. He knows there is right. And whenever man moves to that right-ness, we say it's morality.

And the Greeks had perfected that. In fact, there was a group called the Stoics. You might have heard of the Stoics. They were into self-discipline. And many Bible commentators think that Paul took from the Stoics and was talking here about self-discipline. He's not. He's talking about self-control. And there's a *world* of difference between self-discipline and self-control.

What is self-discipline? A self-discipline is an imposition. That is, it comes from the outside. I impose on myself, or I let somebody else impose on me. It's an imposition upon my inner desires, my inner lusts. I allow someone to impose a law on me – that you shall not do that. And so, here this imposition, something from the outside, comes upon me and says you can't do it. And I say, "Okay, okay, I won't do it." But I really would love to do it. I still want to do it. But I'll be *disciplined*. I won't do what I really want to do. I will do what I am *supposed* to do. That's self-discipline. I bring myself under and I grit my teeth and I say I won't do it. And you'd better give me a good reason why I mustn't do it. And so along with morality and along with self-discipline go the reasons, usually high reasons, why I shouldn't do it. And I'll drag myself. I'll whip myself. "You will not do that!" I am self-disciplined.

Now you see that, as far back as the days of Paul, crept into the church. It's in the church today. I've heard it many times. You can read it any time you want. It comes down to something like this: "After all He has done for you…" Now you can hear it's coming now. You can hear it coming. See, now we've given you a reason. We're going to come to you with all your snake pit of lusts and desires and whip you into shape. "And after all He's done for you, the least you can do for Him is..." And then insert in there the latest fad in the body of Christ. Do you follow what I mean by this? Do you get what self-discipline is? It's something that comes from the outside. You're going to twist your arm and make yourself do what you don't want to do. But you'll do it – for some reason.

I know some people and they are self-disciplined because they feel that's the route to heaven. I tell you this: I heard a man the other day, God bless him. I prayed for that man. I mean that, because he was a preacher, and he was telling the people that when his mummy was dying, he promised her he'd meet her in heaven. And so, since that day, he has tried so hard. He's been disciplined, and he hasn't drunk and he hasn't smoked and he hasn't chewed tobacco, because he wants to see mummy in heaven. That's self-discipline. That's accepted as evangelical preaching, God help us. Do you understand what I'm talking about? Really, I mean!

And then, of course, you go to some churches and they've already got their self-discipline all lined out – that, if you join this church, you can't do this and you can't do this. They've got the list. And you sign at the bottom. Why? To be accepted by the church. So, I'll let someone twist my arm. Self-discipline is saying, "Here is something I shouldn't do, for some reason or other, and so I guess I won't do it." Self discipline is in the world of "you should," "you must," "you ought." You know, those of you that were in the military, you know what it is. You go along with it. I mean, why not? Get off my back, I'll do it. But you forget why, if there ever was a reason. You just do it. Self-discipline.

See, the Pharisees – if any of you are into self-discipline, let me encourage you, the Pharisees were. The Pharisees were *really* into self-discipline. They were very disciplined people. They were disciplined in the way they dressed. They wouldn't dress like heathens. They dressed in a way that they had determined God liked. Poor God, He's brought into all the fashion shows. They decided what God liked and what God didn't like. And so Pharisees dressed very disciplined. And their hours of prayer – you've got to give them A+. I've never yet met anybody that had a disciplined life like the Pharisees. From the minute they got out of bed, almost every hour had some particular expression – a ritual, a prayer, scripture memorization. Who in this audience started at four years old memorizing Leviticus? Every Pharisee did. As soon as you were born into a Pharisee home, four years old and you're memorizing Leviticus. And you move on to Genesis and then Exodus and then Numbers and then Deuteronomy. By the time you're twelve, you can quote the whole jolly lot. That's the beginning of being a Pharisee. By the time you're twenty, you've delved into the Psalms and the Prophets. Man, that's discipline. Strict, rigid discipline. It came into days of prayer, days of fasting, every Wednesday and Friday. Tithing! You didn't only tithe on your money. You tithed on the very leaves on the vegetables in the garden. Did you know that? A Pharisee would go and count the leaves on the herbs that grew in the garden. Every tenth one, he'd pluck it off and put it in the offering plate. You talk about tithing!

But wherever they went, you could feel the results of discipline. It's cold. There is something ice cold about a self-disciplined religion. Highly organized, I'll grant you that. And it looks perfect. It's right – *dead* right. Cold. Distant. And they don't have to say a word. It plays around their mouths – the arrogance, despising. They don't even have to say it: "I thank you, oh God, I'm not as other men." It's coming out of every pore of their skin.

Do you realize they shared that in common with every other religion in the world? And when I see believers today that are self-disciplined, I often have to tell them, "You know, you're not very well disciplined." I mean, if you're going to get into self-discipline, try being a Muslim. I mean go the whole way! Go the whole way! If you want discipline – you say you don't drink alcohol. Well, even the Mormons don't drink coffee. I mean go for it, man. Go for it. Where does this thing end? You'll end up drinking purified water if you're not... If you want discipline, go to the religions of this world, and they have done a perfect job of it.

And it looks so right. Oh, it gets to you. You see a person who's dressed odd and different, and you see a person who, on the hour, every hour, does this, does that; it looks so right. Anyone who's a bit slob-ish, you suddenly feel unspiritual. Paul spoke to this in Colossians 2. He mentions, "Do not handle, do not taste, do not touch..." He says these have "the appearance of wisdom in self-made religion, self-abasement and severe treatment of the body, but are of no value against fleshly indulgence."[2]

"There is a way that seems right to a man, but the end thereof is the way of death."[3] That's the trouble with it. It seems so right. When you look at it, you say it couldn't be wrong. Can a man be wrong because he prays on the hour every hour? Could a man be wrong because he has memorized the Bible? It depends where his heart is at. Yes, he could be wrong. That's why there's a way that seems right. Going off to break the Ten Commandments on the hour every hour does not seem right. There's no doubt where he stands. But, when a person *seems* to be so right, it's hard to say they're wrong.

Jesus went to the Pharisees of His day. In Matthew 23, He says, "You blind Pharisees, first clean the inside of the cup and of the dish, so that the outside of it may become clean also."[4] He has said the cup is not cleaned by scrubbing the outside. And did you notice what He said? Clean the inside *so that* the outside may become clean. That is, you're spending all your time scrubbing the outside. Basically, He said, "Forget the outside. Get to the inside and the outside will take care of itself." So, He is saying that the holiness that He's talking about is not self-discipline. It's something that arises from the inside and moves to the outside.

See, self-discipline, I suppose, in America today, shows up mostly in dieting. I mean that's self-discipline that everybody understands. For some reason – you see, self-discipline always has to have some reason out there. So, for some reason, I guess I'd better diet. The doctor breathing down my neck or a bathing suit hanging in the cupboard that won't fit around my thigh. You know, some reason that I have got to start dieting. So, I impose upon myself these incredible rules. And everything inside me says yes, until the first meal, and then everything says *no*. But I'm disciplined, and I grit my teeth. For a while. Until, apparently, I've got it licked. And then I go and forget the whole thing again. That's always discipline. Because, you see, you don't want to do this. You're accepting the impositions, but you don't *want* to do it. And so, at the first chance, out! You see, you've got all those crazy magazines as you go in the checkout. They're screaming at you. Lose 30 pounds in an hour! New diet! New diet! And people *buy* them! Ah, a new discovery. *I might just do it this time.*

Now I see the church today in America exactly like that. Most believers I know, in the Spirit, are on diets. "I won't do this and I won't do that and I won't do the other. In my heart, I wish I could, but I won't do this. I'm going to be holy. We're going to get this thing on the road." And every passing preacher has got a new fad diet. "Do it my way and you'll be holy in 30 minutes." Come on. "Five steps!" Hey, you do know, don't you, that when you diet and lose weight and gain it right back, you're in a worse state than when you began? And when believers are forever finding new fad ways to try and be holy – try to discipline themselves into holiness – in the long run, you're worse off than when you began. Because, you see, self-discipline is a *sin*. Self-discipline – I mean applied to the things of the Spirit – is a sin. For what is self-discipline? It is but one more action of the flesh.

Now what do I mean by "flesh"? That fills the New Testament. What does it mean? Very quickly, who were you before you came to Christ? I mean, let's take a quick photograph. Who were you? The Bible calls you an "old man." Not old in years. "Old man" means corrupt, decaying, falling apart. So you were old in that sense. What constituted the old man? "*I*, I had determined I would go my own way." "All we like sheep have gone astray. We have turned every one to his own way."[5] That's the essence of it all. I mean forget these big theological words like "original sin." Basically, when all is said and done, it just means man made a choice beyond all choices, a choice out of which every choice would come. "I want it my way," which means I am going to live my life independently of God. I'll acknowledge He's there. I'll tip my cap to Him every Sunday. But I'll do it *my* way. And man died in his spirit. So, the old man, this corrupt man, decaying man, spiritually, is one who is dead in his spirit and has been taken over by his "*I* will do it my way, independently of God." And such a man plays directly into the hands of Satan and is described as being led around by the prince of the power of the air. "The spirit who is now at work in the sons of disobedience"[6] – that's who you were. Do you identify with that? That's who you were. That's the man that is called "dead in sins."

What happened when you were born again? You realized through the preaching of the Gospel that that old man had been taken by Jesus. And when Jesus died, that man died. Everything you were, in rebellion and hostility toward God, was taken to the Cross, and you died. But not only so, Christ came inside of you by His Spirit, and that which was dead in you came alive. You were a new creation. You were born again. And what was not there, is there. Christ now lives inside of you. Your spirit is alive to God, for Christ is in you.

So you still have flesh – this desire to be independent – but it's not you. *You* are Christ in you. *You* are the new creation. That's who *you* are. The Holy Spirit has shed abroad the love of God in your heart.[7] You have eternal life, which is life as God has it. That's who you are. You are a partaker of the new covenant, which says the law of God is written on your heart.[8] That's who you *are*. But I still live in a body of flesh, which means the potential for living independently of God is there. Oh, I'm not the old man. He's gone, he's dead. I, my spirit alive, Christ in me – that's who I am.

But always the pull, always the – what shall I say? – seduction. "Come and do it the old way. Come and be independent. Feel the sweetness of being in control instead of this dependency upon Christ, instead of Christ living in you and Christ living as you." The pull: every temptation you've ever had, really, is a call to live independently of Jesus. I'll get to that again in a moment. But, you see, now that I've come to Christ, if my flesh has got any sense, it's not going to call me to commit murder. It has half an idea I'll say no to that. So the flesh joins a church. The flesh says, "You do realize that, independent of God, you can be good enough for Him. I mean I know we did all that awful stuff before. We didn't have to, you know. We could have done it this way. We don't need God to be holy. Good grief. All you need to do is try a bit harder. I mean we never used to try, did we? Well, let's start trying now. Now you know the rules; we'll play by them. Come on, you can do it." "Just a little discipline," says the flesh. "Independently of God, you can try a little harder. A little prayer wouldn't hurt. Memorize a few Bible scriptures." "I mean, just get your act together," says the flesh. "I can do it. I can be like Jesus. You see, I can go anywhere you want. If you wanted wild parties, we had a jolly good time there, didn't we? Now then we'll do it this way now. Now we'll have wild meetings if you want. We'll do it any way you want; just do it my way. You see, you must understand, I'm your flesh. I am not as bad as you think. I'm a pretty good chap really. Just give me a chance. I can really achieve being like Jesus if you'll only give me a chance." The flesh – I kid you not – that's the flesh. Anything independent of God – the flesh, that's what it wants to do. Oh, you don't have to be bad, bad, bad. You can be good, good, good. If it's independent of God, it's the flesh.

The flesh has got one phrase. It says, "*I, I* will try to please God." [It says,] "That is God's over there. I'm over here." See what we can do to become acceptable to God, more loveable? Do you see what I'm saying? "I, I, I, I, I will try to be good." And the tragedy is there are millions of believers in America who came to receive the forgiveness of sins, knowing it has got to come from the God side. Only God could achieve my forgiveness. And when we accepted his forgiveness and came in, we said, "Thank you very much. Now, after all you've done for me, you'd better sit back, God. Wait till I show you what I'm going to do for you."

I pastored for a long time in Northern Ireland. I look back sometimes to those days, back in the '60s when it was almost like pastoring a Third World country. I mean we didn't have running water and, for a while, we didn't have electricity. And while I was there, the electricity finally came to where we were pastoring. I mean it was a big deal. When the first person in the congregation got electricity, we all went to the house. We were there for the switching on ceremony. Electricity has come! And then it got kind of ho-hum as, one by one, everybody got it. We'd almost forgotten – you know, it was in the church now. Until the last person, the oldest elder we had, decrepit, poor old chap – and he lived way out in the sticks. In Ireland that's the peat bogs, and he lived way out there. And finally, he was the last one to get electricity. And so the board of elders – we all went out there. The last one and the oldest one was going to get electricity. I'd been to dinner there many times before, and just as it got dusk, he would light the paraffin lamps. Well, tonight we sat around. He let it get a little bit darker than dusk. And then in Irish fashion, he gave that nod to his wife – the patriarchal nod, which meant, "Wife, to your duty." And she got up in that semi-darkness and went to the switch. And you could see the anticipation as she put on the switch. And immediately the room flooded with light. Very slowly, the old man got up, went over to the paraffin lamps and lit them. And he says, "You can put it out now." He said to us, "It's going to be a lot easier to light the lamps after this."

When I saw him do that, I said, "There go so many believers." When Jesus comes and the light is turned on, they say, "Now it's going to be a lot easier to keep the law." No. When Jesus comes, it's no more self-discipline. It's no more struggling to keep the law. Jesus doesn't come to make it easier to keep the law. Jesus comes to give us something entirely beyond the law. Never contradicting it. But far, far beyond it. Far, far beyond it.

This was the trouble with the Galatians. They thought they could begin in the power of the Spirit and come to a holiness by self-discipline. No. You have come into something that is unlike any religion in this world. Every religion has a law. You have a Person, the Person who has come to live within. We have the new heart, the love of God shed abroad, and the essence of that law written within. And what is the essence of law? Love. The Ten Commandments are only love written negatively. Do you understand? If I love you, I won't kill you. If I love you, I won't lie to you. It's love in another way.

So, what's self-control? Self-control is listening to my heart, not a law imposed from the outside. It's listening to who I now am in Christ. And what do I hear when I listen to who I am? I hear that I *want*, I *want* God. I *love* Him now and I want to fulfill the love of God that is in me by loving you. When you're first born again, however weak that may sound down inside of you, that is your new heart. I mean that is the new you. You're not who you were. You are who you are. If you listen – "What do I really want?" You want God. You want to express His love to others.

See, if I don't listen to my heart. If I don't – if I listen to what many other believers are telling me or if I listen to my flesh... I sit down with some believers sometimes. It's like sitting at a fat farm when the ice cream man goes by. I mean I hear, "Oh, I am so weak. You know, I get so tempted and I fail God so much. Pray for me. The devil's always after me." And every Sunday night, "Anybody got a request?" One weak, limp hand goes up. "Pray for me. I'm going to be tempted this week." Haven't you ever heard your hearts? You're talking discipline there, and you're saying when the discipline's on, "I feel so weak." Don't you know who you are? You don't talk like that. *Listen* to your heart.

Tell me this – those of you that feel the biggest failure in this place – when it comes to living the Christian life, I mean, you've blown it. Well, let me counsel you. This is what I do when people come to me in private. Let me do it publicly. Listen to your heart. Listen to your heart. That besetting sin that makes you feel such a failure – let's listen to your heart. Do you *want* that besetting sin? I mean, do you *want* it? Tell me, will you go to that besetting sin and say, "You are my friend. I will protect you. I will justify my right to have you in my life"? Now, some of you are looking at me horrified. Of course, if you listen to your heart, you don't want sin. You'll never protect that besetting sin. You'll never justify its existence. You don't want it. Why? Because the grace of God has appeared, instructing you to deny sin.[9] You don't want it. You've got a new heart. Then give yourself a slap in the face. You're not one of the dieters. You're not sitting there, saying, "I've got to try again, but it's a hopeless job. I'm so weak and the devil's going to get me this week." No, you haven't got to try again. Stand up. Stretch. Throw away the diet sheets. It's over. It's gone. Arise and shine and Christ shall give you light![10] Be who you *are*!

And for some reason, you've never realized who you are. This isn't a second experience. I'm only telling you who you are. This is what happened to you when you came to Christ. And you've had your eyes on the flesh, and you've had your eyes on discipline, and you've tried to turn your flesh into something acceptable to God. Well, you can't. All God ever said about the flesh is crucify it. So forget that. He comes and writes on your heart, not on your flesh. And He says, "What's your heart? What's your heart?" And He says, "I've given you a new heart and Christ lives there. The love of God is there." That's who you are!

Now I'm in a position to handle this nonsense. I'm going to make choices. Can't fool me with the flesh anymore. When the flesh calls me, I say, "I know you. You're not me. Ha, ha, ha. Oh no, you've been crucified with Christ. That's my faith confession right now. I'm not confessing it to make it happen. I'm confessing it because it's happened. You're no longer me. I, I, in my innermost self, I – Christ lives in me; that's who I am. I don't live with you anymore. At this moment I live in harmony with who I am, with Christ in me." This is faith. This is real faith. It is daring to believe the facts of the Gospel – the facts that this "I" was crucified with Christ, but *this* "I" is Christ living in me. That's my faith. I am helpless. I know that I cannot, in my flesh, live the Christian life. It's impossible. The fruit of the *Spirit* is self-control, the fruit of me being joined to the Holy Spirit. And so I choose to live life out of my deepest self. I'm going to choose to be who I want to be.

Am I making sense? I'm living out of who I really am. I'm going to choose to be who I want to be. I'm not going to struggle and try to have my flesh imitate Jesus. I'm going to let Jesus be Himself. And I am going to choose to let Him be Himself. So, it isn't changing my flesh. It's *ex*changing. It's not the flesh; that's crucified. I exchange – let Christ live.

Oh, that involves sacrifice. No doubt about that. There are some things I don't do. I do not do them by choice. And I didn't not do them – that's bad, isn't it – "didn't not" -- you know what I mean, though, don't you? I was not stopping doing those things in response to law. That is self-discipline. I asked in my innermost heart, "What do you really want to do?" And I want to love God, and I want to love you. And anything that stands in the way of that, I want to be rid of it. I do. I want to. And, so, if there is something that I am doing that is going to tear your heart up, I'll stop doing that. And if there is something I am doing that will only fuel my desire to forget God, I'll stop doing that. Oh, there's no law that's saying, "You must, you must, you must." I want, I want, I want to please God. Therefore, if that's the case, I must adjust my life around that. You understand that?

In 1 Corinthians 9, Paul gives the illustration of self-control using an athlete. There's a perfect illustration. If Paul hadn't used it first, I would have thought of it first. It's a perfect illustration. What is an athlete? He gives up a lot of things. Why? Because he wants to. He has his eyes set upon a certain goal. He's looking for a gold medal, a certain kind of accolade, and he wants that more than a lot of things. And so he gives this up and he gives that up. It's no sacrifice. Oh, *you* might look at him and say what a sacrifice, but then you're not running the same as he is. It's no sacrifice to him. The biggest sacrifice to him would be not being allowed to run in the race.

A believer who understands who he is in Christ does not have an imposition from the outside. He has the bursting forth of the life from the inside. And because of that, he *will* make sacrifices as far as the outsiders are concerned. As far as he's concerned, he didn't even notice it.

So I'm going to watch what goes into my head. I'm going to watch what I watch. I'm going to watch what I read. Why? Not because there's a church loading me with rules and regulations. Because Christ lives in me, and I want to know Him more than anything else in life. And I want to be able to love you even as Christ loved you. So, therefore, I'm going to watch my life. Because, you see, I want to bring my life to its total fulfillment that I may be the human being God created me, and Christ redeemed me, to be. I want to fulfill my innermost self, who is Christ living in me. I want to know the meaning to life in this existential moment. I want to *live* this moment.

So, you see, there are some things that I'm not going to get involved in. But, you see, the fun of it is, I'm not obeying the law when I do that – unless you call Christ in me the law; that's okay. Self-control is response to the voice of the Spirit within. So, you see, if it was a law to keep, then I would say, "Well, I've kept all those rules, and you didn't. Hee hee hee." Immediately, despising arrogance flickers around my mouth. But, no, no, see, I'm living from Christ in me. And then, you see, it sets me completely free, because there are some things... He knows me; He knows me better than I know I'll ever know myself. And He says, "Malcolm, you can't do that." And I say, "But he's doing it and you're blessing him." He says, "None of your business. He can; you can't," because He knows *me* – and He knows you, too. So, it's okay for you, but not for me. Do you understand that? You're taken out of law; you're into the Spirit. And the Spirit says, "Don't." The Spirit says, "Do." And I learn to live from within, and He never contradicts the Scripture. Never.

But it's no sacrifice, because I have a new heart. And I make choices. It says, "The grace of God has appeared, instructing us..."[11] The Holy Spirit does not come through us like a tornado, *making* us do something. The Holy Spirit never takes away your free will. He gives it back to you. The devil stole it. Sin stole it. You got so used to being a robot – addict to this, addict to that. When Jesus comes, He sets you *free*. And that takes some getting used to sometimes. That's why new believers get into self-discipline so quickly. Because they're used to that. They're used to someone beating them around the head and saying, "Do this." They can't get used to growing up into real human adults. So that I live – I live? You mean I can do this by myself? Go on, go on. I say, "God, you do it for me. Go on, you do it for me. Send us revival. Go on, you do it." He says, "Get on and you do it. *You* make the choice." I live for the first time. I'm free. *I* make a choice. The grace of God came and instructed *me* to deny ungodliness. I didn't think I could. He says, "Go on. You can. Go on." And when I deny it, and when I say no, and I say yes to Him, I suddenly find that I have been empowered with the Holy Spirit so that I can say no to sin.

Do you get this picture? What about temptation? Guess that's another hour, really. Let me tell you this, that temptation is God's method. That's how He establishes us in the Spirit. Now, you looked at me weird. Temptation is God's method. Look, I'm going to get in a plane on Monday morning, and we're going to take off. Do you know how we take off? It's very simple. You need power, but you have to have opposition. You know that? That's why they have those windsocks on the airport. Tells you which way the wind is blowing. You know you can't take off in a vacuum? You've got to have opposition. Power plus opposition equals flight. This is God's method. He allows flesh to call me, so that I make a choice in the power of the Holy Spirit. And then I am established in the Spirit – to the point where with many temptations, you're not even tempted anymore, because He's done.

See, with the self-disciplined person, they never deal with temptation or sin. Never deal with it. They suppress it. "I mustn't do that." That's not dealing with it. That's just saying you mustn't do it. And as soon as whoever gave you the discipline is out of the way, you'll do it. You say, "You know, my teenage boy – he was such a good boy until he went to school. Then he fell apart." No he didn't. He'd fallen apart the whole time. He was just under discipline. Do you understand that? I mean, I know you thought he was a good boy. He's just like any other boy, right? He turned to his own way. But he liked you so much and he felt so sorry for you, he was going to try and be good. And as soon as you weren't there, he's going to be what he wanted to be all the time. Come on, don't look at me like that. You do the same thing when the pastor isn't watching. Off you go. When the cat's away, the mice play.

Suppress, suppress, suppress. See, good Christians aren't angry. So, I won't be angry. I *won't* be angry! *I won't be angry!* You put anger in the basement. And what does it do? It climbs up the basement window and comes back through the front door under another name. Hey, do you know the people who have the most psychological problems? Evangelicals and charismatics. Absolutely messed up in their heads, because they've suppressed and they've suppressed and they've suppressed. That's not dealing with sin. That's just pretending it isn't there.

What do we do? Temptation comes and I say, "No, no, no. I'm a disciplined man. I'm not going to sin. I'm not going to sin. I'm not going to sin." But the flesh – the flesh is so crazy. The flesh says, "You know, I'm getting tired of this. I know it was my idea, but I'm getting tired of this. I think, under the circumstances, it wouldn't be sin if you did it, you know. I've been looking in the books, and I think, under these circumstances, it's okay to do it." I'll give you about 20 times of saying no and, before you get to 21, you've justified – it's okay this time. Always.

If you say no to temptation out of self-discipline, you will fall into sin. And as soon as you've fallen into sin, flesh condemns you. "How could you have done a thing like that?" And the devil takes it up and hurls accusation against you. And you wallow in guilt and self-loathing. "My flesh isn't as bad as that. I don't know what came over me." And you wallow like that. You love penance, every one of you. You're as Catholic as the next. You love penance. Wallow in it. Wallow in it. Come to church looking miserable because I've sinned and I'm feeling it. And then, finally, when you can take your own whipping no longer, you say, "Well, maybe we could try again." And on Sunday night, "Come and give your life to Jesus." "Well, I know I did it last week, but I'll have another try." Here we go. Dedicate and rededicate and re-rededicate my dedications. "And I promise, and I'm beginning to feel good. That's right. I can do this. I can. I know I'm strong enough. I don't know what came over me last time, but this is it, mates. This is it. We're going to do it." And we feel smug. Oh, do I feel... "I made my dedication. Ha ha. He didn't; I did. I did. I know, yeah. we're going to make it this time. They're going to write a book about me. I mean, I'm going to be such a holy man. This is it." And so it goes on, and so it goes on.

Self-control is nothing like that. Nothing. Self-control begins with God, not outside pressure. Self-control is from within, and when temptation comes, I'm not surprised. If God says that my flesh is only good enough to be crucified, I'm not surprised what it comes up with or what it wants to respond to. I'm not surprised. I just say, "Lord Jesus, I know what I'm feeling right now, and it's real feeling. And there's a part of me that feels it wants to do this thing (whatever it is), but I know who I am. That's not me. That me was crucified with you on the cross. Lord Jesus, you are my life, and I am now surrendering to you that you shall live your life in me and through me at this moment." And when I thus surrender and say, "Lord Jesus, take over and live," I am empowered with all power – and love reigns. Love reigns.

And, let me tell you this. If you fail – let's suppose it. I mean, you might fall into temptation. But if you know what I'm talking about, even when you fail, you're not wiped out. Because you know He still loves you. So, when the devil condemns you, when you've fallen, you won't accept it. You say, "No, He loves me. And the blood of Jesus cleanses me from sin. And I know why I failed, you see. That's the point. I never expected me to be able to overcome this. I know I failed because I forgot to trust Jesus. So I'm back to rest again. It's okay."

You say, "But just a minute. What about... You're saying you don't want to sin. Come on, preacher," says somebody back there. "I want to sin." Yeah, I'm not upset by that either. He isn't; He knows you. Let me tell you two things very quickly. If you look in your heart and, honestly, you want to sin, number one, don't. The grace of God never, ever, ever is easy on sin. The person who says, "I'm under grace. I can sin and get away with it," no, you haven't heard the grace of God yet. Even if you find, when you do what I say – listen to your heart and you don't find there that you want holiness – still don't sin. But I'll tell you what to do. Ask of yourself, in the presence of the Holy Spirit, "How, how do I so misunderstand the meaning of life and so misunderstand what it means for you to live in me, that I should want to do this?" And that's okay. You can do that without condemnation. "'Come, let us reason together,' says the LORD."[12] If there's an area of your life where, honestly, you say, "But I find I do want to do that, and I know it's sin," number one, don't do it. For grace never allows you to do it. Number two, He loves you. He loves you, even admitting that. Acknowledge it fully, and sit down and ask yourself, in His presence, "How on earth could I so misunderstand what life is all about that I should want to do that thing which I know is sin?" And, do you know, He'll tell you? He will. And you will enter into a whole new dimension of Christian living. Instead of saying, "I won't do it. I won't do it. I know I want to. I want to, but I won't." You'll get nowhere with that. But if you say, "Lord Jesus, I really want to do that. What on earth's wrong with me? Please show me," He'll show you – without condemnation. That's exactly – and I don't have time to prove it – but that's exactly what James means when he says, "If any of you lack wisdom..."[13] That's not wisdom in general; that is wisdom in the middle of a problem. "God, I don't know what's going on inside of me." "Well, ask," He says. "Ask." And He won't get mad at you. That's what it says.

This is *living*. *This* is *living*. "He who rules his spirit is better than he who captures a city."[14] But if you don't, "like a city that is broken into and without walls is the man who has no control over his spirit."[15] If you're living by discipline, by law, you are of all believers most miserable. But if you are living by the inner control, basically doing what you want to do, because your wants are one with Christ, you'll end up loving.

What's your response? I would imagine, if your response is my response, it's relief. Because, when you think about it, what I've just said, it fits. It fits. That's how truth should be. It clicks. It fits. And there's a tremendous sense of relief. "That's right. It's right. It feels good. It feels right." It is *good* news.

Of course, I know I've upset some people. And it hurts me that I have. You're the self-disciplined people. You got graduated from West Point. Well, do me one thing – that's all. Do me one thing. Concentrate on the areas in your life that your discipline can't handle. And begin to realize that that's really what it's like all the way through. But you can't live this life, and discipline only makes it look as if you can when you really can't. And then listen to what I've just said again.

And if you're undisciplined, the grace of God does not allow you to meander through life doing your "thing." A person who understands the grace of God is not a religious hippie. If you've been undisciplined, believe me, self-control will bring your whole life into focus, and you will now have the focus to love my God and to love all I know, all he puts in my path. "And I shall do that, whatever it costs. Because that's my goal, that's my desire." And He will begin. Mind you, He will instruct you. See, law dumps the whole lot on you at once. Twenty-five rules, sign here, you're in. Grace isn't like that. He comes and He says, "Now, let's begin. Let's show you who you really are." So, to begin with, you're doing things that all the discipline people get all upset about. It's okay; grace is teaching you. And He says, "Let's deal with this. Let's deal with that. Let's deal with this." Gradually, He brings your whole life into focus. That's the grace of God.

Well, there it is. Go and live this life that the grace of God teaches you to live. Can I tell you something? It happened when I was working with some of the "Jesus People." Do you remember the Jesus People? And they came into our church. They had *long* hair. I mean boys, young guys, they had long hair. Some of them didn't wear shoes. None of them wore real shirts. I mean sweatshirts, some with Mickey Mouse on them and others with other things on them. And they came in. They were truly born again. No one really doubted that. But, then, some of the old folk in the church, you know, bless their hearts – I think some of them had seen the grace of God. The trouble is, like so many people, they'd seen the grace of God and then turned their grace into law for their kids. Do you know how that happens? You know God invades me and there's a whole bunch of stuff I don't want anymore, and I turn right around to my kids, who have not been invaded, and I say, "You can't do that." They say, "Why?" I say, "Because I don't do it." Anyway, that's another story.

So, these dear old folk, you know – and they'd seen the grace of God – and they came to me and they said, "These young men – we believe they're born again, but when are they going to get their hair cut? When are they going to start wearing shoes?" I said, "When you give me a scripture and verse for it." They pressured me. They said, "You've gotta go to them and tell them to cut their hair." I said, "No, I won't frustrate the grace of God." I went to them, all right, but not about that. I said to them, "What is the Holy Spirit saying to you about your hair? What's the Holy Spirit saying to you about your feet?" I said, "Just ask the Holy Spirit what's going on." I said, "Check back in a week. We'll talk about it." And, in a week's time, we got together, and we went around the circle. I said, "Well, what's the Holy Spirit saying?" One of the fellas said, "Nothing." The way he put it actually, he said, "I asked the Holy

Spirit, 'Do you like my hair?' and the Holy Spirit says, 'Yep.'" And I came to another one. I said, "What's the Holy Spirit saying about your hair?" He said, "I've got to cut it. And I have to put shoes on." We went around – I forget – it was something like 60 to 40 percent. Sixty percent got their hair cut. But then, when they'd said they're going to cut their hair, I said, "Now we're going back around again." I said to the one who said he had to get his hair cut, "Why did you wear long hair in the first place?" He said, "I hated society. I wanted to show society I was nothing to do with them." And he gave me the whole rebel story. Every one of the 60 percent that wanted to get their hair cut now, every one of them had been rebels against society. The 40 percent that the Holy Spirit said they could keep their hair – they wore it long because it was fashion. So, I learned something there. God goes along more or less with the latest fashion in hairstyles. But if you are wearing clothes or wearing hair or not wearing shoes to be a rebel, God is against rebellion, and He said, "Cut your hair. Put shoes on. Put an IBM business suit on, and get in there."

Do you understand why I said that? My dear church members wanted self-discipline. They said, "Everybody cut their hair. Everybody wears shoes. All look the same." The grace of God says, "No. No." God's not against modern hairstyles. God doesn't want you ladies to wear buns just because that was "in" 900 years ago. Nothing special about that. Now, He's not against modern fashions. What He's against is motives, reasons. See how quickly you can teach a new convert, just born again? "Listen to the Holy Spirit; He'll tell you." That was a risk. I had faith in them – I mean faith in the true them. And as I said last night, I have faith in you. Not faith in your flesh. That's crucified. My faith is you were crucified with Christ. But I believe in Christ in you. And I believe in Christ in you, and I *believe* in Christ in you. And I have come here tonight to call forth the true you, to awaken your faith to know who you *are* – that you might arise and shine, for your light is come. You can go out of this place, not bound by a million rules, trying to learn to walk like a centipede. But to be who you *are*, Christ spontaneously living his life in you.

Addendum Three

"Living Well in Marriage," a handout reproduced by permission of
Ed and Donna Edwards
Living Well
PO Box 720828
Oklahoma City, OK 73172
livingwellokc.org

LIVING WELL IN MARRIAGE

1. **The non-biblical way of relating in marriage** (and in all relationships).
   The Fall has affected the way we relate to others. The natural man looks to others like himself to meet his needs. Giving is based on the belief that we will get something we need from the person to whom we are giving. In marriage each spouse gives out of his own means or out of what he receives from the other.

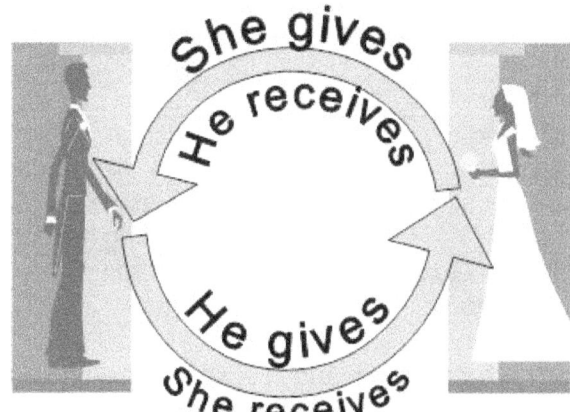

His needs:
Love
Respect
To be accepted
Importance
Safety/comfort
To be admired
Success
Sex

Her needs:
Love
Affection
To be accepted
Cherished
Security/closeness
To be wanted
Communication
Share feelings

What goes wrong:
If one partner stops giving or doesn't give in the way the other wants, then the other partner does not receive. The cycle of giving and receiving stops and the relationship is broken.

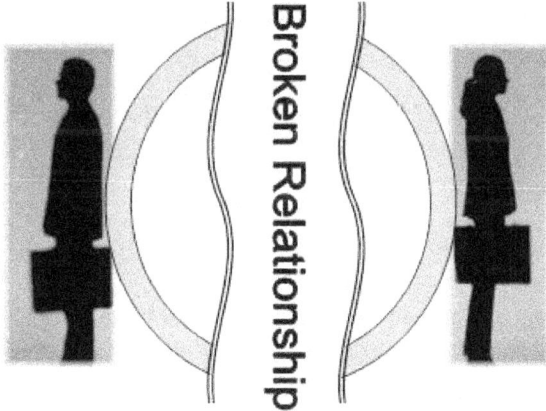

Even if the relationship resumes temporarily, eventually it will break again as long as the couple is in this cycle of giving and receiving. One day, they say "We have just grown apart," or "We live separate lives," and the marriage has died. This cycle creates isolation in marriage instead of oneness. God never intended for your spouse to be able to meet all the needs of your life; he/she is not equipped or enabled to meet your needs. When you look to your spouse to meet those needs apart from God, the person has become your god – the Bible calls that devotion "idolatry."

This cycle can be seen in any relationship but it is seen most clearly in marriage. This way of relating is centered on what we can receive from the other person. It is self-centered.

Marriage before the Fall:	Marriage after the Fall:
Made to be partners	Spouses feel alone and act separate
Wife to be an equal partner	Wife seen as less important person/role
Roles meant to complete and work together	Roles cause disagreement and strife
Needs drew them to God	Needs draw us to people or things
Differences accepted and enjoyed	Differences cause misunderstanding or emotional distance
God Himself met their needs	Control one another to get needs met
Husband a servant leader	Husband misuses his authority
Wife a helper and partner	Wife tries to control
Expressed their thoughts, feelings and desires to one another	Avoid relating to each other out of fear of being hurt or rejected
Marriage is a picture of God's relationship with His people	Pictures man's broken relationship with God

2. **Men and women are created differently.** These differences were meant to complete one another, but sin has used these differences to bring division between men and women. When we choose to ignore the Creator's plan for marriage and do things our own way, conflict results.

Woman	Man
Tries to change her husband	Resists his wife's input or opinion
Seeks security	Seeks safety
Controls by complaining, correcting or withholding affection	Controls by withdrawing, not talking to her, not providing support or protection
Wants to talk things out	Pulls away to think things over
Gives to spouse when she feels cherished	Gives to spouse when he feels needed
Self worth is built on relationships	Finds self worth through his work
She desires romance and affection	He wants his sexual needs met

3. **Giving/Receiving of the Spirit-filled Person.** God wants to use our closest relationships to make us like Him. In Ephesians 5:18-33, God commands us to be filled with His Spirit just before He teaches us about marriage. It is through the power of the Holy Spirit that we are able to give to our spouse even when they do not give to us. We give out of what we receive from God. He is to be the One who meets our needs. The Bible never says to seek another person for love or any other need, but it does say to seek God.

But God does say that we need to have relationships with other people. The need He has created in us to have a relationship with another person is the need to give. He created us to find joy and fulfillment in giving.

The proof of the principle:
Every parent loves their child beyond what they thought was possible from the moment they are born or while the child is still in the womb. The child has done nothing to meet the needs of the parent; the child has only caused physical pain and discomfort up to that point. But the love for the child is based on what the parent **gives** to the child, not what

he/she **gets**. Most parents have done much more to meet the needs of their children than the child does for the parent; yet the greater love and bond is for the child. The bond is from giving our love and meeting the needs of the child. The same can be true of marriage – the greater bond and love come from giving rather than receiving.

> **God's design:**
> God created us to receive from Him, for Him to meet all the needs of our lives.
>
> God has unconditional, unlimited, unending love for us.
>
> Our part is to receive.
>
> When you receive your love from Him, you can give in that same way to your spouse. Your giving is not dependent on what you get from him/her.

a. Marriage is a picture of Christ's relationship with the church. (Ephesians 5:31-32: *As the Scriptures say, "A man leaves his father and mother and is joined to his wife, and the two are united into one." This is a great mystery, but it is an illustration of the way Christ and the church are one. [New Living Translation]*)

   Jesus is the bridegroom, the church is the bride (Matthew 9:15, 25:1-13; John 3:29; Revelation 18:23; 21:2; 21: 9, 22:17).

b. God created us for intimacy with Him. After the Fall, our close relationship with God was broken and we began to go to other people to meet the needs of our lives instead of God.

c. The way we relate to our spouse reveals a lot about our relationship with God. Intimacy in marriage reflects intimacy with God.

d. We are to seek God for our needs. There are no verses in the Bible that say we are to seek out other people to meet the needs of our lives (Psalm 63:1-8; Psalm 84:2; Matthew 5:6; Matthew 6:33). John 4:14: *but whoever drinks of the water that I will give him shall never thirst; but the water that I will give him will become in him a well of water springing up to eternal life.* (NASB)

e. Godly relationships are based on giving rather than receiving. (Luke 6:30, 38; Acts 20:35: *And I have been a constant example of how you can help those in need by working hard. You should remember the words of the Lord Jesus: "It is more blessed to give than to receive." [New Living Translation]*).

f. God's guidelines for all relationships (including marriage) are found in the *"one another"* verses of the New Testament.

The **BIG THREE** of the "one anothers" are love one another, accept one another, forgive one another. If a couple can demonstrate these three principles in marriages, most issues are resolved. But each is shown after it has been received from God, out of the overflow of the heart. (Emphases are added to the following verses.)

- *"As I loved you, so you must **love one another**."*   John 13:34b

- *"**Accept one another**, then, just as Christ accepted you, in order to bring praise to God."* Romans 15:7

- *"**Be kind and compassionate to one another**, **forgiving each other**, just as in Christ God forgave you."*   Ephesians 4:32

g. To follow these "one another" passages, we must first receive from God; then we can give to others out of what we have received (Matthew 10:8; 1 John 4:19).

4. **Marriage is about ministry, not manipulation.** Manipulation is when we try to influence or change another person to meet our own needs or desires. God's first priority for our life and ministry is that we minister to our spouse and family. Ministry is serving the needs of others as a demonstration of God's love for them.

Manipulation	Ministry
Demanding my way	Servant/Leader or Helper
Allow emotions to control response to spouse	Express emotions to God. Ask Him to fill you with His love and care for spouse
Depend on spouse to get my needs met	Depend on God to meet my personal needs, then give freely to my spouse
Insist on my spouse doing things my way or the "right way"	Give up rights and what I expect from spouse Trust God to work in spouse
Try to change my spouse	Accept spouse because God accepts me
Try to keep spouse happy	Encourage spouse to choose right behavior by speaking the truth in love
Hold on to anger and hurt which leads to bitterness and resentment	Forgive hurtful actions and not punish spouse for the wrong done
Judge and point out spouse's failures	Affirm and encourage spouse based on who God has made him/her to be
Try to "fix" or change spouse	Pray for spouse realizing only the Holy Spirit can heal and change him/her
Build walls of self-protection	Trust Christ to protect me emotionally Risk getting hurt or being misunderstood
Speak words that shame or judge	Speak words that build up and bless
Try to get love by "doing"	"Doing" because I am loved by God

PERSONAL EXERCISE

1. What have you been seeking to receive from your spouse?

2. What needs are you hoping your spouse will fulfill in your life?

3. How can God fulfill that need in your life? What needs has He promised to meet?

4. Does God satisfy your life? Do you enjoy God? Why or why not?

5. What can you give to your spouse that you have received from God?

6. What would it look like for you to give without trying to get something in return?

7. How might this impact your spouse's life? What difference would it make in your relationship?

8. Pray and ask God to fill you with an understanding of His love, His acceptance, and His forgiveness so that you can give these freely to those around you.

9. For each of the "one another" verses below, ask the Holy Spirit to show you specific ways you can demonstrate this attitude or characteristic to your spouse (children). Example: What would it look like to show acceptance to your spouse?

10. Ask your spouse to share ways you can better express these character qualities to him/her.

11. Ask God to show you how your spouse is already showing these qualities to you.

"ONE ANOTHER" VERSES

Verses are quoted from New International Version with emphasis added.

- "As I loved you, so you must **love one another**." John 13:34b

- "My command is this: **Love each other** as I have loved you." John 15:12

- "**Be devoted** to one another in love. **Honor one another** above yourselves." Romans 12:10

- "**Accept one another,** then, just as Christ accepted you, in order to bring praise to God." Romans 15:7

- "Therefore, let us **stop passing judgment on one another**." Romans 14:13a

- "**Be kind and compassionate to one another**, **forgiving each other**, just as in Christ God forgave you." Ephesians 4:32

- "**Submit to one another** out of reverence for Christ." Ephesians 5:21

- "Bear with one another and forgive one another if any of you has a grievance against someone. **Forgive as the Lord forgave you**." Colossians 3:13

- "Therefore **encourage one another** and **build each other up** ..." I Thessalonians 5:11

- "And let us consider how we may **spur one another on toward love and good deeds**." Hebrews 10:24

- "Therefore **confess your sins to each other** and **pray for each other** so that you may be healed." James 5:16a

- "All of you, **clothe yourselves with humility** toward one another ..." I Peter 5:5b

- "**Be completely humble and gentle**; be patient, bearing with one another in love." Ephesians 4:2

Addendum Four

"Attitude of Gratitude," a transcript reproduced by permission of
Christian Life Ministries
1948 N. Plaza Dr.
Rapid City, SD 57702
605-341-5305
clmrapidcity.com

ATTITUDE OF GRATITUDE

By Bill Ewing
Transcribed from an audio recording with permission from
Christian Life Ministries
PO Box 9272
Rapid City, SD 57709

Copies of this and other messages produced by Christian Life Ministries may be ordered from
CLM: 605-341-5305
clmrapidcity.com

I think today in our life, in this period of our life, that we have an option. We have an option that can help turn around our lives, turn around the lives of those around us, and we carry within us this tool, this gift. And it's the gift of being grateful, a gift of having gratitude. The root word in the Greek is *charis*. That means to rejoice, to exhibit joy coming out of us. How in the world, in the mess sometimes we're in, can that come out, this extreme joy, this extreme rejoicing? And then what are the effects of it? Normally in the Christian life, in life itself, I believe sometimes we have either one side or the other. You are either for God or you're not. There are two types of wisdom, James says. One wisdom is from above, from God. The other is from the earth, demonic. There are no middle wisdoms. There are no middle places to be. And so sometimes you have to choose this day whom you will serve.

And the same thing works with gratitude, that you and I are either going to have an attitude and a heart of gratefulness and of receiving and of acceptance, or we're going to have a heart of rejection and of complaining and grumbling and whining and murmuring. And there are direct results that happen in our lives and in the lives of those around us because of it.

Today I hope I can at least shed some light on some principles that I think, at least in my life, were some of the most impactful principles that I learned in my life. It really had an impact in my marriage. As I go back to when God began to kind of start revealing some of these things. And I have asked Nancy in her life, I said, "Whatever made that difference where you kind of just made a turn?" and she pointed to this truth, this truth of being grateful and a truth of accepting and a truth of being able to receive things.

And how do you do it? How do you actually do it? Nobody in here gets up in the morning and says, "Today, I'm just gonna see if I can be as grumpy as I can." Now, I don't know if you ever remember the movie "Grumpy Old Men." I really thought that would have been fun to play. You get a chance to literally express some things you just feel. And yet we're going to look at some things today, and I think they'll really be enlightening.

But I want to do something. There are circumstances that come in our life, and Paul, in the book of Philippians, says there are two types of circumstances – those circumstances that we ourselves bring upon ourselves, by choices that we make that somehow have consequences to them, and they come upon us and then we experience the circumstances, the pain and circumstances that come. And Paul referred to those, but he also referred to a word that [means] there are circumstances that fall on you. You didn't do anything about it. Even a little circumstance – Tom loses his voice. He didn't get up in the morning and choose that. It came upon him, living in a fallen world. Those circumstances come on you, and the truths that we're going to talk about today, they do apply to these circumstances. But I want to gear way more importantly on something. And you hear [this] numerous times ... that God is a God of relationships. And I believe if the principle that we see and the truths that we hear are not applied to relationships, we miss so much, because it says, "I have passed from life to death because I have not loved the brethren" (speaker's paraphrase, derived from 1 John 3:14).

But there's something about relationships that makes life all worth it. And so, I'm going to try to focus mostly here with this heart and this spirit of gratitude and rejoicing and receiving as it relates to relationships. We're going to use a few examples. I'll use a few from my life, but we'll use a few examples that have totally, totally reflected and exposed these truths.

Now, God says that we can have two different types, and there are contrasting types [of responses]. He says, "A joyful heart makes a cheerful face," but when the heart is sad, the spirit is also broken. And that's Proverbs 15:13. Also Proverbs 15:15: "All the days of the afflicted seem discouraging, but a cheerful heart has a continual feast" (speaker's paraphrase). Proverbs 15:30: "Bright eyes gladden the heart" (NASB). And, as a matter of fact, it puts health on your bones (Proverbs 15:30b). "A joyful heart is good medicine, but a complaining spirit dries up your bones." (Proverbs 17:22, speaker's paraphrase). It dries up your bones!

And you say, well, sometimes what do we have to be grateful for? What do we have to be thankful for? The people in my life seem to be causing more pain than anything. And I'm going to challenge you – and me. I always do this on the way up here. I've prepared. I've looked at all the different Scriptures. I've tried to apply them, but on the way up here, I said, "Okay, before I walk out here, to whom in my life do I need to apply this – at least begin the application of this – before I get up here and talk to you?" And there's always somebody that comes to mind. And so, we're going to look at some of these.

Now, I'd like to start with a story. I am not going to go into a whole bunch of depth with this story. I'm going to challenge you to go back and, just for yourself, get in the Scriptures and read in the Old Testament. I want to start with a relationship – with Jonathan and David. Now, we read the story and sometimes when you read stories that you have heard and heard and heard so many times before, you miss the emotions of it. You miss the being there and the presence of it, because we always look from the whole picture. But you've got to take a look at this. Here is Saul, the king, and the rightful owner to be king after him is his son Jonathan. This is how it always worked. And so, Jonathan would be rightful king. Everybody would assume he would become the rightful king, but what happens is God comes and anoints this absolute, off-the-charts shepherd boy, David, who according to even his own dad, didn't qualify. He didn't even list him when he was told that "your son will be one of the ones that will take over the throne." The dad lists his sons, and Samuel says, "Is that it?" And he goes, "Yeah, I forgot. Another one is out there in the woods."

Now, what I'm wanting you to see is mostly Jonathan's response. Now, David also begins to apply this principle or this truth or this receiving, grateful heart, but I want you to look at Jonathan. Jonathan has the opportunity to apply what this psalmist says in Psalm 109:17-19. Because grumbling and complaining and murmuring were on their lips continually, then the grumbling and complaining effects began to seep into their body like oil running over their body. As a matter of fact, it says they even wore a belt, and the belt, literally, was "complainer," "whiner," "curser." Cursing was their garment. Because they felt things were not fair. This relationship was not fair. This person you gave me in my life is not fair. It's not what I bargained for. So, there was a murmuring. Jonathan had all the right in the world to do this. But instead, he took a grateful heart, a grateful attitude, one that was continually seeing something different that we cannot see with our own naked eyes. And he began to be grateful and thankful and received David as absolutely sent to him by God, being perfectly suited for him from God. And in doing so, numerous things began to happen in his life and also in David's life.

I'm going to challenge you today that there's going to be one of three places that I'm going to ask you to learn to have a grateful attitude during this season. It moves right in to the holidays. It moves into the Advent, where we're going to be celebrating different things. But you're going to have an opportunity where you sit today in one of three areas that you can say, "Okay, here's where I need to make application of this. I need to begin to apply this to my life – having an attitude of joy."

You know, it's interesting in the Proverbs I read to you, when I went back and looked at the Hebrew words – and I'm just saying this is what I saw. When it said it gladdens the heart, it makes a joyful face, literally what it said is the physical components of your face change. Have you ever been around people that just are giddy; they smile most of the time? And all of a sudden, they look good. They actually look handsome. They look pretty. And then you have people that just frown all the time, and it makes you kind of want to avoid those people. It is amazing – there are lots of times I have said this and probably said it to some of you – when I see people that just carry a smile, I say, "That smile just looks good on you." It does, and it's not fabricated. It actually is real.

And so, when you see Jonathan, you see that Jonathan begins to embrace David. He receives David. He receives with gratitude this person that takes the position that he was supposed to have as king, does not doubt it, but begins to receive it. Now, I want you to understand something as we go on, because this is impossible for us to do. He does not necessarily receive David on David's abilities. He receives David on God's ability.

Come with me way back to the Garden. And we go back to the Garden with Adam. Now, you've got to remember, in the Garden, Adam thought things were really already cool. He was walking in the daily experience with God. God not only walked with him, but inhabited him. He was what the Bible calls "complete." He was whole. And things were all right. I mean he was there to see some of the magnificent miracles that God did in creating things and producing fruit. And whatever it was that Adam had, it just alluded to us that things were just pretty darned good.

And God comes to Adam and says, "Adam, it's just not good that you're alone." Now, first of all, you've got to understand, Adam didn't even know what that meant. He had no idea what He was talking about. And God in his love for Adam, said, "Adam, I'm going to give you an assignment. I want you to go out, and I've empowered you to be able to gather every animal and name every animal that's out here." And in the process of naming every animal out there, do you know what it says? It says he found that, basically, he did not have a partner. He now was made aware of his being alone. And so, God takes him, cuts from him, a woman – basically called "soft man" – and brings her to him and presents her to him, and his response was one of gratitude and receiving, of "Wow, wow! The rest of me. The completer of me!"

Now hold on a minute. I'm sure she looked pretty darned good, but he did not receive Eve on the basis of who Eve was. He had never seen an Eve. He didn't have anything to compare with. He received her and was grateful for her and had a spirit of gratefulness because of who God was. He knew God, and he knew that God had brought him something, so on the basis of who God was, he received. This is also what Jonathan did. Jonathan did not know much about David in this way. He basically received this new next king as from God. He did not look at David's weaknesses and his faults. He looked at

God and said, "The perfect man for the job," because he has been anointed by Samuel to be the king. And Jonathan totally began to become grateful.

Now, I give you that background, because I want to read some Scriptures here, and then I want to give you at least some things that I have seen in my own personal life and in the lives of others and what I've seen the Scriptures say about what actually happens when you begin to develop a grateful attitude and what happens, not only in your life, but in the life of the person that you are expressing that gratefulness for. There are two huge effects that I believe are absolutely unexplainable when we apply that grateful heart, that receiving heart – because you either receive or you reject; there's no in between.

Yesterday I was driving downtown and I saw an old, old man, and he had difficulty walking, and I looked over and his gait was a little bit familiar. And I looked and I realized this was an old, old teacher of mine. It dated me after I saw how old he was. But I remember I was thinking of this message, and I said, "You know, the interesting thing – I do not know anything about this person's spiritual life, but this was one teacher in my life that literally accepted me as I was." And because of that, I looked forward to being in that class. I remember going to that class, always eager to be there. I think the best of me came out, because I was received. And I've also been in places where I have been rejected, and in that rejection, I didn't want to be in the presence of the person rejecting me. And I think it stifled me in so many different ways.

But here's principle one: When we are grateful and we accept – accept and receive totally this person – I believe we liberate that person that you're receiving to become all that they were intended to be in relationship to you. Now, I am *not* saying that you limit that person and that you and I have the ability of limiting that person from growing in faith. God and that person have that. You don't have that kind of power. But it liberates them to be, in relationship with you, all that that they were intended to be. This happened with Jonathan and David. David began to be to Jonathan and Jonathan began to be to David more than you can ever imagine. It says more than even a lover. They began to free them. And the more that that begins to take place, that person becomes free. And the more they become free, all of a sudden, you're seeing that they're freed up and now they're liberated, and they're no longer bound.

A personal example that happened in my life a long, long time ago is I grew up with a dad – he's since passed away. When my dad died, my dad was probably one of my best friends on this planet. But I grew up in kind of a tough time, because my dad was an alcoholic. And he wasn't the alcoholic that sometimes would get drunk and then fall asleep. He was the alcoholic that would be drunk most of the days of his life. And I was always trying to do something of going and finding where he was in a bar and trying to get him in the car to bring him home before something would happen. Whether that was wrong or right, I just don't ask the questions anymore. But then, as we grew older, and he began to have a little bit more control there, there was just always a spirit of rejection that I had towards my dad because of his drinking problem. And these truths began to be unfolded in my life. And I thought, you know what, let's give it a try here.

And so, I began to take the verses that had been laid out here. And it says, "Receive ye one another in the same manner that Christ Jesus has also received you" (Romans 15:7, speaker's paraphrase). And I remember saying, "God, where was I when you received me? Where was I?" *Therefore, accept, receive one another, just as Christ has received you.* And I said, "You know what, I was more than an alcoholic before you. I was a rebel against you. I absolutely lived isolated from you, and you embraced me. You received me. Everything about me, you took into yourself." And you said, "Now receive ye one another." I'm going to try, I'm going to apply this to my dad, and I said, "I'm going to receive my father in the same manner that God received me, and I'm going to start being grateful for him." I am not saying that his drinking and alcoholism were fine. I'm saying that I needed to receive. This was what I had on my plate. This is the father that I had, and I said, "I can either reject him, which I've been doing, or I can receive him as a perfect, perfect father to me and what is needed in my life."

And when I began to be grateful and thankful – the moment I would start to be that way – something would unfold, and I would start to see neater things about my dad that I had missed, just lots of things. Those that knew him pretty well knew he was fun to be around. He had a great sense of humor. He was witty. He was clever. I had missed all of that by being rejecting and being ungrateful. But the more I began to be grateful, the more I began to see I freed him to be to me the father that he could be to me. I'm not talking about the drinking, but the father.

I remember my sister called me one time before she moved back here, and she was somewhat leery of coming back because Dad was here. And she asked me about it, and I said, "Man, he's become my best friend. It's incredible what I'm beginning to see in him." And she goes, "Well, when did he change?" And I said, "You know what, I'm not sure he did." I believe that as God gave me this truth of having a grateful heart and a grateful spirit, I believe that I'd now freed him, unlocked him to let him be and flow into my life all that a father could be for me, and I began to be freed, but I set him free to become [a father] to me. And I would say he would probably have told you I was one of his best friends.

But not only does being grateful allow that person to be set free, the second thing that I think it does is, as I receive and I embrace and I become grateful – grateful in my heart towards that person – it also begins to change things in my life that I have attempted to change most of my life. But now as I begin to receive them, I now begin to change. Let me stretch this into the present.

I don't know if my wife's here, so I can go ahead and be free here too! I've had an issue my whole life, and I've explained it away – and I've always had verses to explain everything away with my wife, which has never gone over well ever. I am very careful and I'm very good at being in the right place at the right time. If you ask me to be there, and it's just me, I will be there a little early or I will be there at the time. I can get timing pretty much down to an art. I know how long it takes to get to somebody, and I'm usually pulling up on time. Not my wife. Matter of fact, my wife will be late for her funeral. She'll come late. And I have tried to change her every way possible. I've even told her how rude it is and how unpolite and how disrespectful it is, and it has helped zero in 44 years.

And I'm still in the process, but I can either reject her for that behavior – and I'm not saying the behavior is right or wrong; that's between her and God – or I can just begin to embrace her. This is the woman that I have, and if I'll just start to receive her and quit trying to change her where she's constantly being told, with verses being misused and spiritual abuse thrown on her, and just receive her, and maybe even say, "Hon, is there anything I can do to help you get ready," rather than be in the car, revving it up. And the more I began to do that, the more relaxed she gets, the more I get to see kind of who she is designed to be for me. That woman can absolutely, absolutely blow me away of how God knew what I needed. I'm seeing things about her I never, ever, ever saw when I said "Yes" at the altar.

But here's one of the things it's slowly doing. Now, please, don't hear something I'm not saying. I also have a sin of relational idolatry. I like people to think well of me. That's okay to like it, but sometimes I *need* it. I'm a people-pleaser, and I don't want people to be displeased. So, as I'm going along and George invites me and Carol invites me to their house, I don't want to show up late and have them be disappointed in me. So, I'm on time, a lot of time not because I'm so thinking of the other people, but I'm on time because I don't want you thinking poorly of me. Put that together with Nancy. And so, I end up late at many events. I learned over in Europe, when you go over to Europe, they're not so anal about this thing. They say, "You want to get together?" "Yeah, let's get together Wednesday morning." That means Wednesday morning. *We* get together – "Well, let's get together at 7:51 and 13 seconds" over here because we've got to be in a hurry. You see, I have tried numerous times to let it be okay that somebody thinks poorly of me, as long as God doesn't. And I try and I fail and I try, and it seems that your opinions sometimes mean more than what God's opinion is. And even though I'll take Ephesians 6:6 and say, "Not by way of eye-service, rendering service unto men, but rendering service unto the Lord" (Ephesians 6:6-7, speaker's paraphrase), for God alone is my audience. Even though I try that, it just doesn't seem to work, and I try to change it. I've got to be there on time. But being married to Nancy and accepting her and receiving her and being grateful for who she is and her little idiosyncrasies that she has, has made me able to get to a place where I have no choice but to say, "God, you're the one that matters."

It is effective in people's life. It's effective in others. It frees those people to become everything they're meant to be to you. And the Scripture says that everything created by God is good. Nothing is to be rejected. It's always to be received with gratitude. "Owe nothing to anyone except to love one another; for he who loves his neighbor is fulfilling the entire law" (Romans 13:8, speaker's paraphrase). For love does no wrong to anyone. And I love this – it says, "Every good thing given and every perfect gift is from above, coming down from the Father of lights, with whom there is no variation or shifting shadow" (James 1:17, NASB). And that basically means this, that everything in your life, every person in your life – your boss, your children, your parents, your spouse, your brothers, your siblings, your church members, your parishioners, your pastors, your preachers, your musicians – those are all perfect gifts that came down from God for the very purpose to do a work in your life. You can reject and complain and murmur and gripe about them and get in your circles and gripe, or you can say, "God, how about we, at this season, start developing a spirit of gratefulness and let me begin to receive who you have placed in my life. And let's let it have its full effect in my life." And I promise you, you will not be disappointed. It will transform your relationships. It will free that person to become to you all that you desire.

Tom's here. Tom's the one up here, the musician that didn't have a voice today. Tom knows this story, so I think I have freedom [to tell it]. When I first came to faith, I was obnoxious, to say the least. I tried to share Christ with anybody that moved. And I didn't do it in a really gentle way. Tom says – and I don't believe this – that I took a match, lit it, and burned his arm and said, "That's how hell will feel." I think he's delusional. [In the background, Tom says, "That was a true story!"] Okay. He says it's true. But in the meanwhile, that I'm growing in my faith one way, and Tom is headed in the other direction. He's hair-ing out. He's kind of using drugs. He's playing music. He thinks he's from Europe. And the more that he was living like that, I began to be irritated with him. And I had to live next door to him. I would just look at him and say, "Oh, that guy just bugs me!" And I was developing almost a hatred. Because I was either receiving Tom or I was rejecting him. And at that time, he was being rejected, and he was experiencing that rejection.

But something began to happen, and God began to show me something. And the more that I began embracing Tom, that this is a neighbor that I have and this is a person you've placed in my life, and as we began to see that unfold, I can say today that that person has had great impact in my life as I began to be grateful for him, receiving him. When I stopped trying to change him and began to receive him – "This is Tom, and he's perfect for me in our relationship" – it is amazing. I think in his life, he would say it has freed him to be himself around me, never feeling judged. It freed him, and the things that I would have changed about him God has used to make a difference in my life. And now I can say he is one of my best friends on this planet. That happened in this principle of applying a grateful spirit, a grateful, receiving spirit, rather than a rejecting, complaining spirit.

In Psalm 109, it said because they loved cursing, because they loved complaining, because they loved murmuring, the murmuring and the cursing began to come upon them to where that person began to be a curse. And blessing was far from them because they wouldn't bless with their tongue and they wouldn't bless with their heart. So, I'm challenging you in three areas of your life.

You've got one of three areas that I encourage you to apply this grateful spirit principle. Number one is that we have to begin first by doing this: That Jesus died for you and you have a chance to either reject what he did or you have a chance to receive what he did. And the receiving means to take fully into yourself that which was done for you. And if you will receive that, you have the right now to become children of God (John 1:12). So, you have, first of all, to settle that issue. Have I accepted and received, and am I grateful for Jesus Christ, and have I embraced him into my life? And if so, then the living God comes and inhabits your life, and you begin to be whole. And I promise you this, what he can do for you is off this planet. You will absolutely be marveling. The Scripture says, "I will create a wonder in you that will never, ever be satisfied." (Exodus 34:10, speaker's paraphrase). It's a wonder, a marvel. God says all things have been created for you to see, things we have no idea are out there. That's one.

Here's number two: If you've made that decision, then something happened to you and me. We have been crucified with Christ. We have been nailed to the cross with him. We have been buried with him. And that old man – it says "consider him dead" – but many of you will not receive that person who you are, and you need to embrace what God did when he transformed you into this new creation, made beautiful after the righteousness of God (Romans 6:11; Ephesians 4:24). Many of you have never received you. You've rejected yourself because of your own little idiosyncrasies. You look in the mirror and you're trying always to complain and murmur about yourself. Maybe you need to apply this grateful attitude toward yourself. And sometimes it's good to just stand in front of the mirror and say, "God, I am grateful for that person you've made me to be – with all of its little quirks." I sometimes – rarely – will listen to myself after I've talked, because I have a hard time listening to myself. Sometimes I have to listen to myself and say, "Hang in there. Receive that's who you are. Well, I don't know, but I wish I'd presented it differently. I wish I was more like this person." And I need to receive me. Because if I don't receive me, I will not be grateful for or receive you.

And then the third thing in closing today is this: Somebody in your life you are rejecting. You have not been grateful. You've been more complaining and grumbling and whining about somebody in your life. And I would ask you to do this: Put that person on the altar and say, "God, this is what I've done. I agree with you that I have not received them as your perfect gift into my life. I have rejected them, and I have been trying to change them for a long time." Put them up there and say, "God, let's give this a shot." And if you'll to that, you're going to see something amazing happen.

In closing, this is an illustration that just drives me crazy. I used to play baseball, and something that just irritated me – you've probably been one of the irritators if you've been at a game – and the pitcher's out there pitching and he's having a hard time throwing strikes. So, what do we yell at him?

"Throw strikes!" You think the guy's not trying to do that? "I never thought of that, to throw a strike. I've walked the last three, not even thinking I should have thrown a strike." Unbelievable. Or this: "Be happy!" "Oh, no, I just think I don't want to do that. I'm just gonna give it a shot now." We tell people all these things. "Well, stop worrying." If you're worrying about something, let me just tell you, "Stop worrying!" How well does that work? It doesn't. There are some things that make it possible to make it happen. If you want to say something wise to the pitcher, go out to the pitcher and say, "Hey, your stride is way too deep and that's what makes the ball go up. Shorten your stride a little bit, and I think you'll be able to bring the ball down," and that's a little more effective.

There are three things that I think are absolutely essential for you to be able to *apply* what I've talked about, and if you don't understand these things, you won't apply it. You'll just have heard this message, it sounded good, but you won't be able to do it. Number one is that this is about a relationship between you and God. If you don't know God as loving – that his loving kindness is filled with mercy – you won't be able to apply this message. And secondly, if you don't know that God is sovereign; that is, he didn't get shocked about who your parents were, he didn't get shocked when out of the womb came somebody and so he said, "Oh my, that person wasn't supposed to go to that home!" If you don't understand that God's sovereign, you won't be able to apply this message. He's in control. He's in absolute control. All the people in your life, he knows about them and he's in control, he's sovereignly controlling, and he's a loving God.

And then the third thing is: You and I were never made for this earth. We have another land that we're going to, and this may be all about that next kingdom and that other land. And if you can embrace those three things, you will be able to then move on in to have a grateful spirit for every person that comes into your life. And you will set people free around you. And when you do that, you become attractive in every way – your face changes, your body changes, your health changes.

Pray with me. Father, you already demonstrated this perfectly to us. You received us and we were a mess. There were so many things you could have changed about us, and you just took us as we were. And I pray that we would be able to do the exact same thing in other people's lives. And we're going to trust you to make that possible. Amen.

Addendum Five
Answer Keys

Chapter 3: Homework

1. Fill in the blanks in the following study of New Testament verses regarding the Person and work of the Holy Spirit.

    a. Romans 5:5 — *God's love is poured out into our hearts by the Spirit.*

    b. Romans 8:6 — *A mind controlled by the Spirit is filled with life and peace.*

    c. Romans 8:11 — *The Spirit lives in those who are in Christ and gives eternal life to their bodies.*

    d. Romans 8:15-16 & Galatians 4:6 — *The Spirit convinces us that we are children of God.*

    e. Romans 8:26 — *The Spirit helps us pray.*

    f. 1 Corinthians 3:16 & Ephesians 2:22 — *The Spirit dwells in the midst of his people.*

    g. 1 Corinthians 6:19 — *You are a dwelling place of the Spirit.*

    h. 1 Corinthians 12:4, 11 — *The Spirit distributes different kinds of gifts to believers in Christ.*

    i. 2 Corinthians 1:22 & Ephesians 1:13-14 — *The Spirit is a "down payment," assuring our eternal future.*

    j. 2 Corinthians 3:17 — *Where the Spirit is, there is freedom.*

    k. Galatians 5:16 — *If we live by the power of the Spirit, we will not act in fleshly ways.*

    l. Galatians 5:22-23 — *The Spirit produces "fruit" in and through us.*

    m. Ephesians 3:16 — *Believers are strengthened by the power of the Spirit, who is within them.*

    n. Ephesians 6:17 — *The Scriptures are the sword the Spirit wields against the devil.*

    o. Philippians 3:3 — *Believers serve (or worship) God by the power of the Spirit.*

    p. 1 Thessalonians 1:6 — *The Spirit gives joy to believers even in the midst of "severe suffering."*

    q. 2 Thessalonians 2:13 — *The Spirit saves and sanctifies believers.*

    r. 2 Timothy 1:14 — *The Spirit enables us to continue in the faith.*

    s. Titus 3:5 — *The Spirit saved us through the washing of rebirth and inner renewal.*

2. Read John 14:16-20 & 26-27 and 16:13-15 and write out who the Holy Spirit is to you as a believer.

    Example answer: *The Holy Spirit is my advocate and helper, who lives in me and is actually Christ living in me. The Spirit teaches me all I need to know and reminds me of what Jesus has said. He provides me with peace and calms my fear and troubled thoughts. The Spirit is guiding me into the truth of God and tells me what God says and what doesn't line up with what God says (in Scripture). The Spirit told the Apostles what to write in the New Testament. He glorifies Jesus and makes known to me the glory and truth of Jesus.*

Chapter 11: Homework

Freedom from…

Acts 13:39; Romans 6:6-7, 14, 17, 22 — sin and slavery to sin

Romans 8:1; Colossians 1:22 — condemnation and accusation

Romans 6:23; Colossians 1:14; 1 Thessalonians 1:10 — the penalty of sin (death)

John 8:12; Ephesians 5:8; Colossians 1:13 — darkness

Galatians 5:13-16, 24 — bondage of the flesh

John 14:1-3; Romans 8:2; Hebrews 2:14-15 — fear of death

Romans 7:6, Galatians 3:13, 23-25 — the law

2 Peter 1:4 — the corruption of this world

2 Corinthians 2:11; 10:4-5 — the schemes of the devil

1 Thessalonians 5:9 — God's wrath

Freedom to…

Jeremiah 31:34 — know God

John 1:12; Romans 8:15-16; Galatians 4:6-7 — be God's child

John 14:15; 1 John 5:3 — obey God

Galatians 2:20; Ephesians 2:8 — live by faith

Romans 6:22; Titus 2:11-12 — live a godly life

2 Corinthians 5:21; Ephesians 4:24 — be righteous and holy

2 Corinthians 3:18 — become more and more like God

John 14:16-20, 1 Corinthians 6:19 — be a dwelling place of the Holy Spirit

Ephesians 3:12; Hebrews 4:14-16 — confidently approach God

Ephesians 1:11-12, 2:10 — live according to the purpose for which you were created

John 3:16; 1 John 2:25 — enjoy eternity with your good and loving Creator

Addendum Six
Facilitator's Guide

FACILITATOR'S GUIDE

NOTE: This guide is designed to be used by absolutely anyone. Facilitating group meetings of people who are all reading this book at the same time does not require that you've read this book ahead of time or have any particular level of biblical knowledge.

If you have already read this book and want to facilitate a group study, you may want to hold an **"Interest and Information Meeting,"** to spark interest and weed out those who are not interested in this sort of book. In addition to giving your own review of the book, it is suggested you go over: (1) the information presented on the book's back cover, (2) the chapter titles, and (3) the main points from pages 1-7. It's best to keep the presentation portion of the meeting to about 30 minutes and allow about 30 minutes for audience questions, some of which you may not be able to answer, which is perfectly fine.

First Meeting – Everyone has a book, but not everyone has started reading it yet

- Open the meeting with prayer. (Pray out loud for God's guidance in all that takes place during the meeting.)
- Starting with you, have each group member briefly introduce him/herself by giving the following information:
  - Name
  - The two to five most important people in his or her life
  - One thing he or she wishes others knew about him/her right off the bat rather than finding out by becoming better acquainted over time
- Discuss the format for each of the subsequent meetings, as follows:
  - Facilitator opens the meeting with prayer
  - Brief discussion of those parts of the assigned chapter that stood out to group members
  - Discussion of the assigned chapter's Reflection questions
  - Discussion of the assigned chapter's Homework Follow-up questions
  - Review the assignment to complete prior to the next group meeting: Read the next chapter, completing the Reflection questions, Homework, and Homework Follow-up questions in that chapter.
  - Close with conversational prayer. (No one has to pray out loud. Eventually the facilitator closes the prayer time.)
- Read out loud the "Small Group Guidelines" on page 7.
- Engage in group discussion by having each participant, starting with you, tell what he or she hopes will be the benefits of going through this book.
- After discussing that question, go over with the group what needs to be completed before you meet again:
  - Read pages 1 through 17.
  - Do the Homework that is provided on the bottom of page 15 through the top of page 16.
  - Complete the Homework Follow-up questions on page 16.
- Close with conversational prayer, explaining that no one has to pray out loud and that you will eventually close the prayer time.

Second Meeting – Discussion of Chapter 1

- Open the meeting with prayer.
- Starting with you, have each group member briefly state those parts of the reading assignment that stood out to him/her.
- Starting with you, have each group member answer the Reflection questions on page 14. Explain that no one has to answer any given question but everyone is encouraged to do so. Every person who desires to answer reflection question #1 should do so before you move on to discussing reflection question #2, etc.
- Starting with you, have each group member answer the Homework Follow-up questions provided on page 16. (Have all the participants who want to answer a question do so before going on to the next question.)
- Go over the assignment for the week, as follows: Read Chapter 2, completing the Reflection questions, Homework, and Homework Follow-up questions in that chapter.
- End the meeting with conversational prayer.

Third through Thirteenth Meetings – Discussion of each week's assigned chapter

- Open the meeting with prayer.
- Starting with you, have each group member briefly discuss those parts of the reading assignment that stood out to him/her.
- Starting with you, have each group member answer each of the Reflection questions provided in the chapter that was read during the week. Have everyone who would like to do so answer one question before moving on to each person answering the second question.
- Starting with you, have each group member answer the Homework Follow-up questions provided in the chapter that was read during the week.
- Go over the assignment for the week, as follows: Read the next chapter, completing the Reflection questions, Homework, and Homework Follow-up questions in that chapter.
- End the meeting with conversational prayer.

Acknowledgments

In the 1960's, Jim Craddock, an area director for Campus Crusade for Christ, was challenged by Christian psychologist Henry Brandt to explore the Scriptures for answers to the many problems Jim was observing in the family lives of fellow believers. Jim's dedicated and intense study of the Bible led him to establish Scope Ministries International, which offered to countless people insights and discipleship leading to Christ-centered emotional healing. (Although Scope is no more, the legacy of Jim Craddock is carried on by his wife Doris and daughter Christi Taylor through His Truth Transforms International.)

I was one of the broken people who sought counsel at Scope Ministries, and my experience there resulted in such transformation that I decided to join Scope's staff so that I could participate in extending to others the freedom I had found in Christ. Many of the concepts presented in this book are inspired by the writings and teaching of Jim Craddock and others on Scope's staff, such as Doris Craddock, Terry Coy, Steve Johnson, Judi Boyer, Marci Maddux, Donna Edwards, Richard Patzke, and Dub Rogers. This book exists because they were faithful in diligent Christian service and because Scope offered an environment in which I could minister to women in the context of small groups. I took that experience with me when I moved to Kansas City in 1996 and continued teaching, speaking, and conducting small groups for Christians who wanted to experience more fully the freedom they already had in Christ.

In 2008, *The Weight of Grace: Experience the Freedom from Overeating You Already Have* was published. That "big pink book" was very obviously addressed to women with a particular set of struggles. Over the last several years, I occasionally heard from ministry leaders who conducted Weight of Grace small groups and readers of *The Weight of Grace*, asking if I had materials that presented the concepts covered in that book but applicable to struggles other than just overeating and dieting. After prayerful consideration and relief from some vocational and family obligations, I reworked and added to *The Weight of Grace* with a wider audience in mind, resulting in *Experience the Freedom You Already Have in Christ*.

I would like to sincerely thank my many cheerleaders during the writing of this book, especially my husband. Mike has been my greatest supporter and biggest fan. I cannot thank him enough for his unwavering encouragement and unconditional love. Also, many thanks to Penny McAdams of Shepherd's Call, editor Sharon Smith, and dear friends Judi Boyer, Cymantha Brooke, Robin and Karen Noad, Brenda Robinson, Bethany Risher, Cheryl Thiesfeld, and Michelle Smith, who have all provided great feedback, encouragement, and prayer support.

I would also like to express my deep appreciation to all the women and men who have so honestly and bravely shared their struggles and victories with one another in small groups and with me in one-on-one discipleship meetings over the past 35 years.

Of course, my greatest thanks go to the Lord Jesus Christ, who has extended to me the grace and mercy that not only enabled me to overcome many years of torment from painful emotions and shame-filled behaviors, but also continually provided inspiration and affirmations that kept me on track through the process of writing *Experience the Freedom*. And I know that it will only be through Christ's ministry in each reader's life that any of the information presented in this book will have a meaningful impact.

NOTES

Will *You* Benefit from Reading this Book?

1. "Do You Know Your ABC's?" is not original to me; however, the authors asked that they not be credited. I have adapted the original slightly in order to fit the context of this book.

Chapter 1: Freedom from What ... and How?

1. John Newton, Chris Tomlin, and Louie Giglio, "Amazing Grace (My Chains Are Gone)" (Brentwood, TN: Capitol CMG Publishing), 2006.
2. John 8:32.
3. Question posed to me by a reviewer of my previous book. He didn't get it. I was FREE!
4. Lawrence O. Richards, *Expository Dictionary of Bible Words* (Grand Rapids, MI: Zondervan Publishing House, 1985), 185.
5. Colin Brown, Ed., *Dictionary of New Testament Theology*, Vol. 3 (Grand Rapids, MI: Zondervan Publishing House, 1975), 822.
6. This exercise is based on "Age Span Sheets," a handout created by Scope Ministries International.
7. Adelaide A. Pollard, "Have Thine Own Way, Lord" (Public Domain), 1906.

Chapter 2: Freeing Truth about God the Father and God the Son

1. Leland Hayward, Oscar Hammerstein, II, and Richard Rodgers, "Do-Re-Mi" (New York: Williamson Music, Inc.), 1959.
2. Genesis 1:1.
3. John 1:1.
4. 1980 confession of a friend.
5. Gerhard Kittel and Gerhard Friedrich, Eds., *Theological Dictionary of the New Testament Abridged in One Volume by Georffrey W. Bromley* (Grand Rapids, MI: William B. Eerdmans Publishing Company, 1985), 2.
6. Jim Craddock and Christi Craddock Taylor, *FatherCare* (Oklahoma City: His Truth Transforms International, 1993), 55.

Chapter 3: Freeing Truth about God the Spirit

1. B. B. McKinney, "Holy Spirit, Breathe on Me" (Brentwood, TN: Broadman Press c/o Music Services), 1965.
2. John 14:16-17.
3. Comment of a prayer group participant in approximately 2001.

Chapter 4: Freeing Truth about Who You've Become and Why You Still Sin Anyway

1. John Newton, "Amazing Grace," 1779.
2. Ephesians 2:4-5.
3. Pronouncement by my pastor in 1973.
4. Bill Gillham, *Lifetime Guarantee* (Eugene, OR: Harvest House Publishers, 1993), 97.

5. Matthew S. Harmon, "What Does Saint Mean?" Grace Theological Seminary, December 21, 2021, https://seminary.grace.edu/what-does-saint-mean/#:~:text=In%20its%20most%20basic%20sense, Jesus%20Christ%20is%20a%20saint.
6. Scope Ministries International, Inc. *Pneumanetics* (Oklahoma City: Scope Ministries International, Inc., 1992), 5-6.
7. Bill Gillham, 21.
8. Ibid.
9. Judi Boyer, "The Flesh," email message to author, March 6, 2024.
10. Jim Craddock, "Becoming Who You Already Are," a one-page handout reprinted by permission of His Truth Transforms International, Oklahoma City, OK.
11. Bill Bright, "Would You Like to Know God Personally?" (Orlando, FL: New Life Publications, 1968), 12.

Chapter 5: Freeing Truth about How Your Beliefs Motivate Your Behavior

1. Paul Anka, Frank Sinatra, C. Francois, and Revaux, "My Way" (1967). *Vocal Popular Sheet Music Collection.* Score 3598. https://digitalcommons.library.umaine.edu/mmb-vp-copyright/3598.
2. Proverbs 14:12, ESV.
3. Small group member regarding why she continued to eat and eat even though she felt overly full.
4. This example is borrowed, with permission, from: Scope Ministries International, Inc. *Pneumanetics* (Oklahoma City: Scope Ministries International, Inc., 1992), 6-6.
5. Lawrence O. Richards, 185.
6. Scope Ministries International, Inc., *Pneumanetics* (Oklahoma City: Scope Ministries International, Inc., 1992), 6-7.
7. David Baker, "Love is Something You Do" (Waco, TX: Word Records), 1970.
8. Scope Ministries International, Inc., *Pneumanetics*, 9-7.

Chapter 6: Freeing Truth about Your Emotions

1. Morris Albert and Louis Gaste, "Feelings" (Lyrics © Editora e Importadora Musical Fermata do Brasil Ltda., Peermusic Publishing), 1975.
2. Psalm 77:2a.
3. What I always said when I was binge-eating and my roommate asked me if I was upset about something.
4. Aspects of this chapter are adapted, with permission, from "Emotions," Session 7 of *Pneumanetics* (Oklahoma City: Scope Ministries International, Inc., 1992), 7-9 – 7-14.
5. Colin Brown, Ed. *Dictionary of New Testament Theology*, Vol. I (Grand Rapids, MI: Zondervan Publishing House, 1975), 111.
6. Scope Ministries International, Inc. *Pneumanetics* (Oklahoma City: Scope Ministries International, Inc., 1992), 7-11.
7. An excellent aid is the poster, "How Are You Feeling Today?" It is available from Creative Therapy Associates, Inc., 800-448-9145 or www.ctherapy.com.
8. Handout originally published by Scope Ministries International, Inc. Contact His Truth Transforms for permission to reproduce: 405-603-2020.

Chapter 7: Freeing Truth about Some Specific, Especially Troubling Emotions

1. Bill Berry, Peter Buck, Mike Mills, and Michael Stipe, "Everybody Hurts" (Chicago: Universal Music Publishing, Inc.), 1992.
2. Ephesians 4:26, KJV.
3. What I said to my sister countless times when we were kids. As an adult, I realized it had been my *choice* to become angry.
4. Since the mid-1970s, I have seen several versions of this diagram in many settings, such as Christian seminars and classes, and am unsure of its original source. One version appears in: Scope Ministries, *Be Transformed* (Oklahoma City: Scope Ministries International, Inc., 2001), 7.4.
5. Attribution regarding the "Serenity Prayer" is debatable. See, for example, Fred Shapiro, "Who wrote the Serenity Prayer?" yalealumnimagazine.com, Jul/Aug 2008, https://www.yalealumnimagazine.com/articles/2143-who-wrote-the-serenity-prayer?.
6. Grant Colfax Tullar, "The Weaver."
7. I cannot locate a recording or transcript of Jack Taylor's "The Principle of Receiving"; however, a message making the main points I recall from Mr. Taylor's message is transcribed and provided in Addendum Four of this book, starting on page 211.
8. Lawrence O. Richards, 185.

Chapter 8: Freeing Truth about Guilt, Shame, and Punishment

1. Matt Boswell and Matt Papa, "His Mercy Is More" (Nashville, TN: Getty Music), 2019.
2. Romans 8:1.
3. Statement made by a small group participant during a discussion of the forgiveness Jesus offers.

Chapter 9: Freeing Truth about Living by Rules and Standards

1. Les Emmerson, "Signs" (Los Angeles: Sony/ATV Music Publishing LLC, Warner Chappell Music, Inc.), 1970.
2. Romans 7:8.
3. A question I asked my biblical counselor in 1979.
4. With permission, portions of this chapter were inspired by "Session 11 - The Torah Syndrome," of *Pneumanetics*: (Oklahoma City: Scope Ministries International, Inc., 1992), 11-1 - 11-38.
5. Bill Gillham, untitled conference, Tahlequah, Oklahoma, June 1990.
6. Scope Ministries, *Be Transformed* (Oklahoma City: Scope Ministries International, Inc., 2001), 8.9.

Chapter 10: Freeing Truth about Relationships

1. Joe Brooks, "You Light Up My Life" (Santa Monica, CA: Universal Music Publishing Group), 1977.
2. Matthew 6:33.
3. How many fairy tales end; in other words, not true!
4. Corrie ten Boom, *The Hiding Place, 35th Anniversary Edition* (Grand Rapids, MI: Baker Publishing Group, 2006), 12.

Chapter 11: Freeing Truth about Bad Things People Have Done to You

1. Jimmy Webb, "Shattered" (Santa Monica, CA: Universal Music Publishing Group), 1985.
2. Psalm 56:8.
3. What a church counselor told me when I told him I'd been sexually molested as a child.

Chapter 12: Where Do You Go from Here?

1. Joe Hamilton, "I'm So Glad We Had this Time Together" (Los Angeles: Jocar Inc.), 1967.
2. Galatians 5:1a.
3. Confession of a small group participant during the group's final discussion time.
4. Corrie ten Boom, 12.
5. Joni Eareckson Tada, "God's Sovereignty in Tragedy," joni&friends.org, April 28, 2020, https://joniandfriends.org/4-minute-radio-program/gods-sovereignty-in-tragedy/.
6. Unnamed GotQuestions contributor, "How Did the Apostle John Die?" GotQuestions.org, accessed April 9, 2024, https://www.gotquestions.org/apostle-John-die.html.

Addendum One: *FatherCare*

1. J. I. Packer, *Knowing God* (Downers Grove, Illinois: InterVarsity Press, 1973), 14.
2. Gerhard Friedrich, ed., *Theological Dictionary of the New Testament*, Vol. 5 (Grand Rapids, Michigan: Wm. B. Eerdmans Publishing Co., 1967), 272.
3. Packer, 14-15.
4. William Barclay, *The Daily Study Bible: The Letters of John and Jude* (Philadelphia: The Westminster Press, 1958), 87. Used by permission of St. Andrew Press.
5. Kenneth S. Wuest, *Word Studies in the Greek New Testament*, Vol. 4 (Grand Rapids, Michigan: Wm. B. Eerdmans Company, 1966), 142.
6. Friedrich, Vol. 8, 2.
7. Wuest, Vol. 1, 134.
8. William Barclay, *The Daily Study Bible: The Letter to the Romans* (Philadelphia: The Westminster Press, 1958), 109-112. Used by permission of St. Andrew Press.
9. Packer, 41.
10. J. Oswald Sanders, *Enjoying Intimacy with God* (Chicago: Moody Publishers, 1980), 19-20.
11. Ibid., 20.
12. Packer, 41.
13. Sanders, 13-14.

Addendum Two: "Self-Disciplined Religion"

1. Titus 2:6, personal paraphrase.
2. Colossians 2:23, NASB.
3. Proverbs 14:12, personal paraphrase.
4. Matthew 23:26, NASB.
5. Isaiah 53:6, KJV.
6. Ephesians 2:2b, personal paraphrase.
7. See Romans 5:5b.
8. See Hebrews 10:16.
9. See Titus 2:11-12.
10. See Ephesians 5:14.
11. See Titus 2:11.
12. Isaiah 1:18a, NASB.
13. James 1:5, NASB.

14. Proverbs 16:32b, personal paraphrase.
15. Proverbs 25:28, NASB.

About the Author

For 16 years, Paula Neall Coleman served as the executive assistant to the founder and president of a biblical counseling center in Oklahoma City. For over 30 years, Paula has led Bible-based small groups while writing, speaking, and teaching about how, for the Christian, understanding the truths about God and "being yourself" as a "new creation in Christ" is the answer to many of the painful struggles Christians face. She is also the author of *The Weight of Grace: Experience the Freedom from Overeating that You Already Have*. For more information, visit experiencethefreedom.net.

www.ingramcontent.com/pod-product-compliance
Lightning Source LLC
Chambersburg PA
CBHW080434110426
42743CB00016B/3160